The Hudson

The Hudson

An Illustrated Guide to the Living River
Second Edition

Stephen P. Stanne

Roger G. Panetta

Brian E. Forist

RIVERGATE BOOKS
AN IMPRINT OF RUTGERS UNIVERSITY PRESS
NEW BRUNSWICK, NEW JERSEY

A Project of
Hudson River Sloop
Clearwater, Inc.

Library of Congress Cataloging-in-Publication Data

Stanne, Stephen P., 1950–
    The Hudson : an illustrated guide to the living river / Stephen
P. Stanne, Roger G. Panetta, Brian E. Forist. — 2nd ed.
        p.   cm.
    "A Project of Hudson River Sloop Clearwater, Inc."
    Includes bibliographical references and index.
    ISBN-13: 978-0-8135-3972-0 (hardcover : alk. paper)
    ISBN-13: 978-0-8135-3916-4 (pbk. : alk. paper)
    1. Natural history—Hudson River (N.Y. and N.J.)   2. Stream
ecology—Hudson River (N.Y. and N.J.)   3. Hudson River
(N.Y. and N.J.)—History.   4. Hudson River (N.Y. and N.J.)—
Environmental conditions.   I. Panetta, Roger G., 1939–
II. Forist, Brian E., 1956–   III. Hudson River Sloop Clearwater,
Inc.   IV. Title.
    QH104.5.H83S74   2007
    508.747'3—dc22
                                                                2006011843

A British Cataloging-in-Publication record for this book is
available from the British Library.

Manufactured in the United States of America

Credits

Text: Chapters 1, 2, 3, 6, 11, and 12 by Stephen P. Stanne; chapters 7, 8, 9, and 10 by Roger G. Panetta; and chapters 4 and 5 by Brian E. Forist.

Illustrations: Unless otherwise credited, drawings for chapters 1, 2, 5, and 6, and all photographs by Stephen P. Stanne; drawings for chapter 3 by Cara Lee; and drawings for chapter 4 by Cynthia Saniewski.

Hudson River map by Nora Porter, CHP Productions.

Picture research for chapters 7, 8, 9, and 10 by Nora Porter.

Contents

Preface to the Second Edition   ix
Preface to the First Edition   xiii
Acknowledgments   xvii

Chapter 1   **A Physical Overview of the Hudson**   1

Chapter 2   **Energy Flow and Nutrient Cycles in the Hudson**   13

Chapter 3   **The Hudson's Habitats and Plant Communities**   27

Chapter 4   **The Hudson's Invertebrate Animals**   43

Chapter 5   **The Hudson's Fishes**   59

Chapter 6   **The Hudson's Birds and Beasts**   77

Chapter 7   **Exploration, Colonization, and Revolution**   93

Chapter 8   **The Romantic River**   109

Chapter 9   **Industrialization and the Transformation of the Landscape**   117

Chapter 10   **Conservation and Environmentalism**   131

Chapter 11   **Resolving River Conflicts**   139

Chapter 12   **Is the Hudson Getting Cleaner?**   161

Afterword   183
Sources and Notes   185
Glossary   195
Suggested Readings   201
Index   205
Map of the Hudson River   inside back cover

Preface to the Second Edition

When work began on *The Hudson* some fifteen years ago, we intended to create an introduction to the river that combined environmental science and history in a manner useful to teachers and students, a mission reflected in the original working title: *A Hudson River Primer*. Given the opportunity to revisit that goal with this new edition, there was a temptation to greatly expand its coverage. The Hudson has rightfully become even more prominent in the public eye. It is now an American Heritage River, the backbone of the Hudson River Valley National Heritage Area, the site of a Rivers and Estuaries Institute intended to be a world-class research facility, a magnet for anglers seeking trophy striped bass, a key element of urban redevelopment plans, and a continued inspiration to artists. Hand in hand with all this attention, research and scholarship have generated a wealth of new data and interpretation of the Hudson, and a corresponding trove of fresh material to include in a revised book.

This new edition is longer, but not by much. We decided to stand by our original intent to provide a broad overview, and to re-emphasize the importance of interdisciplinary examination of the river. The Hudson Valley is a unique and special place, and integrated knowledge of its ecology, natural and human history, and culture is essential to understanding its distinctiveness.

Scientific information in the book has been updated, as has the status of the various environmental battles that have embroiled the valley and its residents. Our revisions reflect recent scientific emphasis on including the watershed in studying the ecology of the river, and on the interplay of native species and exotic interlopers. Historically, we examine more closely the impacts of the first European interlopers to settle here: the Dutch.

The Hudson is based on the research, scholarship, and expertise of a host of scientists, historians, environmental advocates, civil servants, and others. Many kindly and generously reviewed the manuscript or answered questions critical to developing the text. In addition to contributions acknowledged in the first edition, we greatly appreciate input to the revised work from M. Peter deVries, U.S. Geological Survey (chapter 1); Dr. Stuart Findlay, aquatic ecologist at the Institute of Ecosystem Studies (chapters 2 and 3); Kathy Hattala and Andy Kahnle, biologists in the Hudson River Fisheries Unit, N.Y. State Department of Environmental Conservation (DEC) (chapter 5); Dr. Erik Kiviat, executive director of Hudsonia Ltd. (chapters 3 and 6); John Sansalone of the DEC's Division of Water (chapter 12); Dr. David Walker, professor of earth and environmental sciences, Lamont-Doherty Earth Observatory of Columbia University (chapter 1); and Byron Young of the DEC's Bureau of Marine Resources (chapter 4).

The drawings, photographs, paintings, prints, and other illustrations are essential to this book, and we again thank the artists, photographers, and institutions (credited elsewhere) who, on a volunteer basis or for nominal fees, provided this material.

The authors are fortunate to be surrounded daily by people committed to understanding, managing, and protecting the Hudson. This book's interpretation of the river is in part grounded in interaction with these individuals, especially Fran Dunwell, Nancy Beard, Scott Cuppett, Barbara Kendall, Tom Lake, Kristin Marcell, Karen Strong, and Beth Waterman of DEC's Hudson River Estuary Program and Betsy Blair and her staff at the Hudson River National Estuarine Research Reserve.

We appreciate the continued support of the Hudson River Foundation, where Clay Hiles, Dr. Dennis Suszkowski, Helena Andreyko, and Dr. John Waldman (now at Queens College) have provided wise counsel to the project.

Fordham University supported our decision to prepare this revision in several key ways. We are indebted to Dr. Gerard Reedy, S.J., Dean of Marymount College of Fordham University, not only for his recognition of the importance of Hudson River scholarship but also for his consistent encouragement and commitment to the study of the river. The University Librarian, Dr. James P. McCabe, has nurtured and expanded the Hudson River Collection and, with the library staff, provided a welcoming atmosphere for river scholars. The Beacon Center for Rivers and Estuaries has been a strong advocate for interdisciplinary study and has supported collaborative projects to document the history of the Hudson, which have deepened knowledge of rivers and estuaries.

Clearwater provided essential administrative and logistical support to the revision effort. Our thanks go to Gregg Swanzey, Andy Mele, and especially Hal and Debbie

Cohen, who were able to retrieve the original manuscript files from prehistoric floppy disks, saving us much work.

We are grateful to Dr. Audra Wolfe, Marlie Wasserman, and Suzanne Kellam of Rutgers University Press for their assistance in shepherding this second edition through the production process.

Finally, work on this new version of *The Hudson* required even more patience and understanding from our families than did the first edition. We truly appreciate the sacrifices they made without complaint on behalf of this project.

Preface to the First Edition

In studying a river, the place to begin seems obvious: find its source. Take out a map and follow the twisting blue line as it narrows, heading upstream past each tributary, until it ends in a lake or wetland, or perhaps dwindles to nothing in a mountainside valley.

But those with a more historical frame of reference may want to start with discovery of the river by humans. From there one can follow the growth of human society and endeavor along the river over the ensuing centuries.

To a geologist, whose vision of time extends back millions of years, a few centuries is nothing, nor does a river's present source necessarily constitute its beginning. The river may be where it is because of forces operating on a scale much grander than the swirl of its currents.

To a biologist, leery of chicken-and-egg questions about what came first, the beginnings may not matter as much as a deeper understanding of one of the many diverse and fascinating groups of organisms that inhabit the river.

To a teacher, what is important about studying a river, particularly one that is the defining feature of an area's natural landscape and that has figured prominently in a region's—indeed, a nation's—history, is that it can support curricula in any or all of these disciplines, and many more besides. In addition, a local river has real shape and associations in students' lives and minds, an advantage a teacher can use to make inquiry and learning even more effective and substantive.

No better example exists than the Hudson River. Get up close and its teeming life and shifting currents provide a compelling introduction to the natural sciences, while artifacts along its shores provide a glimpse of our forebearers' daily lives. Pull back a bit, study the landscape in which the river flows, and feel for yourself the inspiration that guided major developments in American art. Widen the field of view even more, place the Hudson in its geographical setting, and gain a clearer picture of American history while examining the river's pivotal role in Revolutionary War strategies or in providing a route of migration and commerce into the expanding frontier. Study the precedent-setting battles waged over Hudson River environmental concerns to understand our political and legal process, and realize that these controversies offer an interdisciplinary link back to the close-up view of the river's biology.

The Hudson was originally envisioned as a basic reference for teachers studying the Hudson River with their students. It remains that, but it also fulfills the larger role of providing information to anyone inclined to be a student of the river, whether or not the inquiry takes place in a formal classroom.

This is a book of elementary principles, providing an overview of the Hudson's natural and human histories between the head of tidewater at Troy and the briny ocean at its mouth. It is not a complete field guide; only common or distinctive species were selected for brief descriptions. The many forms of life to be seen in the river could be fully described only in a multivolume work. Besides, field guides concern themselves primarily with identification of organisms or objects, not so much with the physical phenomena and biological relationships which tie them together. This book does attempt to convey a sense of the great diversity of life in the Hudson, weaving descriptions of representative organisms into discussions of the ecological ties that bind them together.

Similarly, this book cannot cover all the basic tenets of sciences that have application to studying the Hudson—from astronomy, botany, and chemistry all the way to zoology. But those interested in specific sciences will find examples from the Hudson to illustrate the workings of important phenomena, theories, laws, and principles from many disciplines.

The Hudson's content draws on the research and writing of, among others, historians, naturalists, scientists, and government officials. However, it is not intended to be an academic or scientific work; thus we have not cited the source of every fact or observation that originated in earlier works. Key references are acknowledged in the Sources section at the end of the book. The most encompassing and widely available of those references, along with other worthwhile books, are also cited in the annotated Suggested Readings section.

Any book dealing with science must confront the bugaboo of terminology. Scientists sort out phenomena, particles, organisms—whatever it is they study—and assign names or terms to the categories they create. In his authoritative *Freshwater Invertebrates of the United States,* Robert W. Pennak quotes Lewis Carroll's *Alice in Wonderland:*

> "What's the use of their having names," the Gnat said, "if they won't answer to them?"
> "No use to *them,*" said Alice; "but it's useful to the people that name them, I suppose."

While the terminology created may seem daunting to the layperson, it is a necessity for scientists who must be very precise in their descriptions.

We have made an effort to limit terminology, but there are scientific terms that are very useful in discussing the Hudson River in any detail. Most will be defined where and when they first appear in the text, as well as in the appended glossary. While these twenty-five-cent words may twist the tongue and seem pretentious, they are often more efficient than wasting breath or text in repeated descriptive phrases or sentences. For instance, we will discuss algae that live self-sufficiently on the stems and leaves of underwater plants. Don't let the fact that we will discuss epiphytic algae put you off.

In studying history, a major obstacle is the memorization of dates, the names of people and places, and similar facts. Like scientific terms, they have their place in discussions of the Hudson. But pay attention to them as you pay attention to minutes passing on a clock, reference points against which major themes of American history play out on the stage provided by the Hudson. Just as species descriptions illustrate biological diversity and junctures in the network of ecological relationships, so do accounts of specific events of the Hudson's history, with their associated dates, people, and sites, illuminate the interplay of far-reaching social, political, and cultural ideas and movements.

In years of leading teacher workshops dealing with Hudson River studies, we have learned that educators attend them not only—or even mainly—because they expect the practical reward of being able to enrich their curricula or programs. Most participate because they are fascinated by the Hudson and feel that it is a vital part of their lives and communities. For all those who dwell along the Hudson, it is our hope that this book will reinforce that fascination and strengthen that sense of the Hudson's vitality and importance.

Acknowledgments

The authors and Clearwater wish to acknowledge and thank the Hudson River Foundation, the Henry L. and Grace Doherty Charitable Foundation, and the Norcross Wildlife Foundation for grants in support of the research, writing, and production of *The Hudson*. The views expressed herein do not necessarily reflect the beliefs or opinions of the donors, who assume no liability for the contents or use of the information. Additional funding was provided through general support from the J. M. Kaplan Fund, the Joyce Mertz-Gilmore Foundation, and Clearwater's members.

The support of the entire Clearwater staff was critical to our production efforts. We would like to express special appreciation to Nora Porter and the late Ken Yeso, whose contributions of creativity, time, and energy to this project went far beyond any work listed in the credits. Thanks also to Hannah Kalkstein for her editing assistance, Bridget Barclay, Julie Neander, and Don Kent for research and review of chapters 11 and 12, volunteer Jane Kellar for her hours at the copy machine, intern Julia Wilson for her consistency checks, and John Mylod for his patience.

This book was greatly improved by the knowledge and critical eye of expert individuals outside Clearwater who generously donated time from their busy schedules to review chapters relevant to their fields of knowledge. We owe particular thanks to Nancy Beard, Citizen Participation Specialist, Hudson River Program, N.Y. State Department of Environmental Conservation (DEC) (chapters 11 and 12); Dr. Jonathan J. Cole, Aquatic Microbiologist at the Institute of Ecosystem Studies (IES) (chapters 2 and 3); Frances F. Dunwell, Special Assistant to the Commissioner and Hudson River Coordinator, DEC (chapters 11 and 12); Dr. Erik Kiviat, executive director of Hudsonia Ltd. (chapters 3 and 6); Thomas R. Lake, Hudson River Fishermen's Association (chapter 5); Cara Lee, environmental director at Scenic Hudson (chapters 11 and 12); Dr. Michael Pace, Aquatic Ecologist at IES (chapters 2 and 4); Dr. David Strayer, Freshwater Ecologist at IES (chapter 4), and Dr. John Waldman, Research Associate at the Hudson River Foundation (chapter 5).

Equally generous and expert are the teachers who reviewed and helped to shape the book in ways benefiting those who teach about the Hudson. Our thanks go to Meg Clark-Goldhammer, Lisa Fitzgerald, Gary Post, Paul and Vincent Rubeo, Suzanne Tichner, and Al Vinck.

Other individuals patiently answered questions during our research: Dr. Joanna Burger, Rutgers University; Dr. Donald Cadwell, N.Y. State Geological Survey; Dr. Stuart Findlay, IES; Ward Freeman, U.S. Geological Survey; Tony Goodwin, Adirondack Mountain Club; Kathy Hattala, DEC; Andy Kahnle, DEC; Kate McCaig, Liberty State Park, N.J.; Russell Mt. Pleasant, DEC; the late Jim Rod, National Audubon Society; Larry Sarner, N.J. Department of Environmental Protection; and Dr. Russell Waines, State University of New York at New Paltz.

We are most grateful to the artists, photographers, and institutions (credited elsewhere) who, on a volunteer basis or for nominal fees, provided materials for use in illustrating this book. In addition, we would like to thank Val Ruge for providing access to her extensive collection of Hudson River prints and allowing us to use many images.

Clay Hiles and Dr. Dennis J. Suszkowski of the Hudson River Foundation, Dr. Terry Shtob, formerly of the Foundation, and the late Sam Kalkstein provided much appreciated general review and suggestions for improving this book. Thanks also to Uta Gore, river educator, Sr. Brigid Driscoll, President of Marymount College, and Dr. Bessie Blake, Dean of the School of New Resources, College of New Rochelle, for their support of Hudson River studies.

Finally, thanks to Dr. Karen Reeds of Rutgers University Press for her patience and interest in seeing this project come to fruition, and to Paul Fargis of Stonesong Press for advice and assistance in the endeavor.

The Hudson

Chapter 1

A Physical Overview of the Hudson

The Chapter in Brief
The Hudson River flows 315 miles from Lake Tear of the Clouds in the Adirondacks to the Battery in New York City. Its course and shoreline topography result from erosion by water and glacial ice over the past sixty-five to seventy-five million years. The river is influenced by ocean tides to Troy, 153 miles north of the Battery. Diluted seawater typically ranges upriver to a point between the Tappan Zee and Newburgh, depending on the volume of runoff from the Hudson's watershed. The lower Hudson is an estuary, a type of ecosystem that ranks among the most productive on the planet.

The Hudson's Origins

To begin a study of the Hudson River at its source, lay out a map of eastern New York State and trace the blue line north from New York Harbor along the cliffs of the Palisades, under the ramparts at West Point, through the sunset shadows of the Catskill Mountains, past the capital city of Albany, and on into the Adirondacks. There, at the confluence of two creeks near Henderson Lake, the name Hudson River disappears; the map offers the option of following Calamity Brook northeastward or the outlet from Henderson Lake westward.

Looking for the highest body of water feeding the Hudson, turn northeast and face the heart of the High Peaks region. Continue upward along Calamity Brook, the Opalescent River, and little Feldspar Brook to find, as Verplanck Colvin did in 1872, a tiny lake perched 4,322 feet up on the southwest side of Mt. Marcy, New York State's highest peak at 5,344 feet. Colvin, an indefatigable explorer and surveyor of the Adirondacks, described his discovery as a "minute, unpretending tear-of-the-clouds—as it were—a lonely pool shivering in the breezes of the mountains." Thus the

Hudson's source was named—Lake Tear of the Clouds.

The Water Cycle

The clouds that so often cap the Adirondacks, the snow that falls on Mt. Marcy's shoulder, the raindrops that dimple the surface of Lake Tear, the fog that condenses in tiny droplets on spruces lining Feldspar

Lake Tear of the Clouds, source of the Hudson, nestles high on the southwest shoulder of Mount Marcy, New York State's highest peak.

In this simplified illustration of the water cycle, rain falls to earth (1) and runs off into streams flowing seaward (2) or enters the ground (3). As groundwater moves towards the ocean, it feeds streams and lakes and is taken up by plants (4), from which it is transpired into the atmosphere as water vapor. Evaporation from the sea (5) and other surface waters also supplies water vapor to the atmosphere. There, the vapor condenses to form clouds (6) and eventually falls to earth again as precipitation.

In the water cycle, that function is carried out by the sun, which provides energy to evaporate water and move it from place to place in the atmosphere, and by gravity, which causes precipitation to flow as runoff across the land and as groundwater under the land's surface.

The Hudson's Watershed

From Lake Tear to the Battery at the southern tip of Manhattan, the Hudson follows a course 315 miles long. Joining it along the way are many tributaries, the largest being the Mohawk River, which flows in from the west at Cohoes. The area of land drained by the Hudson and its tributaries totals 13,390 square miles, mostly in eastern and northern New York State. Small portions of this area, the Hudson's watershed, reach into Vermont, Massachusetts, Connecticut, and New Jersey.

Brook, and their union in the runoff that eventually becomes the Hudson—all are manifestations of a much larger "stream" of water. These visible forms are linked to water hidden in the ground and pulled up in the stems of plants to the leaves, from where it is transpired into the atmosphere. There it joins water vapor invisibly rising from great oceans and tiny puddles, moving with weather systems from continent to continent or from a valley to its bordering hills, and once more taking forms that we can see—clouds and precipitation. This unending movement of water, seen and unseen, constitutes the water cycle.

The water cycle is a circulatory system supporting life on earth much as arteries and veins support human existence. Like blood, water transports substances needed by living organisms of the Hudson and its valley. In our bodies, the heart is the pump that circulates blood through the system.

Gathering waters from Adirondack tributaries, the Hudson rushes through its gorge at Blue Ledge, near the village of North Creek.

Besides gathering rivulets into creeks and creeks into a river, the watershed sustains the Hudson ecosystem with essential nutrients that fertilize aquatic plants and with autumn's faded leaves and other organic matter to be recycled in food chains. The watershed's contributions are greatly influenced by human land use, sometimes with less desirable outcomes. These include pollution from, among many sources, factory pipes, parking lots, farm fields, malfunctioning septic systems, and suburban lawns.

The watershed, particularly the portion drained by the Mohawk, is also the major source of clay, silt, sand, and other sediment entering the Hudson. Some settles out in the river, becoming a foundation for the establishment of plant and animal communities, and some remains suspended in the water, giving the Hudson a muddy appearance. This turbidity is especially noticeable after major rainstorms, when heavy loads of sediment in runoff give the river the appearance of café au lait. These particles tend to settle and fill in certain stretches of the river, notably at Haverstraw Bay and from Kingston north to Albany. In these areas, the ship channel must be maintained by dredging—digging out bottom mud—since under federal law, the channel between New York and Albany must be kept at least 32 feet deep. This allows large barges and ocean-going ships to reach the Port of Albany.

An Arm of the Sea

In length and watershed area the Hudson does not rank highly among American rivers. Yet numbers do not tell the full story, as one can appreciate when gazing across wide bays at Newburgh, the Tappan Zee, and Haverstraw, the latter being where the Hudson is widest, about three and a half miles east to west.

Bordered on the west by the northern portion of the Palisades, Haverstraw Bay is the widest spot on the Hudson.

Such expansive grandeur results from the fact that for nearly half its length, the Hudson is an arm of the sea. In plunging over a dam at Troy, the river falls to a level only a few feet above that of the faraway Atlantic Ocean, entering a long narrow trough in which its flow is governed less by

The Troy Dam marks the upriver limit of tidal influence on the Hudson. A lock here allows boat passage via the river to and from the New York State Barge Canal (successor to the famed Erie Canal) and the Champlain Canal.

the pull of earth's gravity than by the pulse of ocean tides responding to the gravity of the moon.

The lowest portions of the Hudson's valley south of Troy were drowned when sea level rose at the end of the most recent ice age. The deepest spot known is at World's End near West Point, where a recent river-bed mapping project found bottom 177 feet down.[1] The Hudson's gorge through the Highlands is its deepest stretch, with many charted depths over 100 feet.

The Hudson Fjord

With its great depths and cliffs slanting steeply into the river, the Hudson's route through the Highlands reminds many observers of the strikingly scenic fjords of Norway. Fjords are troughs eroded below sea level, often to great depths, by glacial ice. They are deepest not at their mouths but upstream, where the ice was thickest and its erosive power the greatest. A shallower, less eroded sill of bedrock is usually present at the mouths.

The bedrock underlying the lower Hudson is largely buried below layers of sediments, some deposited by the river, others dropped by the ice sheets or their meltwaters. These deposits fill a much deeper gorge scoured out by the glaciers. Drilling during construction of aqueducts and bridges across the river found that the deepest portions of this gorge lie at least 750 feet below sea level at the northern entrance to the Highlands, and 740 feet down at the Tappan Zee. Nearer the ocean, geologists have found a shallower sill: bedrock is less than 200 feet down at the Verrazano Bridge. Thus, this portion of the Hudson qualifies as a fjord.

Shaped by the Ice Sheets

Other aspects of topography along the Hudson's course reflect the enormous

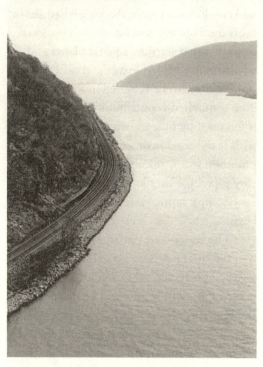

The Hudson's established channel through the Highlands was gouged to greater depths by glacial ice, which also steepened the slopes plunging down to the river.

power of the Ice Age's continental glaciers. At the peak of glaciation, the metropolitan New York area was buried under as much as 3,000 feet of ice. So much water was frozen in ice sheets worldwide that the Atlantic Ocean was about 400 feet lower than it is today. To reach the sea the Hudson flowed an additional 120 miles across a wide coastal plain.

As these glaciers began to melt 20,000 years ago, tremendous volumes of water were released, carrying with them great loads of sediment—the remains of rock and soil pulverized by the moving ice. Surges of meltwater and accompanying turbidity currents (underwater landslides generated by the buildup of sediment deposits) carved the Hudson Submarine Canyon, a deep gorge at the edge of the continental shelf southeast of New York Harbor. A sub-merged valley running across the continental shelf—a feature not seen off other East Coast rivers—links the Hudson's mouth to the canyon. This valley may have been cut when glacial meltwaters from the prehistoric Great Lakes and Lake Champlain, their St. Lawrence River outlet blocked by the ice sheets, flowed torrentially down the Hudson to the Atlantic.

The glaciers also built up some landscapes. Debris eroded from areas to the north was piled up by the ice sheets at the limits of their advance. At this terminus the rate of melting equaled the speed of advance; like Cinderella, left without conveyance as her carriage turned back into a pumpkin, the debris brought south was dropped, forming rows of low hills, as ice turned to water. Such deposits constitute the backbone of Long Island and Brooklyn. The Hudson breaches one of these glacially created ridges, called a terminal moraine, at the Narrows between Brooklyn and Staten Island.

Other shoreline features owe their origins to the continental glaciers. As the ice sheets began melting back, the newly freed water collected behind moraines, glacial debris, and melting ice masses in the region's valleys, creating large lakes such as glacial Lake Hudson, which occupied the valley north of the terminal moraine at the Narrows.[2] Rivers swollen by meltwater carried gravel and sand into the lake. At their mouths, where the currents slowed, this material was dropped to form deltas. Much of Croton Point is such a delta, built up by the ancestral Croton River.[3] In the still waters of the lake, tiny particles of rock flour—soil and rock ground up by the glaciers—gradually settled to the bottom, forming deep beds of clay. These beds later supplied the raw material for the brick industry that flourished along the Hudson.

As the post-glacial thaw continued, sea level rose. About 12,000 years ago, the ocean breached the terminal moraine across Long Island and Staten Island, draining the glacial lake and allowing the tides to roll north.

Of Time and River Flowing

Though its origins are poorly known and disputed, the river's general course was probably set sixty-five to seventy-five million years ago, long before the great glaciers' advance. The region's landscape at the time was very flat, similar to that seen today near the coasts of the southeastern states. The rocks that would later be sculpted into the Highlands and Palisades were buried under coastal plain sediments, over which the ancestral Hudson made its way to the ocean. The river and its tributaries wore away those sediments, exposing and cutting into bedrock. The erosive power of the current allowed the ancient Hudson to carve a gorge even through hard, resistant rocks such as the gneiss and granite that ultimately were exposed to form the Highlands.

Gaps in the ridges of the Palisades and New Jersey's Watchung Mountains suggest that until ten million to fifteen million years ago the Hudson followed a course different from its present route between the Tappan Zee and the Atlantic. It crossed the Palisades at the Sparkill Gap, located a few miles south of the Tappan Zee Bridge, and continued southwest across the Watchungs near Paterson, New Jersey. The river then parallelled the Watchungs south for about 15 miles before turning eastward and re-crossing them on its way to the ocean, perhaps as a tributary of the Delaware River. Later in prehistoric time the Hudson probably flowed south from the Sparkill Gap along the Hackensack Meadowlands to the sea.

It is possible that the river abandoned the Sparkill Gap as the headwaters of a small stream running east of the Palisades

At the low-lying Sparkill Gap, the Hudson once flowed westward through the Palisades and on to the sea past the site of present-day Paterson, New Jersey, instead of Manhattan.

eroded its watershed, extending its boundaries to the north. At some point this erosion reached the ancestral Hudson, giving it a new, lower outlet to the sea. Eventually all the waters of the river were diverted into this new course past Manhattan Island and on to the ocean. Another hypothesis suggests that glacial deposits blocked the Sparkill Gap, forcing the Hudson to erode its present course east of the Palisades.

The geological handiwork of water and ice over millions of years created a waterway which offered immense advantages to the humans who eventually settled in its valley. In a time before railroads, superhighways, and jumbo airliners, water-based transportation was the easiest, fastest, most comfortable, and most capacious way of moving goods and people long distances. The river's surface was unbroken by rapids or waterfalls for over 150 miles inland. Its erosive power had created the gorge through the Highlands, the only sea-level passage through the Appalachian Mountain range. This fact figured prominently in De-Witt Clinton's vision for a water route linking America's expanding west to its Atlantic coast, a vision realized in the Erie Canal. And in the days before steamships, when vessels depended on the motive power of

wind or muscle, the Hudson offered yet another boon to those trying to get from one place to another: tidal currents.

A River That Flows Two Ways

Tides were not always favorable to the sloops once so common on the Hudson—the currents would usually move in the direction opposite to the one desired for half of each day. But when there was little wind (frequently the case during Hudson Valley summers), vessels could anchor to wait out an ill tide, and then get a much-needed boost in the desired direction when the tide turned in their favor.

Tides occur in patterns set by a celestial dance involving the earth, the moon, and, to a lesser extent, the sun. The most obvious of these patterns is the daily tidal cycle along the Atlantic coast, in which two high tides and two low tides occur over roughly twenty-four hours. While a complete explanation of how tides work is beyond the scope of this book, a simple overview will be helpful in understanding the Hudson.

The Pull of the Moon . . .

The moon is large enough and near enough to exert considerable gravitational pull on

The effects of ocean tides in the Hudson are evident at Poughkeepsie, where the average high tide is three feet higher than the average low tide.

the earth. In the oceans, this attraction literally causes water to bulge out towards the moon. This bulge remains positioned under the moon (actually a little behind it due to inertia and friction) as the earth spins on its axis. Thus, while beachcombers on the Atlantic coast watch the moon rise, they are being inexorably carried into a mound of water, evident in the rising tide lapping around their feet.

This bulge raises the ocean's level above the level of water in the Hudson; as a result, seawater starts rushing into the river. At the Battery on Manhattan's southern tip, strollers gazing out at the Statue of Liberty might notice that the Hudson's current is pushing northward, in from the sea towards the mountains, and that the water is rising along pilings lining the shore.

Hours later, after the beachcombers and strollers have gone to bed, the Atlantic coast has passed under the moon and reached the backside of the bulge. The tide is now falling, and as the ocean's level drops below the level of water in the river, the current at the Battery reverses and starts flowing toward the sea once more. The native tribes of the valley described this in one of their names for the river: *Muhheakantuck*, meaning "river that flows two ways."

For reasons best explained in cited references, a second tidal bulge forms at a point on the earth opposite the moon. In between the two bulges are areas where the ocean's level is lower, resulting in low tides. Thus, in the twenty-four hours it takes the earth to spin around its axis, a

Moonrise over the Esopus Meadows just south of Kingston.

This diagram shows, in greatly exaggerated form, the tidal bulge created by the gravitational mechanics of the moon and earth (as viewed from above the North Pole). High tides occur on the portion of earth facing the moon and on the portion directly opposite.

Moon   Earth

6:00 P.M., DAY 1: In between, where the lighthouse stands at 6:00 P.M. on day 1, the tide is low. But earth's rotation is carrying the lighthouse into the bulge under the moon . . .

12:00 A.M., DAY 2: . . . and at midnight 6 hours later, the tower is largely submerged by a high tide.

6:00 A.M., DAY 2: By 6:00 A.M. on day 2, earth's rotation has taken the lighthouse out of the bulge. A low tide laps at the tower's base.

12:00 P.M., DAY 2: At noon, the lighthouse reaches the crest of the bulge on the opposite side of earth and is again experiencing high tide.

6:00 P.M., DAY 2: By 6:00 P.M., earth's rotation has brought the lighthouse back to where it was 24 hours earlier. During those 24 hours, the lighthouse went through two high tides, the typical pattern along the East Coast (see note 4).

given point on the Atlantic coast will usually experience two high tides and two low tides, one following the other roughly every six hours.[4]

. . . and of the Sun

In addition to this daily rhythm, tides vary cyclically over the twenty-eight day lunar month—the time the moon takes to circle once around the earth. The lunar month is marked by the phases of the moon. More extreme tides (higher highs and lower lows) occur when the moon is in its new or full phase; these are the spring tides. During the moon's first and last quarter, the range between high and low tide heights is minimal; these are the neap tides.

Spring and neap tides reflect the interaction of the sun's gravitational attraction with the moon's. One might expect the sun to have greater tidal influence because it is so much bigger than the moon and exerts a correspondingly stronger gravitational force. However, this force decreases with distance, and the sun is much further away from the earth than the moon. On balance, the sun's effect in raising tides is only about half that of the moon's.

Up and Down, Back and Forth

The rise and fall of the tides affects the river all the way to the dam at Troy, 153 river miles north of the Battery. In fact, the Hudson's maximum tidal range (the difference in level between average high and low tides) is observed at Troy: 4.7 feet. Tidal range is least along the mid-Hudson, averaging only 2.7 feet at West Point.

Like high and low tides, reversals in current direction follow roughly a six-hour schedule. The current draining the river south towards the ocean is called the *ebb*; that pushing north from the ocean is called the *flood*. Extreme rain and accompanying runoff will sometimes suppress the flood current in northern reaches of the estuary.[5] Persistent, strong northerly or southerly winds can also affect the timing and strength of tidal currents.

The velocity of the Hudson's currents varies depending on the strength of tidal forces at a given time, location along the river, the volume of runoff entering the estuary, and weather conditions. Currents are swiftest near the George Washington Bridge (average flood 1.9 mph; ebb 2.6 mph) and further north around Catskill (flood 1.9 mph; ebb 2.4 mph).

An adventure like Huckleberry Finn's raft trip down the Mississippi would be quite a different experience on the Hudson below Troy. Instead of progressing steadily downstream, a rafter on the Hudson might admire the scenery while drifting southward on an ebb current for about six hours, then view the same scenery again as the flood current pushed the raft back upstream for the next six hours, and endure it yet again as the ebb current took over once more. The ebb current is generally stronger than the flood; thus our Hudson River rafter would eventually reach New York Harbor.

How long would the trip take? That depends on the *flushing rate*—the time it takes water entering the estuary at Troy to reach the harbor. The rate varies greatly, depending on freshwater runoff. In very dry summers with minimal runoff, the raft's net movement downriver might only be 1.5 miles per day. At that rate, it would take 102 days to float from the head of tide at Troy to New York Harbor. On the other hand, a major rainstorm can cause heavy runoff that presses against and shortens the duration of the flood current while strengthening the ebb. This speeds up the flushing rate, perhaps to 5 miles per day, reducing the rafter's trip to about 30 days.

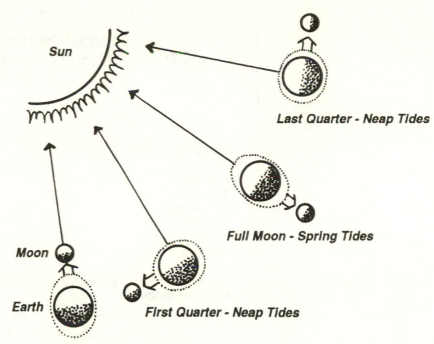

Last Quarter - Neap Tides

Full Moon - Spring Tides

First Quarter - Neap Tides

New Moon - Spring Tides

At any given time different parts of the river will be experiencing different tides. Since the Hudson's tides are generated in the ocean, there is an increasing lag in the timing of a specific event as one moves away from the sea. The crest of a high tide which occurs at the Battery at 12:00 noon will not reach Poughkeepsie until about 4:30 P.M., and Albany around 9:00. The accompanying table shows lag times based on high and low tides at the Battery. Tide predictions are available in printed tide tables, on the internet, and in the almanac accompanying the weather report in major newspapers.

The Hudson Estuary

Tides are not the only evidence of ocean influence in the Hudson. Swimmers escaping summer's heat with a dip in the river at Croton, or sailors hit with a faceful of spray as they tack across the Tappan Zee might have their tastebuds surprised by the tang of salt water. They learn by experience that

Spring tides occur when the moon is new or full. The sun, moon, and earth are all in line, so that the sun's pull works with the moon's to create a more extreme tidal bulge evident in higher high tides and lower low tides.

Neap tides occur at the moon's first and last quarters, when sun and moon are at right angles relative to earth. The moon raises the high tides alone, without help from the sun; thus these highs are lower than normal. However, the sun's pull does act on the low tide area of the bulge, causing higher low tides.

HUDSON RIVER TIDE TIME DIFFERENCES BETWEEN THE BATTERY IN MANHATTAN AND POINTS UPRIVER

	High water hrs. / mins.	Low water hrs. / mins.
George Washington Bridge	+ 0 50	+ 0 46
Tarrytown	+ 1 49	+ 1 57
Peekskill	+ 2 28	+ 3 03
Newburgh	+ 3 46	+ 4 03
Poughkeepsie	+ 4 34	+ 4 46
Kingston	+ 5 20	+ 5 34
Catskill	+ 6 41	+ 6 58
Albany	+ 8 55	+ 9 21

These differences are predictions from standard tide tables; they will vary depending on runoff and weather.

(Data from National Ocean Survey Tide Tables.)

the lower Hudson is an estuary, a semi-enclosed coastal body of water freely connected to the sea, in which salty seawater is mixed and diluted with fresh water running off the land.

The Salt Front

Fresh Hudson River water contains some salt, typically about 20 parts per million (ppm).[6] In moving downriver one reaches a point where salinity starts to rise above that background level. This is the salt front—the leading edge of seawater entering the river. While the term suggests a sharp line of demarcation, seawater at the front is greatly diluted and only slightly saltier than fresh water; the difference is not apparent to the eye or to most taste buds. Salinity increases downriver from the salt front, reaching about 35,000 ppm (more commonly expressed as 35 parts per thousand—ppt) of salt in the waters of the open ocean. By the way, the word "salt" is used loosely here; it includes all the dissolved chemicals in seawater. Sodium chloride—common table salt—accounts for about 78 percent of the

mix; magnesium chloride another 11 percent or so.

The Hudson estuary supplies drinking water for a number of communities, and the location of the salt front is a matter of interest to them.[7] The United States Geological Survey defines the salt front's location as the spot where the concentration of chloride reaches 100 ppm. Ecologists studying estuaries have a different convention, defining water as fresh until the salt reaches a concentration of 500 ppm (0.5 ppt). The lower convention is preferred in relation to drinking water since public health laws set a limit of 250 ppm of chloride in drinking water supplies, mainly for reasons of taste. However, individuals on low-sodium diets do need to pay attention as the salt front nears drinking water intakes.

The salt front's movements up and down the Hudson (and thus the salinity at any point) are chiefly controlled by the volume of freshwater runoff from the watershed, which tends to follow a seasonal pattern linked to weather conditions. Rainfall and melting snow and ice in spring send runoff surging against the salty ocean water, pushing it well downriver. As freshwater flow slackens through the summer months, salt water penetrates further upriver, only to be driven seaward again as rainfall increases in late autumn. In winter, extended periods of subfreezing weather occasionally lock fresh water up as ice and snow, reducing runoff and allowing the salt front to creep upriver.

Superimposed on this seasonal pattern are daily movements of the salt front with the ebb and flood tidal currents, the former causing the salt to retreat towards the Atlantic, the latter pushing it upriver.

So how far up the Hudson does the salt front travel? In a year with typical amounts and patterns of precipitation, the salt front reaches Newburgh Bay, 60 miles north of the Battery, during summer or early fall. Drought conditions reduce freshwater runoff, allowing the salt front to push further north. In dry spells during the mid-1960s, 1985, and 1995, salinities exceeded 100 ppm at Poughkeepsie, 75 miles upriver. Spring runoff and major storms can push the salt front well below the Tappan Zee Bridge, and sometimes south to Manhattan.

Salinity from Top to Bottom

One would expect salinity in estuaries to increase from the salt front toward the ocean. Less obviously, salinity often increases from surface to bottom at a given place in an estuary. Salt water is denser than fresh water; in response to gravity it spreads upriver underneath fresh water flowing seaward at the surface—a phenomenon called estuarine circulation. In an idealized model of an estuary, with a small, steady input of fresh water and no obstructions in the channel, gravity would draw the denser salt water upriver almost to the point where the river bottom rises to sea level. It is this circula-

tion pattern, not tidal action, that moves the salt front up the Hudson.

In the Hudson estuary, such layering—called stratification—occurs in partial fashion according to runoff conditions, geographic location, and tide cycles. During times of high freshwater flow, salinity at the bottom is, on average, about 20 percent greater than at the surface. In low flow periods, the average difference is reduced to about 10 percent.

However, these averages mask much variation. Through the Highlands salinity is fairly uniform from top to bottom because turbulence disrupts the smooth flow of the layers and mixes them together. The turbulence is caused by the river's twisting course through the mountains and bottom irregularities like reefs and deep holes. The Hudson's waters generally remain well-mixed into Haverstraw Bay. From the southern end of the Tappan Zee to New York Harbor the channel straightens out, promoting stratification. In this stretch of the river salinities at the bottom can be three or four times greater than those near the surface.

The cycle of spring and neap tides also plays a role in stratification. The swifter currents typical of spring tides disrupt the layers, mixing the fresh and salt water layers. The slower currents during neap tides allow stratification to occur.

Salinity and Productivity

In many estuaries, the layering of outgoing fresh water over intruding salt water contributes to high biological productivity. The richest estuaries rank among the most productive ecosystems on the planet, matching tropical rain forests and coral reefs. They are typically more productive than either the freshwater systems draining into them or the oceans beyond their mouths. Estuaries frequently generate or collect more nutrients and organic material than they can

The volume of freshwater runoff into the Hudson determines the salt front's location. Typically, runoff is greatest—and the front is farthest south—in spring. Freshwater flow is least—and the front is farthest north—during the drier summer months. Ocean water at the salt front is greatly diluted by fresh water; salinity increases as one moves toward the sea.

In many estuaries, fresh water flows seaward over denser salt water intruding inland. Though some layering can be observed in the Hudson from the Tappan Zee south, friction between the layers creates turbulence, which mixes them and moderates differences between salinities near the surface and in the depths. Such turbulence and mixing are intensified by the back and forth motion of tidal currents and by irregularities in the river's bed and course.

use, a surplus eventually exported to nearby coastal waters.

In some estuaries, stratification of fresh and salt water promotes high productivity through creation of a nutrient trap. The landward movement of seawater underneath fresh water tends to keep nutrients in an estuary, and they do not sink readily into the denser lower layer. In addition, friction between the layers creates turbulence that keeps nutrients suspended in well-lit surface waters. There algae and other tiny organisms can readily take advantage of these vital substances and grow in great abundance.

However, research suggests that this physical trapping phenomenon does not play an important role in promoting productivity in the Hudson estuary. Scientists have discovered that the most productive regions of the estuary are not located where stratification of salt water and fresh water is greatest.

Nonetheless, the Hudson estuary is clearly a productive ecosystem; the huge rafts of waterfowl floating on its surface and tremendous schools of striped bass that annually appear in its waters are eloquent evidence of this. The factors that do account for this wealth of life and the ways in which this biological productivity is defined and measured are the subject of the next chapter.

Chapter 2

Energy Flow and Nutrient Cycles in the Hudson

The Chapter in Brief

Ecologists often describe ecosystems in budgetary terms, tracking inputs, outputs, and available quantities of energy and nutrients. Solar energy, captured by green plants, is bound up in food molecules that travel through food webs made up of herbivores, carnivores, and detritivores. In the Hudson, much of the energy stored by plants enters food webs as detritus after the plants die. Energy is *not* recycled through food chains, but is ultimately converted into forms unusable by living creatures. Carbon, nitrogen and phosphorus are recycled. Most of the detritus, carbon, nitrogen, and phosphorus available to organisms in the Hudson estuary come from sources outside the estuary; human sewage is a major source of these substances. Growth of organisms can be controlled by scarcity of a single limiting factor, even if other vital substances are present in abundance.

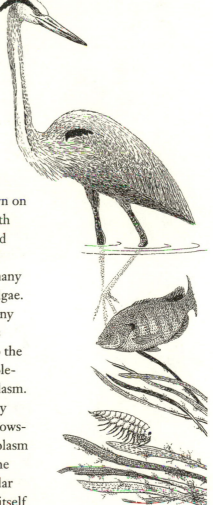

Ecological Budgets

Budgets and the bottom line often dominate headlines. How much money is coming in? From what sources? How much is going out? To where? What limits does lack of resources place on society?

Over the past few decades many scientists have adopted a budgetary perspective in looking at nature's structure and function. They use budgets to track and describe the flow of energy and vital nutrients in ecosystems, the functional units encompassing interacting living organisms and all aspects of the physical environment inhabited by these organisms. The study of relationships between living organisms and their environments constitutes the science of ecology.

In his classic *Fundamentals of Ecology*, Eugene Odum noted that the words "ecology" and "economics" have the same root—the Greek word *oikos*, meaning "house"—and he pointed out that "economics deals with financial housekeeping and ecology deals with environmental housekeeping." Perhaps the most basic item in a household budget is food, and the most important task of human housekeeping is keeping oneself or one's family fed. The flow of food is also key to ecological housekeeping—and a good place to start discussion of Hudson River ecology.

Food Chains: A Deli-style Approach

On a cloudless September morning the rising sun clears the hills along the Hudson's eastern shore and shines down on the shallows of the Green Flat just north of Saugerties. Its rays light a bed of wild celery, the plant's long, tape-like leaves gently undulating in the current. On many leaves are green, hair-like growths of algae. As sunlight enters each algal cell, the tiny plant's photosynthetic machinery starts humming, converting light energy into the chemical energy of sugar and other molecules which build and maintain protoplasm.

Nosing along one of the wild celery leaves is a half-inch-long amphipod, browsing on the algae, digesting plant protoplasm and converting it into animal tissue. The amphipod's algal food also fuels muscular activity, as when the creature launches itself off the leaf, swimming away from the bright sun and towards a thicker, more shadowy patch of vegetation.

A bluegill sunfish, alert and hungry, spots the amphipod spiraling downward and with a quick burst of speed intercepts it, gobbling it down whole. Still hungry, the sunfish slowly swims downcurrent to explore a couple of sticks reaching upward through the surface and out of its watery world.

With only the slightest motion of its head, the great blue heron zeroes in on the bluegill approaching its legs. Experienced, not over-eager, the bird waits patiently for the fish to come within range, spears it with a motion too quick for the eye to follow, pulls the bluegill out of the water, and swallows it. A quick shake of its head, a few steps towards a likely-looking patch of pondweed, and the heron resumes the alert wait familiar to anglers everywhere.

Producers and Consumers

The example above describes one of many food chains in the Hudson River ecosystem. The food chain concept allows us to understand important aspects of organisms' roles in ecosystems.

The various meals in this Hudson River food chain and in the vast majority of food chains in earthly ecosystems (including those that put food on our tables) are repackaged solar energy. Whether a diet includes amphipods, steak, algae, or tofu, the energy contained in those items came from sunlight.

Green plants like the algae in the example above have earned the label *primary producers,* since they can capture solar energy and convert it into chemical energy, stored in the compounds which make up living protoplasm. Animals and other organisms that cannot make food directly from light must meet their energy needs by consuming these compounds; thus in ecological jargon they are labeled *consumers.*

Amphipods and other plant-eaters, familiarly called *herbivores,* are primary consumers since they are able to use the chemical energy stored in plant tissue. That energy must be modified through incorporation into animal tissue before it can be used by predators like the bluegill sunfish and great blue heron. Such animals, commonly known as *carnivores,* are categorized as secondary and tertiary consumers according to how far removed they are from the primary producers.

Weaving Food Chains into Food Webs

While it is useful to draw connections between a producer, primary consumer, secondary consumer, and so on to illustrate a food chain, most organisms belong not to one but to many food chains. Bluegills eat (in addition to amphipods) insects, worms, and small fish. Sunfish, in turn, are menu items not just for great blue herons but also for kingfishers, bass, and other predators, whose diets include many kinds of fish, amphibians, and other small creatures. Draw lines connecting all these organisms and the result is a complicated web showing who eats whom—a food web.

Cloth woven of many threads is much stronger than a single strand of thread. So it is in ecosystems, where an interwoven web of food dependencies is more stable than a few independent food chains. If one element drops out of a food chain—perhaps a disease kills off bluegills—then the chain is cut with dire results for consumers higher up on the chain. If one organism disappears from a food web, those creatures that eat it may turn elsewhere for nourishment. Of course, while food webs are less fragile than linear food chains, removal of several

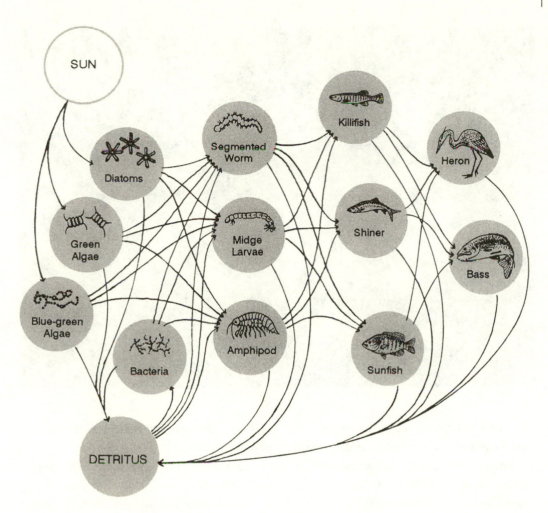

Complicated as it looks, even this food web linking Hudson River organisms is greatly simplified. Sunfish and shiners, for instance, eat a greater variety of creatures than can be shown here, and a host of other animals eat algae.

members can wreak havoc even with such interwoven networks.

Grazing Food Chains

In the food chain described above, the primary consumer is the amphipod eating living green plants, a situation characteristic of grazing food chains. Other examples would be muskrats chewing on cattails in the Tivoli North Bay, copepods eating algal cells drifting in the Tappan Zee, and white-tailed deer grazing on saltmeadow cordgrass in the Piermont Marsh.

One might well ask how another sort of food chain could exist. Aren't green plants and algae at the base of almost all food chains? The answer is yes; however, in some

ecosystems, including the Hudson estuary, their energy is not used by herbivores chewing on living plants but later, as plant tissues die and decompose.

Detrital Food Chains

Imagine a Hudson River cattail marsh at the end of the growing season. Winter is coming; the cattails are turning brown. Looking at this scene in terms of food, we might think "What a waste! Here's an abundant crop going uneaten, fated to be plowed under when winter's ice scours the marsh. Think of all the starving muskrats in China!"

Besides the fact that there are no muskrats in China, this view of uneaten food,

This decaying plant material in a Hudson River marsh is one example of detritus.

of limited value at a family dinner table, reflects an incomplete understanding of the workings of an estuarine ecosystem. While little of the living plant tissue here was grazed by herbivores during the growing season, there are hordes of organisms ready to feast on those brown cattail leaves as they bend, tatter, and break apart in the clutches of ice and wind. Green or brown, they are a source of food energy.

Dead and decaying organic material—plant parts, bodies of animals, undigested food excreted by living organisms—is called *detritus*. Like living tissue, this material contains energy ultimately derived from sunlight. Detritus becomes food for small invertebrate animals grouped under the label *detritivores* and for *decomposers*—the bacteria and fungi. As they feed they carry out the process of decomposition. From a human viewpoint, this process might seem to be chiefly a matter of cleaning up unsightly remains. Ecologically the process is important as a means of freeing up nutrients and

carbon in detritus and making them available for reuse in the ecosystem.

Detritivores are abundant in the Hudson—mussels, clams, small crabs, worms, and amphipods among them. But, you may ask, wasn't the amphipod acting as an herbivore in the food chain example earlier in this chapter? Yes; the feeding habits of some animals include plant and animal material, sometimes both dead and alive. Such animals are labeled *omnivores*.[1]

Larger detritivores break decaying material into smaller pieces and alter it in passage through their digestive systems so that it becomes more susceptible to bacterial and fungal breakdown. Detritus that supports large numbers of bacteria is preferred by many detritivores. They obtain additional nourishment from eating the bacteria with the decaying organic matter, just as peanut butter adds nutrition to the cracker on which it is spread.

While carrying out the process of decomposition, these small invertebrates and bacteria provide another pathway through which energy can move up a food chain; the invertebrates become food for predators like the sunfish. Ecologists distinguish food chains in which the links between producers and consumers include detritus as detrital food chains.

Food Chains: A Gourmet Approach

Food chains are sometimes simplistically described as cycles—endless circles in which matter incorporated into plant tissue passes through herbivores and carnivores, is decomposed, and is taken up by plants once more. In traveling through a food chain, molecules of organic matter—compounds that are composed largely of carbon and associated with living organisms—are rearranged and ultimately broken down, with their building blocks being recycled back into the system.

While true, such a description ignores the most important function of food chains: they are pathways by which chemical energy in organic molecules is distributed throughout ecosystems. This energy *cannot be recycled*; it is ultimately transformed into heat energy of no further use to organisms in an ecosystem.

Energy flow through food chains obeys the two laws of thermodynamics. The first law states that, though energy may change form, be transferred from one location to another, or be used to do work, it is neither created nor destroyed; none is lost or gained in any of these processes. The second law states that in any energy transfer or transformation, some of the energy assumes a form not useful in doing any more work.

Energy "Loss" at the Molecular Level

These laws affect food chains in several ways. Food chains do not create energy; they only transform solar energy into chemical energy, contained in the forces that bind molecules together, and route it through a succession of further transformations. Energy is not destroyed when food is eaten along this route; the molecules are altered in ways that release energy or transfer it to bonds in different chemicals. After each transformation the total amount of energy remains the same, but a certain portion has become low-grade heat energy no longer usable in the food chain.[2]

Since the total amount of energy transformed into heat increases with each step in the chain, the available amount of useful chemical energy dwindles as we get further away from the primary producers. Putting the food chain in budgetary terms, the top consumers get the smallest piece of the food energy pie.

Energy "Loss" at the Organism Level

The impacts of thermodynamics at the molecular level may seem abstract. It is easier to understand how energy is also lost to a food chain by the activities of the organisms in the chain, starting with green plants and algae. They must use much of the solar energy they capture to meet their own growth and maintenance needs. Only the remainder is available to food chains.

Think also of what happens to the energy contained in the amphipod meal eaten by the bluegill sunfish (and allow a little more time between that meal and the bluegill's demise at the feet of the heron). Some of the energy contained in the amphipod is in body parts that the fish cannot digest; this energy is lost through excretion of digestive wastes. Of the energy assimilated by the fish, much is used up in activity: swimming, opening its gill covers to breathe, and making chemicals that its body needs to function. What is left builds tissue; it is this small remainder that goes to the heron when it eats the sunfish.

Ecologists have estimated that in going from one level to the next higher one in a food chain, the amount of food energy available is reduced by a factor of ten. Thus in the algae-amphipod-sunfish-heron example above, only one-thousandth of the energy available from the algae would ultimately reach the heron.[3]

Productivity and the Hudson's Energy Budget

With such reductions occurring as energy flows through food chains, it helps to start off with a big budgetary pie—a large stock of chemical energy collected by the producers. This energy pie is called *primary production;* the rate at which energy is stored is called *primary productivity.* The magnitude of this productivity has a major role in determining the diversity and numbers of organisms that an ecosystem can support.

Within estuaries, the greatest portion of the primary production pie often comes from the smallest of the producers—tiny algae called phytoplankton that drift on the currents. This was once true in much of the Hudson, and still is in the saltier reaches of the estuary below Haverstraw Bay. But in the tidal freshwater Hudson, primary production by phytoplankton has greatly declined since 1992, when the population of the newly-arrived, non-native zebra mussel exploded. The mussels feed by filtering algae from the water, and their invasion drastically reduced phytoplankton populations there. Zebra mussels are absent from the saltier reaches of the Hudson.

Cutting Budgetary "Waste"

As mentioned in chapter 1, estuaries like the Hudson can be very productive environments, in part because they use net production (total capture of solar energy minus the amount of energy used by plants and algae to meet their own needs) very efficiently.

Detrital food chains are one means by which this is accomplished. In some ecosystems, detritus is lost to inaccessible "sinks"—buried deep in sediments, perhaps. The Hudson, though, is inhabited by numerous and diverse bottom-dwelling detritivores. Like skilled pinball players keeping that silver ball in play, these organisms keep the energy-rich organic molecules and nutrients of detritus circulating in the ecosystem and minimize the burial and loss of these valuable commodities deep in the river bottom.

Budgetary Subsidies

The contributions of detrital food chains to the Hudson's energy budget loom even larger when scientists look at the sources and quantities of organic, carbon-based molecules available to consumers in food webs here. The estuary receives a subsidy in the form of organic carbon washed into the Hudson from its watershed, and detritivores and decomposers are the agents through which that material becomes part of the food web.

This subsidy is considerable. In the tidal freshwater Hudson near Kingston, organic carbon compounds from the watershed constitute about 90 percent of the potential food resources available to bacteria, detritivores, and other consumers. Only 10 percent comes from primary production by the algae and green plants growing there.

The timing of that 10 percent contribution from estuarine plants may make it more significant than its size alone would indicate. This contribution comes during the warmer months of the growing season, when biological activity in the estuary reaches a peak and needs fuel. Populations

As energy moves through a food chain, the amount available to organisms at each successive level decreases. Ecologists show this graphically as a pyramid of energy, in which the greatest quantity of energy is found in the plants at the bottom, and only a small amount remains for predators at the top.

of invertebrates like the amphipod are exploding, and countless young fish hatched after spring spawning runs are growing and eating hungrily.

Much of the detritus from the watershed enters the river in spring runoff, when high flows tend to carry it out of the estuary rapidly, reducing its value to the system. Nonetheless, the organic carbon compounds in this detritus represent an enormous amount of food energy, giving detrital food chains a major role in the Hudson ecosystem. In the mid-Hudson, production by bacteria—the store of chemical energy stockpiled among countless numbers of these tiny cells as they consume detritus—is roughly twenty times greater than production by algae.

In the saltier lower part of the estuary, production by phytoplankton does constitute the largest part of the food budget. The bacteria upriver have reduced the watershed's subsidy of organic carbon compounds by roughly 50 percent, but given the dense population surrounding this section of the Hudson, there is an additional subsidy of note here—human sewage. In the early 1970s, the organic carbon available to food webs from sewers exceeded that produced by phytoplankton. By the 1990s, construction of treatment plants had cut this subsidy to roughly one quarter of its previous level.

Tidal currents indirectly provide another energy "subsidy." In a Hudson River marsh, for instance, the currents bring food into the system and carry wastes away. Many animals—mussels and barnacles, for instance—can live well staying in one spot, not using up any energy in movement. Thus a fairly high proportion of their energy intake goes into building tissue and subsequently becomes available to creatures—waterfowl, for example—further up the food chain.

The Bottom Line

So what is the bottom line? How much energy is available to the Hudson's food webs? This figure is difficult to pin down in such a large and dynamic system. The productivity of several plant communities—phytoplankton, submerged aquatic vegetation, and marshes—and amounts of organic material washed in from the watershed vary greatly by location and from year to year.

Measurements in the tidal freshwater Hudson since the zebra mussel invasion suggest that phytoplankton there produce about 10,000 tons of organic carbon annually. In the saltier reaches from Haverstraw Bay south, phytoplankton production is much greater, perhaps as much as 92,000 tons per year. Submerged vegetation, found mainly in the freshwater Hudson, is estimated to produce about 5,000 tons of carbon on an annual basis. Yearly

Primary production by phytoplankton is lower in the freshwater tidal Hudson and in New York Bay than in other nearby estuary systems. But primary production is only part of the picture. Detritus entering the river nourishes immense numbers of bacteria, which are a major source of energy for organisms farther up the food chain. The freshwater tidal Hudson ranks highest among these estuaries in bacterial production.

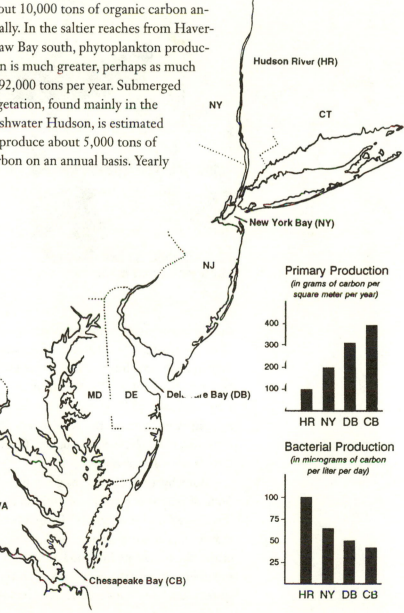

Hudson River (HR)

NY

CT

New York Bay (NY)

NJ

MD   DE   Delaware Bay (DB)

VA

Chesapeake Bay (CB)

Primary Production
(in grams of carbon per square meter per year)

400
300
200
100

HR NY DB CB

Bacterial Production
(in micrograms of carbon per liter per day)

100
75
50
25

HR NY DB CB

This pie chart shows the tidal Hudson's overall income budget—its sources of organic carbon. Keep in mind that contributions from each source vary from place to place. For example, phytoplankton production is low in the freshwater tidal river, high in the lower, saltier Hudson. *(Microphotograph by Dennis O'Leary/ Micro-Optical Methods.)*

THE HUDSON'S INCOME BUDGET
Sources of Organic Carbon

sewage - 7%

submerged aquatic plants - 2%

watershed and marshes - 41%

phytoplankton - 50%

subsidies from outside the mainstem include approximately 2,000 tons of organic carbon from tidal freshwater marshes each year into the river, 82,000 tons from the watershed, and 15,000 tons from sewage. Adding everything up, the Hudson estuary runs on a yearly budget of roughly 206,000 tons of organic carbon.[4]

But why are these figures given in units of weight of organic carbon? Isn't this discussion about energy? Remember that food chains distribute chemical energy—the forces binding food molecules together—among the organisms in an ecosystem. Carbon atoms are the basic build-

ing blocks bound together in these molecules. By measuring amounts of carbon, scientists size up the amount of energy available from these molecules and from the organic material of which they are the constituents.

The Carbon Cycle

Unlike energy, carbon atoms can be recycled through food chains. In describing this carbon cycle, the best place to jump in is the point where solar energy and atoms of carbon, along with other elements, are brought together through photosynthesis by algae and green plants.

During photosynthesis, carbon in the compound carbon dioxide (chemical formula CO_2) is chemically combined with hydrogen from water molecules (H_2O) to form the compound glucose ($C_6H_{12}O_6$). Molecular oxygen (O_2) is released during the process. The presence of light and chlorophyll—the chemical that makes green plants green—is required for photosynthesis to occur.

The carbon in glucose can move along two paths. Glucose is a form of sugar which can be quickly digested and broken down to provide energy. It is also a building block used in constructing more complex compounds, a process which involves linking together more carbon atoms.

Plants and animals make use of the energy in glucose through respiration, a process which is essentially the reverse of photosynthesis. Oxygen is used in breaking glucose apart, releasing energy, carbon dioxide, and water. Carbon dioxide released by respiration can be reused in photosynthesis, cycling carbon atoms back into the food chain and freeing oxygen to be used in respiration again.

Use of glucose and its carbon atoms in building more complex molecules can delay the cycling of carbon. This delay might be as long as the life of the sunfish in our food chain example, up to the point where the blue heron uses the energy in molecules of sunfish tissue, or where bacteria and other detritivores use the undigested remains of the fish to meet their metabolic needs. Respiration by the heron and detritivores ultimately will break down the complex molecules, releasing carbon dioxide for reuse in photosynthesis.

Nutrient Budgets and Cycles

While the element carbon is the most important building block of living tissue, other

$$6CO_2 + 6H_2O + \text{light energy} \xrightarrow[\text{of chlorophyll}]{\text{in the presence}} C_6H_{12}O_6 + 6O_2$$

$$C_6H_{12}O_6 + 6O_2 \dashrightarrow 6CO_2 + 6H_2O + \text{energy}$$

Photosynthesis and respiration cycle oxygen as well as carbon. Oxygen released by photosynthesis is used in respiration, producing carbon dioxide to be taken up during photosynthesis, which makes oxygen available again. This oxygen cycle is one of the most oft-cited examples of the interdependence of plants and animals.

elements are required in lesser amounts. The most significant of these nutrients are the elements nitrogen and phosphorus.[5] Their abundance or scarcity is often key to determining the productivity of a particular ecosystem. For example, nitrogen and phosphorus are the most important ingredients in fertilizers applied by homeowners trying to establish lush green lawns and by farmers eager to increase crop yields.

Nitrogen, Nitrogen Everywhere, But . . .

In trivia contests and science exams, people are often surprised to find out that the most abundant gas of the atmosphere—79 percent of it, in fact—is not oxygen or carbon dioxide but nitrogen. However, this form of nitrogen (N_2) cannot be used by most living things. To be useful biologically it must be *fixed:* combined with oxygen and hydrogen to form compounds such as ammonia (NH_4^+) and nitrate (NO_3^-) which are taken up by living organisms.

Fixation can occur in a variety of ways. In the atmosphere, nitrogen is combined with the hydrogen and oxygen of water using the energy of lightning and cosmic rays. The resulting ammonia and nitrate fall with rain into the Hudson, as does a much larger contribution of nitrates from air pollution.

Natural atmospheric fixation supplies very limited amounts of usable nitrogen to most ecosystems. A more important source is fixation by living organisms, especially bacteria that live on the roots of plants known as legumes, other bacteria living freely in the soil, and blue-green algae (actually a specialized group of bacteria, called *cyanobacteria*, which photosynthesize in much the same way as do green plants—

see chapter 3). Blue-green algae are common in the Hudson, but their contribution to the estuary's nitrogen budget, though not known for certain, is probably small.

Even more than is the case with the river's carbon budget, most of the usable nitrogen available to the Hudson ecosystem is not fixed in the river itself. Large amounts of nitrate enter the estuary in runoff from the watershed. However, the greatest inputs of nitrogen to the Hudson River come from human sources, especially wastewater from municipal sewage systems (chiefly in and around New York City and Albany), and deposition from atmospheric pollution caused by burning fossil fuels.

The Nitrogen Cycle

Once in the estuary, nitrogen is taken up by plants and cycled through the food chain. Like carbon, it is bound up in different molecules at each step, and either excreted in waste products or incorporated into

In the nitrogen cycle, here shown in simplified form and without accounting for human inputs, the main reservoir is gaseous nitrogen in the atmosphere (1). Some nitrogen is fixed by lightning and other atmospheric processes (2) to reach ecosystems in rainfall and runoff (3), but most is fixed by microorganisms: soil bacteria, bacteria associated with leguminous plants, and blue-green algae (4). Fixed nitrogen is taken up by plants and cycled over and over in food webs (5). Nitrogen in runoff (6) from terrestrial ecosystems is a major source of this nutrient in aquatic systems. Fixed nitrogen may be transformed back into a gas by bacteria (7) or buried deep in sediments (8).

tissue that is ultimately broken down by decomposers. In both cases the nitrogen is then available for reuse in the ecosystem.[6]

The greatest amounts of biologically useful nitrogen enter the Hudson with spring runoff. Since this is also the beginning of the growing season, the nutrient is in high demand by plants, which bind up a large amount of nitrogen until fall, when their tissues die and decomposers release the nutrient.

Fixed nitrogen exits the Hudson ecosystem in several ways. Much of the excess supply is exported into the New York Bight, an area of the Atlantic Ocean between Long Island and New Jersey and reaching seaward to the edge of the continental shelf some 80 to 120 miles offshore. And while the abundant detritivores of the Hudson's bottom keep much of the nitrogen in play in the food chain, this nutrient can be incorporated into decay-resistant tissue and buried deep in sediments out of the

reach of the decomposers. Finally, some fixed nitrogen is bacterially altered back to the molecular form (N_2) which enters the atmosphere.

The Phosphorus Cycle

Phosphorus is often the critical nutrient controlling productivity in freshwater aquatic ecosystems, simply because it is less abundant and available than nitrogen and carbon. Unlike those elements, phosphorus does not circulate in the atmosphere as a gas. Thus the sources from which an ecosystem can obtain phosphorus (when humans are not present) are limited: erosion, weathering, and leaching of rock containing phosphate; and reuse of phosphate already present in organic matter.

In the Hudson, organic detritus is an important natural source of phosphorus, just as it is for carbon and nitrogen. And like these other nutrients, phosphorus is released by the decomposers, quickly taken

Phosphorus is not found in a gaseous form; it weathers from rock, reaching ecosystems in runoff (1) or leaching into soil (2) to be taken up by plants and cycled and recycled through food webs (3). Runoff from ecosystems on land (4) is the most important source of phosphorus in aquatic systems. Eventually it is lost deep in sediments (5), which eons later may be solidified into rock and lifted above water, exposing the nutrient to weathering once more.

Human activities have increased the amounts of biologically useful nutrients entering the environment, degrading the health of ecosystems by providing too much of a good thing.

Used too freely, fertilizers containing phosphorus and nitrogen may increase crop yields or make grass more lush at the expense of nearby waterways that receive runoff from farms and lawns.

High-temperature combustion — in automobile engines and power plants, for example — fixes nitrogen, which eventually falls from the atmosphere into terrestrial and aquatic ecosystems.

Dense urban populations may discharge large volumes of sewage into aquatic systems, over-enriching them with nitrogen, phosphorus, and organic carbon.
(Courtesy New York City Department of Environmental Protection/Marion Bernstein.)

up by plants, and moved through the food chain until it becomes part of detritus again and is released once more by the detritivores. Like nitrogen, phosphorus is taken up by plants at the start of growing season and released with dieback in the fall. The Hudson ecosystem loses phosphorus to sediments and to the Atlantic.

Research suggests that phosphorous may be in short enough supply to limit the growth of algae in the Hudson north of Poughkeepsie, particularly in late summer and fall. In other sections of the estuary, however, phosphorous is in ample supply due to contributions from the region's human population.

Human Subsidies to the Hudson's Nutrient Budgets

Millions of people live in the Hudson Valley, people at the top of food chains which bring in vast quantities of foodstuffs from around the world. Their digestive wastes— sewage discharged into the river—are major contributors of nitrogen, phosphorus, and organic carbon to the Hudson estuary, particularly in the densely populated metropolitan area of New York City. Additional nutrient contributions that people make to the river include runoff from fertilized fields and lawns, laundry water containing phosphate detergents, and nitrate, originally emitted in automobile exhaust, that enters the river from the atmosphere.

It is logical to think that such subsidies benefit the Hudson ecosystem; after all, these nutrients are vital to the growth of plants and animals. But more is not always better. The increased productivity made possible by greater supplies of nitrogen and phosphorus may enrich aquatic systems through a process called eutrophication. The process is often characterized by blooms—rapid expansions of algae and other plant populations. However, when these large masses of algae ultimately die off, their decomposition can deplete a waterway's oxygen supplies, killing much of the life in the water. Recent episodes of serious oxygen depletion in the New York Bight and in western Long Island Sound are thought to be linked to such overenrichment.

Sewage has historically caused severe oxygen depletion in parts of the Hudson, though not, except in localized instances, because of algal blooms due to its nitrogen and phosphorus content. Instead, sewage discharges have directly nourished populations of bacteria, elevating them to the point where their activities have reduced dissolved oxygen levels (see chapter 12).

Limiting Factors

Plants and animals depend on many nutrients for growth and health. Of these many nutrients, the one in lowest supply relative to the needs of a given organism or group of organisms in an ecosystem is a *limiting factor*. No matter how abundant the other nutrients may be, populations of the given organism will not be able to grow beyond the levels allowed by the limiting factor.

Nutrients are not the only examples of limiting factors. The Hudson's turbid-ity limits the penetration of sunlight into the water, which in turn limits populations of algae (and primary productivity). The river's turbulence may also play a role here, swirling algae to depths where there is not enough light for photosynthesis and thus limiting their growth. Scientists estimate that the average algal cell in long narrow reaches of the tidal freshwater Hudson may spend from eighteen to twenty-two hours of each twenty-four hour day in light too dim to support photosynthesis.

In the more saline estuary below the Tappan Zee, nutrient levels are high enough that the Hudson could be considered to be hypereutrophic, raising the question of why more algal blooms are not observed here. In addition to light limitations imposed by turbidity, a rapid flushing rate may be a factor. Compared to other estuaries, water moves very quickly through this reach of the Hudson to the sea, carrying phytoplankton out of the system before blooms can occur.

Other examples of limiting factors include current velocity, the type of material found on the river bottom, and the presence of predators. The next chapter will discuss habitats and the limiting factors characteristic of different habitats.

Chapter 3

The Hudson's Habitats and Plant Communities

The Chapter in Brief

Habitats created by erosion, deposition, and other forces support distinct communities of plants and animals according to the mix of physical and chemical factors present, including depth, light penetration, extent of tidal flooding, salinity, and exposure to waves and ice. The effects of these factors are often modified by the living organisms of the community occupying each habitat. In open water, phytoplankton drift near the surface where light is sufficient for their growth. Wetlands covered by shallow water or intermittently flooded by tides contain stands of submerged vegetation, marshes, and tidal swamps. The types of plants dominating each of these communities are distinctive, identifying the community and determining its contribution to the Hudson's overall productivity.

What is a Habitat?

To a commuter idled in traffic on the Mid-Hudson Bridge, the river might seem featureless, save for a few boats or buoys. A picnicker at Tallman Mountain State Park, looking out over the Piermont Marsh between bites of potato salad, might see only an undistinguished expanse of "grass." But in both cases closer study reveals a variety of habitats created by the chiseling of erosion, the soft sculpting of sediment deposition, and the energies of living organisms, all working on the material supplied by the region's geological development.

A habitat is the environmental setting which supports an individual organism or a community of organisms—a group of populations living in a particular area and interacting with one another. The habitat of an individual organism includes other organisms found in the environment as well as nonliving elements.

To many, the obvious differences between the river's habitat types are structural—features such as landforms, substrate (the type of material on the bottom), and water depth. Other factors may be less apparent but equally important in determining which, if any, plant communities develop in a given site. For example, at first glance the Piermont Marsh might look much like the Tivoli North Bay marsh. However, the Piermont site is flooded by brackish water; the Tivoli marsh by fresh water. As a result, the marsh communities at these sites have a different mix of plant species, and since the diversity of rooted plants increases as salinity decreases in estuaries, the Tivoli North Bay marsh also has a greater diversity of such plants than Piermont.

The plant communities that develop in each habitat often mediate its functions within the Hudson River ecosystem. These might include contributing energy to the river's food web, cycling nutrients, buffering the impacts of stressful forces, and providing shelter or other necessities for animal life.

The Channel

The term "channel" describes the deep, open water portion of the river. Its extent and depth vary greatly along the tidal Hudson. Near Poughkeepsie the Hudson is a channel virtually from bank to bank; narrow shoals tucked along each shore quickly drop off to depths of 50 to 60 feet. On the other hand, much of Haverstraw Bay, the river's widest spot, is less than 20 feet deep, and its deepest regions are naturally only 25 to 30 feet deep. A channel 32 feet deep, 600 hundred feet wide, and over 2.5 miles long is dredged through the bay to allow passage of large ships and barges.

The channel generally experiences the full force of tidal currents in the Hudson. Otherwise, its depth and large volume of water moderate the extreme conditions—summer heat, winter ice scour, and wave action, for example—that assail the shallows. Some fishes take refuge in this habitat when such extreme conditions exist.

The channel's depths are not the Hudson's most biologically productive habitat. A key factor here is light penetration, or rather, lack of it due to the Hudson's turbidity. The euphotic zone—the depth of water to which there is enough light for plants to grow—is quite shallow, generally 5 to 10 feet but ranging from 2 feet in late winter to 13 in fall.[1] The point where the bottom rises into the euphotic zone marks the shoreward limit of the channel habitat. With insufficient light for plant growth below this point, primary productivity in the channel's depths is low.

Life at the Very Bottom: The Benthic Community of the Channel

Though plants cannot grow at the channel's bottom, a diverse community of animals known as *benthos* (bottom-dwellers) lives just above, on, and in the bottom sediments. With green plants absent, herbivores are lacking here but there are bacteria and many detritivores feeding on particles of detritus drifting in the water or deposited on and in bottom sediments. They capture the carbon and energy available in that material for the estuary's food webs. Clams and worms are examples of such organisms, which in turn feed carnivores including fish and crabs. The animals of the channel's benthic community are described in chapters 4 and 5.

Life Adrift: The Planktonic Community

In thinking of the Hudson's plant communities, one pictures leaves, stems, and branches waving in the currents or reaching skyward through the water's surface. But out in the open water, drifting in the euphotic zone near the surface, is another community—an aquatic "pasture" of countless microscopic plants capturing the sun's

The Hudson's channel is often not in the middle of the river. This ship, bound for Rensselaer with a cargo of gypsum, is hugging the west side of the river as it approaches the Rip Van Winkle Bridge. The map shows why: the channel runs along that shore to avoid shoals in the middle and along the river's east bank. *(Map from National Ocean Survey Chart 12347.)*

energy, using that energy to live and grow, and providing food in turn for zillions of tiny animals that graze here. This is the plankton community of the Hudson—plants and animals that, being weak swimmers or unable to move on their own, drift at the mercy of the currents. Animals of this community are called *zooplankton*; they are described in chapter 4. The algae and other tiny photosynthetic organisms are called *phytoplankton*.

As pointed out in the previous chapter, phytoplankton supply significant amounts of carbon to the Hudson, but their contributions depend on location, climate, and other factors. In the freshwater tidal river, zebra mussels have reduced phytoplankton numbers by 80 percent, and their production by 75 percent. In the saltier lower estuary, phytoplankton production in the 1990s was far greater than in the 1970s. The earlier decade was unusually wet, promoting high flows that washed plankton out of the river.

These tiny plants obviously make up in numbers and rapid growth what they lack in size. Though present throughout the year, their numbers and productivity peak in summer and are lowest in winter. Approximately 90 percent of their annual primary production occurs from May through October, the result of more daylight, warmer temperatures, and minimal flow through the estuary at that time. Populations tend to be highest in bays, shallows, and other areas where downstream flushing action is minimal.

The most abundant organisms in the Hudson's phytoplankton community are microscopic, single-celled algae that drift as solitary cells or in colonies with more or less distinctive patterns of growth. Most often they reproduce asexually by simply splitting into two cells. Cells may undergo this fission process several times a day, al-

lowing phytoplankton populations to build rapidly given the right conditions.

The plants we lump together as algae are genetically an extremely diverse group; indeed, most of the genetic diversity in the entire plant kingdom is within this group. For example, the genetic differences between diatoms and green algae (described below) are far greater than those between grasses and trees or pumpkins and corn. And the group commonly labeled blue-green algae are actually photosynthetic bacteria quite different from other plants; they are more properly called cyanobacteria. So although we talk about algae as a group, keep in mind that the blue-greens are about as different from the diatoms as intestinal bacteria are from oak trees.

Botanists classify the major groups of plants into a series of divisions, which are equivalent to phyla in the classification of animals. The algae most common in the Hudson, green algae and diatoms (sometimes called yellow algae), belong to separate divisions—Chlorophyta and Bacillariophyta, respectively. Though the major groups of algae are sometimes designated by color—yellow, green, red, etc.—members of each group vary widely in their actual hue.

Diatoms. Of the algae found in the Hudson's phytoplankton community, diatoms appear with the greatest regularity. Diatoms characteristically have a cell wall made of silica. This wall is formed into two pieces which fit together like the two halves of a pillbox.

Diatom populations peak in early summer and fall, though they are exceeded in abundance then by blooms of green and blue-green algae. Though overall numbers are less in the colder months, diatoms dominate the phytoplankton community during that period.

Representative Genera of Diatoms

Melosira cells, long and cylindrical, sometimes join end-to-end to form tubelike chains. Often there is a constriction in each cell where the two halves of the cell wall overlap. Frequently the half above the constriction is intricately ornamented, whereas the lower half is not. Many marine and freshwater *Melosira* inhabit the estuary, different varieties becoming prominent as the year progresses.

Asterionella species form starlike colonies in which a number of elongated individual cells are joined together at one end by a gelatinous mass. Freshwater and saltwater species are present.

Cyclotella cells commonly appear as solitary small disks decorated with radial grooves near their edges. Most *Cyclotella* are marine, but representative species are found throughout the estuary, some appearing one after the other in distinct progression during the growing season.

Representative Genera of Green Algae

Pediastrum is colonial, with anywhere from 2 to 128 individual cells often arranged in a circular geometric pattern. Several species occur in the river, some dominant in the phytoplankton community near Poughkeepsie during summer.

Scenedesmus species are also colonial, cells arranged side by side in multiples of 2: 4, 8, and sometimes 16 or 32. The genus is widespread in fresh water; some two dozen species have been found in the Hudson.

Ankistrodesmus, needle-shaped and usually somewhat curved, appears as solitary cells or in loosely formed masses without any particular growth pattern. This group is most common in summer and north of the Tappan Zee Bridge.

Green Algae. Green algae are characterized by an abundance of the green pigment chlorophyll localized in cell parts called *chloroplasts*. Their cells also have distinct nuclei, as do diatoms. Green and blue-green algae dominate the Hudson's phytoplankton community in summer. Though most common in fresh water, there are some saltwater species of green algae.

Cyanobacteria (Blue-green Algae). Like the rest of the bacteria (more formally called procaryotes), cyanobacteria lack most true cell organelles such as nucleii or chloroplasts. However, the photosynthetic machinery of these special bacteria is very much like that in algae and the rest of the plant world. Their chlorophyll pigments are generally localized near the cell wall.

Blue-greens (Cyanophyta) are very numerous in the Hudson, both as phytoplankton and on mud, pilings, and other surfaces. Most species grow in filamentous colonies—that is, the colonies form long strands.

Dinoflagellates. While included here as members of the phytoplankton community, dinoflagellates (division Pyrrophyta) actually show characteristics of both plants and animals. These one-celled organisms possess two whiplike flagella which give them mobility. Many species have chlorophyll and carry on photosynthesis. Others are predators that feed on other dinoflagellates. A number can provide for their nutrition in either fashion.

Some dinoflagellates produce poisons toxic to many marine organisms and to humans. Blooms of such dinoflagellates are often the cause of the notorious red tides, during which people must avoid eating shellfish or other organisms which may

Representative Genera of Cyanobacteria (Blue-green Algae)

Anacystis species occur in fresh and brackish reaches of the river. They form amorphous, free-floating colonies in which spherical cells are embedded in a gelatinous substance.

Anabaena is filamentous, growing in solitary strands or in colonial masses. It is common in fresh and brackish portions of the Hudson estuary.

Representative Genera of Dinoflagellates

Ceratium might remind you of a science-fiction spaceship. The plates of its cell wall form two or three horns of different lengths sticking out in one direction and a single horn projecting in the opposite one. Most *Ceratium* species are saltwater organisms; one freshwater form is found in the Hudson.

Prorocentrum lives in saltier portions of the estuary. A spine projecting from one end of the cell identifies the forward end of this organism.

have accumulated the toxins. These blooms seem to depend on the presence of particular nutrients, and some scientists believe that contributions of nutrients from sewage and other human sources are increasing the frequency of red tides and other problematic algal blooms along our coasts.

Reefs

No coral lives in the Hudson; the term reef applies to rock outcrops in the riverbed. Reefs are limited in extent here, and their rocky substrate is inhospitable to rooted plants, so their contributions to the river's overall energy budget are minimal. Anglers favor them, since fish will seek shelter around them. The Hudson's reefs are perhaps best known as sites of shipping accidents involving oil spills; an infamous example is Diamond Reef, an underwater tower of rock reaching from 60-foot depths to within 5 feet of the surface midriver near New Hamburg.

Flats and Bays

Tidal flats are expanses of mud or sand in the river's shallows. Portions of these areas may be regularly exposed by falling tides, but the term also includes shoals that remain submerged even at low tide. Along shore, flats can occur as narrow belts or broader expanses like the Esopus Meadows, extending over half a mile into the river. North of Kingston, flats are sometimes found midriver, requiring mariners to pay heed to buoys marking the navigational channel.

Open river flats can be difficult habitats for rooted plants to colonize, being buffeted by the full force of storm waves, boat wakes, and ice scour. These forces stress and uproot plants; thus one may see only bare mud on portions of such flats exposed at low tide. Plant communities most often found here are submerged rooted plants,

epibenthic algae, and occasionally low marsh vegetation.

Flats are often broadest near points or breakwaters that jut out into the channel. The water shoreward of the tips of such features moves more slowly than water in the channel. As water slows, its ability to carry sediment decreases; particles settle out on the bottom. This effect is most marked in coves or small bays located

This reef extends northward from Esopus Island off Hyde Park. At low tide it is a favorite perch for gulls, cormorants, and other birds.
(Map from National Ocean Survey Chart 12347.)

In Croton Bay, nestled inside the long peninsula of Croton Point, the river's tidal currents are slowed, allowing sediment to accumulate. Portions of the bay's flats are exposed by very low tides. *(Map from National Ocean Survey Chart 12343.)*

Environmental Conservation Law, for example, defines freshwater wetlands as "lands and waters of the state which contain any or all of the following: (a) lands and submerged lands commonly called marshes, swamps, sloughs, bogs, and flats supporting aquatic or semi-aquatic vegetation" and goes on to specify plant species fitting into those categories. Separate regulations governing tidal wetlands use a similar definition.

In wetlands, different plant communities and species grow in response to the frequency and degree of flooding by water. It may seem too obvious to point out that flooding depends on the height of the substrate above or below the water's surface, but it is important to realize that seemingly minor differences in elevation can make a big difference in the mix of plants growing in a given area.

between two adjacent headlands. The more sheltered conditions here often allow marsh and swamp plant communities to become established.

Sediment deposition in many coves along the Hudson has accelerated since they were cut off from the main river by railroad causeways constructed in the mid-1800s. This is only one of many impacts humans have had on these habitats. Such impacts, further discussed in chapter 11, are of particular concern because shallow-water habitats are among the most productive in the Hudson ecosystem.

Wetland Communities

The term "wetlands" broadly refers to shallow-water habitats and plant communities that develop there. New York State's

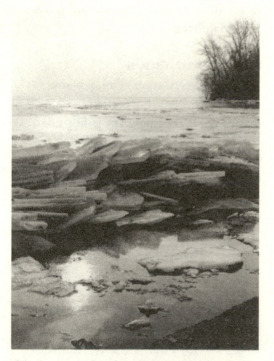

While the extent of ice formation on the Hudson varies with the severity of its winters, in most years there is ice north of the Highlands. Carried back and forth by tidal currents, ice floes scour river flats like these at Esopus Meadows.

Upland
Irregularly Flooded
Upper Intertidal
Lower Intertidal
Subtidal

storm & high spring tides
mean high tide
mean tide level
mean low tide

The Hudson's water level fluctuates with the tides. Their daily and monthly rhythms—and to a much lesser extent the effects of flooding due to heavy precipitation—set growth conditions for wetland plants. Descriptions of where given wetland plants are found often refer to zones of tidal flooding as follows:[2]

Subtidal—below low tide level; submerged
Intertidal—between average low and high tide levels; this zone will be alternately submerged and exposed to air over the course of a day; often subdivided into lower and upper zones, the dividing line being the *mean tide level* (the average of high and low water height)
Irregularly flooded—above average high tide level, this area is flooded occasionally by spring high tides and storm-driven tides;
Upland—area beyond the reach of all but the highest storm-related tides.

Wetland plant communities may develop in all of these zones. However, in the Hudson rooted vegetation is scarce at depths greater than 10 feet. The upland limit is land beyond the reach of the highest tides and floods, where plants adapted to drier soils will dominate.

Over time, many wetlands can evolve into dry land through a process known as ecological succession. Succession is often described as an orderly change in species composition and community type over time. In wetlands, stands of rooted aquatic plants slow currents, allowing sediment and organic material to be deposited, and building the substrate to a higher and drier level. Their own detritus also contributes to this process, setting the stage for their demise as other plant species adapted for drier conditions move in.

However, ecologists have become somewhat uncomfortable with a broadly applied view of succession as an orderly and quite predictable process. In many communities there are a variety of factors—severe disturbances such as fire and storms, for example—that alter, retard, or interrupt the process so regularly that the notion of orderly change has little basis in reality. In the case of the Hudson, no one has demonstrated that—in the absence of human intervention—tidal wetland communities develop into dry land as predicted in the usual descriptions of wetland succession.

Algal Communities
Many of the algae found in the phytoplankton community can also be found growing in shallow-water benthic communities

within the euphotic zone. Algal colonies become visible when they attach to and build up on substrates in the water. The dark greenish band sometimes seen on mud-banks in the intertidal zone is composed of epibenthic algae—those that grow on the river bottom. The hairy green growth covering the stems and leaves of underwater plants is also formed by algae; this habit of growth is described as *epiphytic*.[3]

Blue-green algae are particularly prominent on mud flats in the intertidal zone. Many blue-greens are very hardy, able to endure extremes of temperature and wetting or drying. This hardiness gives them a real advantage in colonizing this habitat with its changeable conditions.

Attached algal communities, especially in the Hudson, have not received as much study as rooted plant communities. Generalizations about such communities here are thus a little risky. Scientists doing research in estuaries in Georgia estimated that "mud algae" accounted for as much as a third of annual primary production there, making up for what they lack in size by their ability to carry on photosynthesis even in the colder months when rooted plants have died back. But that figure might well be lower in the Hudson estuary, where winters are more severe. Other studies of algae in the soil of tidal marshes suggest that the algal communities reach peak diversity and densities just before and after the growing season for rooted vegetation, which probably shades algae out. Epiphytic algae, on the other hand, reach maximum densities during the growing season when they are abundant on the leaves and stems of submerged vegetation.

Submerged Aquatic Vegetation

These rooted plants grow completely submerged in the subtidal zone. Rather than

Wild celery, native to the Hudson, is the most abundant species of submerged aquatic vegetation in the fresh-water tidal river.
(Courtesy of the Hudson River National Estuarine Research Reserve.)

being tough and woody to reach for sunlight, their leaves and stems are limp and sometimes buoyant, supported by the water and able to float upward towards the surface and light. Most of these plants are freshwater species; the two most abundant—wild celery and water chestnut—cover nearly 25 percent of the river bottom from Kingston to Catskill.

Per unit of area, the productivity of submerged aquatic vegetation is not as high as that of emergent marsh plants such as cattails, but dense and extensive stands contribute substantially to the river's energy budget. Wild celery beds also increase dissolved oxygen levels significantly through

Water chestnut, a non-native species from Eurasia, often chokes freshwater shallows, blocking boat access and shading out submerged aquatic plants below its floating leaves.

Representative Species of Submerged Aquatic Plant Communities

Wild celery (*Vallisneria americana*) has long (to 3 feet, but usually less) ribbonlike leaves that grow in tufts, often closely spaced in dense stands. Though considered a freshwater plant, wild celery is found downriver to the brackish Tappan Zee. This plant is a favorite waterfowl food.

Water chestnut (*Trapa natans*), not the esteemed vegetable of Chinese cuisine, is an exotic species first introduced as an ornamental plant. Its rosettes of floating leaves often crowd together in mats, sometimes miles long, on flats where wave action and currents are minimal. Its seed is the sharp-spined, nutlike "devil's head" found in vast numbers on the river's banks.

Eurasian water milfoil (*Myriophyllum spicatum*), another nonnative species, is considered a pest like water chestnut. Often growing in dense stands in fresh water, it replaces native plants that are more important as food for waterfowl. Milfoil's bushy stems and feathery leaves are habitat for great numbers of invertebrates and young fish.

Pondweeds commonly grow mixed in with a variety of other plants rather than in single-species stands. Some rank highly as waterfowl food. Pondweeds come in many forms; those shown in the next three illustrations, selected from kinds widely distributed both in fresh and brackish water, illustrate this variability.

Curlyleaf pondweed (*Potamogeton crispus*), a species introduced from Europe, has few stems and its leaves have a curly, wavy margin.

Clasping pondweed (*Potamogeton perfoliatus*) has oval leaves, the bases of which clasp around the plant's stem.

Horned pondweed (*Zannichellia palustris*) has linear, threadlike leaves.

photosynthesis. Underwater vegetation is an important habitat for many invertebrates—insect larvae, crustaceans, and snails among them—and for young fish seeking both invertebrate cuisine and shelter from larger fish also looking for meals. The leaves, stems, and underground parts of many submerged aquatic plants are prime foods for waterfowl.

This community has been greatly altered by nonnative species. Most notorious is the water chestnut, brought to North America by botanists, one of whom wrote: "But that so fine a plant as this, with its handsome leafy rosettes, and edible nuts, which would, if common, be as attractive to boys as hickory nuts now are, can ever become a 'nuisance,' I can scarcely believe."[4]

In large water chestnut beds, dissolved oxygen concentrations can drop to very low levels, since oxygen from photosynthesis in the floating leaves diffuses into the air. While a few animals do eat the newcomer—the water lily leaf beetle eats the leaves and chipmunks gnaw open the seed pods—they cannot keep it in check. Human attempts to control water chestnut have included herbicide application and removal by mechanical means. The former is ecologically problematic, the latter expensive. Small areas such as boat landings can be cleared by hand. Besides, water chestnut beds do have positive attributes, among them an abundance of invertebrates that can exceed the number found in wild celery beds.

While extensive mats of water chestnut catch the eye, submerged beds of the native wild celery cover more area. Aerial surveys in the mid 1990s found 4,453 acres of wild celery compared to 1,421 acres of water chestnut. These acreages vary from year to year, but the native consistently occupies more territory than the alien. Wild celery beds have probably increased in density and extent since the zebra mussel invasion; the mussels filter out phytoplankton, improving water clarity and increasing light penetration. Even so, at the peak of its growing season, the biomass of the Hudson's water chestnut plants equals that of wild celery.

Marshes and Swamps

Growing in the intertidal zones of the Hudson's more sheltered flats and bays are *emergent* plants—those that push their leaves and stems above the water's surface. Where trees and other woody plants dominate, the wetland community is called a *swamp*; where cattail, reeds, and other *herbaceous* (nonwoody) plants dominate, the community is a *marsh*.

Marshes are probably the most productive wetland communities (per unit area) in the Hudson. They are fertilized by tidal

currents, which bring in nutrients needed during the growing season. The nutrients are taken up in plant tissues during spring and summer. While some are retained in underground parts of these plants, a large percentage of these stored nutrients is released back into the river during fall and winter as leaves, stems, and other above-ground tissues die back.

Low marsh. Low marsh occupies the lower intertidal zone, where plants must endure extremes from complete submersion to baking in the hot sun.[5] In winter, this zone is scoured by ice; in warmer months, carp and snapping turtles do a fair amount of digging into the bottom in some locales. Few plants are adapted for this regime, so species diversity in this community is lower than in adjacent shallows or higher marsh. The plants that colonize this area most successfully are freshwater species; in saltier reaches the lower intertidal zone is largely devoid of rooted vegetation, excepting a few stands of saltwater cordgrass.

The above-ground parts of most of these plants die back and decay rapidly in fall, and may be a major source of

Spatterdock is the dominant plant in this area of low marsh at Kingston Point. The photograph was taken at low tide; at high tide, these plants will be completely submerged.

Representative Plants of Low Marsh Communities

Spatterdock (*Nuphar lu-
teum*) forms extensive
stands low in the intertidal
zone in fresh water. It has
large, heart-shaped leaves
up to 3 feet long by late
summer and sports a single
yellow flower on a long
stalk. Spatterdock offers
cover but is not grazed much
by larger marsh animals; the
seeds are eaten by various
creatures. It supports invertebrates eaten by fish, birds,
and other animals.

Pickerelweed (*Pontederia
cordata*) leaves are similar
to spatterdock's but smaller
and more elongated. Like
spatterdock, the plant
forms dense stands, but
usually higher in the
lower intertidal zone. In
summer a spike of small,
closely packed violet blue
flowers crowns the plant.
Its rhizomes are eaten by
muskrats, the seeds by
ducks and other birds.
This freshwater plant also
grows in downriver sites
where tributaries lower
the salinity.

Arrow-arum (*Peltandra
virginica*) has arrow-shaped
leaves with a pattern
of veins unlike that of
pickerelweed, with which
it often grows. The fruiting
structure, commonly found
floating in the Hudson, is
an oval ball full of green
berries with clear, jelly-
like coatings. Ducks eat
the berries and shoots of
arrow-arum. Also found in
the upper intertidal zone,
this plant is very sensitive
to wave action, even that
produced by small boats.

Common three-square (*Scir-
pus pungens*) is most common in the northern reaches
of the tidal Hudson, where
flats are more likely to
have the sandy substrates
it prefers. This plant, grass-
like in appearance and up
to 4 feet tall, is one of
many sedges found along
the river. Sedges are distinguished from grasses by
their stems, which are triangular in cross section.

Wild rice (*Zizania aquatica*)
grows to 10 feet or more
in fresh and slightly brackish water, most commonly
near the mean tide level
and with a more diverse
mix of plants than occurs
lower in the marsh. Though
this grass can form dense
stands, its abundance has
varied along the Hudson
over the past few decades.
Wild rice is an excellent
wildlife food. There have
been efforts in the past
to raise wild rice commercially here, notably in
the Constitution Island
Marsh.

nutrients to the estuary at that time. By
winter the flats on which they grow appear bare.

High marsh. High marsh is found in the intertidal zone above the mean tide level.
This is the community many people vi-

sualize when they hear the word marsh; a
wetland dominated by reed and grass-like
plants, perhaps suggesting a rankly growing corn or wheat field. The comparison
is an apt one, for this wetland community rivals the productivity of intensively
cultivated field crops. While muskrats,

Representative Plants of High Marsh Communities

Saltmeadow cordgrass (*Spartina patens*), also called salt hay grass, was once a common livestock food. The species is usually found above the mean high tide level, where it may be flooded only a few times a month. Up to 3 feet tall, it often grows in distinctive, matted whorls resembling cowlicks. This *Spartina* requires salty water and forms small salt meadows in the Piermont Marsh.

Saltwater cordgrass (*Spartina alterniflora*) tolerates fresh water better than *Spartina patens*; it is common at Piermont and present at Croton Marsh. This species, up to 5 feet tall, also occurs lower in marshes than saltmeadow cordgrass, to mean tide level and sometimes lower in the intertidal zone. Growing along tidal channels and marsh edges facing the open Hudson, it provides food and habitat for birds, fish, and crustaceans.

Swamp rose-mallow (*Hibiscus moscheutos*), up to 6 feet tall, is not a dominant high marsh plant but has found a niche among the more abundant grasses and grasslike species. In summer the rose-mallow has showy pinkish or white flowers 4–6 inches across. Though found in freshwater marshes elsewhere, along the Hudson it is most common in brackish marshes from the Highlands south.

Purple loosestrife (*Lythrum salicaria*) is a Eurasian immigrant that competes with native species in disturbed wetlands. Eaten by deer and insects, loosestrife has a bushy form which provides songbird nesting sites. In midsummer, spikes of pinkish-purple flowers crown the 5–7-foot-tall plant. Dense stands of loosestrife are most common high in the upper intertidal zone of freshwater marshes and around the landward edges of brackish marshes.

Narrow-leaved cattail (*Typha angustifolia*) is a dominant plant in marshes as far south as Piermont. Cattail rhizomes are a prime muskrat food, and many birds and animals find shelter and nest sites in dense cattail stands. Average height is about 6 feet.

Common reed (*Phragmites australis*) is also known by its generic name *Phragmites*. Its stalks, up to 14 feet tall, are tipped with a feathery flower cluster, purplish in late summer, fading to silvery tan later. *Phragmites* populations are increasing along the estuary, often at the expense of cattail. The reed quickly colonizes areas of exposed soil high in the intertidal zone, and has capitalized on human disturbances of wetlands.

This photograph of the Tivoli North Bay marsh, taken at low tide, shows the cattail-dominated high marsh community thinning out in the lower intertidal zone along the channel, which must endure longer periods of flooding.

geese, insects and other creatures may significantly graze high marsh plants locally or periodically, most of this productivity enters the Hudson's energy budget through detritus food chains. The tough leaves and stems of many high marsh plants make them unappealing to most herbivores. But after being fragmented by waves, ice, and wind, these tissues become prime food for invertebrates, bacteria, and fungi, which feed animals higher in the river's food webs.

Most of the dominant high marsh plants have strong underground networks of rhizomes (underground stems); these stabilize the underlying soil against erosion by currents and waves.[6] The tough, closely growing stems and leaves also absorb the punch of waves and resist winter storms and ice, often remaining standing through their rounds with that difficult season. Partly because of this buffering ability, the Hudson's high marsh communities offer breeding, nesting, and wintering habitat for many birds and mammals. In similar marshes on open coasts buffeted by severe storms, this shock absorber role is particularly important even to humans, whose shortsighted filling and development of marshes can

both destroy the buffer and put structures directly in harm's way.

Tidal Swamps. In many of the Hudson's marshes the upper intertidal zone ends against a steep slope, making the transition to dry land very abrupt. But in some of the river's freshwater marshes the landward slope is more gradual, and a tidal swamp community dominated by woody plants can be found near the average high tide level and above into true upland.[7] Its elevation is such that plants here usually endure only brief periods of flooding at high tide. The woody species typical of this community will also grow singly or in clumps on small bits of such high ground elsewhere in the marsh.

The Hudson's freshwater tidal swamp communities have not received much study,

The trees and shrubs of this tidal swamp border a small marsh near Norrie Point in Hyde Park.

Representative Plants of Tidal Swamp Communities

Red maple (*Acer rubrum*) or swamp maple has red flowers that impart a hazy rose color to wet woodlands in early spring. In early fall, its foliage turns brilliant red. Large specimens can exceed 100 feet in height.

Red ash (*Fraxinus pennsylvanica*) and black ash (*Fraxinus nigra*) have compound leaves with several leaflets on one stalk. Red ash leaves have 5–9 leaflets (usually 7), each attached to the main stalk by its own little stem; black ash has 7–11 leaflets lacking such stems. Wood from these trees is used in basket making.

Willows (*Salix* species) take forms ranging from the 70-foot-tall black willow tree to the shrubby pussy willow. Many hybridize, making species identification difficult. Generally, willow leaves are long, narrow, and arranged alternately along branchlets. Species that become large trees usually have several thick, irregularly shaped branches reaching skyward from their bases instead of one trunk. Their bark is rough and deeply furrowed.

Smooth alder (*Alnus serrulata*), is a tall (to 20 feet) water-tolerant shrub in the birch family. Its bark pattern is the reverse of familiar birch bark, with light dots on a dark gray background. Alders have distinctive catkins—scaly spikes that bear inconspicuous flowers lacking petals. The catkins persist through the winter, the more oval ones (which bear female flowers) looking much like small, dark pine cones.

Silky dogwood (*Cornus amomum*) is typically densely branched, each branch tapering to twigs covered with silky hairs and usually dull reddish purple in color. This shrub's leaves are arranged opposite one another along the branches. Clusters of bluish berrylike fruits develop from small white flowers at the tips of the branches.

Jewelweed (*Impatiens capensis*) or touch-me-not is an herbaceous plant found throughout the upper intertidal zone. Three to five feet tall and somewhat shade tolerant, it is prominent in the tidal swamp community. The tubular orange flowers, about an inch long, develop into a pod that, when ripe, will burst open at a touch, explosively scattering the seeds.

but they contain a rich assortment of plant and animal species. Of the many herbaceous plants found among the more prominent trees and shrubs, quite a number grow widely in the upper intertidal zone but are seldom dominant anywhere.

Tributaries

The Hudson's tributaries vary greatly in size and impacts on the main stem, and a complete description of their ecology is beyond the scope of this book. However, they are of major importance to the Hudson, de-

The Rondout Creek, a major tributary of the Hudson, enters the river at Kingston. Many largemouth bass move from the Hudson into the Rondout for the winter.

livering much of the detritus and nutrients that sustain the estuary's food webs. These streams also route sediment and numerous pollutants into the river.

Tributaries serve as critical habitats for many river organisms on a seasonal or localized basis. Some fishes swim in from the ocean and enter tributaries to spawn—alewives and sea lampreys, for instance. A few river residents, smallmouth bass and white suckers among them, ascend these creeks on the same mission. Largemouth bass move from the open river into tidal portions of larger tributaries for the winter. Where the Hudson is brackish, plants with low tolerance for salt water can maintain a foothold in fresh water entering from these streams.

A Caveat

Having taken many pages to distinguish and describe the Hudson's various habitats and plant communities, we must now add a caveat. When you actually paddle through these communities, you may find that the distinctions between them are not always as clear as might be inferred from the text. The diversity of microhabitats in marshes, for instance, allows plants typical of one community to appear interspersed among the species of another community. Our tendency to draw lines separating the natural world into discrete categories is helpful and often necessary, but in real ecosystems these lines are sometimes blurred.

For example, New York's tidal and freshwater wetlands laws differ in procedural points, making their application problematic on the Hudson, which is both tidal and fresh for much of its length. The regulatory solution was to draw a line at the Tappan Zee Bridge: for legal purposes, wetlands above the bridge are freshwater wetlands; below, tidal wetlands. As tidal currents carry them back and forth under the bridge, phytoplankton do not notice any difference.

So while learning to distinguish these communities, remember to appreciate the inextricable links between them and the often subtle gradients along which one community is transmuted into another.

Chapter 4

The Hudson's Invertebrate Animals

The Chapter in Brief
The Hudson River is home to diverse ecological communities, of which invertebrate animals are important members. Invertebrates in the zooplankton community consume detritus, bacteria, and phytoplankton, and in turn are food for other larger organisms. Some are planktonic at all life stages, others at one or two of several stages. At the bottom of the river, invertebrates dominate the benthos. Benthic invertebrates include many detritivores as well as herbivores, carnivores, and omnivores. Zooplankton and benthic communities include representatives of nearly every invertebrate phylum. Among these are species of great commercial value, and also species that cause significant damage to human fisheries and infrastructure.

Animals without Backbones

Invertebrates are animals without backbones, an apparently simple definition. But dig a little deeper—beyond large, showy invertebrates such as butterflies, crabs, and lobsters—and they start to seem complicated. Most are small and hard to study casually. Many have a daunting multiplicity of appendages and sensory organs—or seemingly none at all. Names are often in unfamiliar Latin and Greek rather than plain English. Their behavior patterns may seem alien or even repulsive compared to that of more familiar warm, fuzzy creatures. And there are so many: 97 percent of the world's animal species are invertebrates.[1]

In ecosystems, including the Hudson River, these animals play roles that correspond in importance to their numbers. They are vital links in food chains. For instance, very few of the Hudson's fish subsist primarily on plants; the food energy captured through photosynthesis reaches fish mainly through invertebrates that dine on plants and detritus. A number of invertebrates show up on human menus as well: lobsters, crabs, clams, oysters, and squid.

And once one has gotten beyond an initial dislike for creepy-crawly critters and their strangeness, one finds among them some fascinating creatures of great beauty.

A Collection of Communities

In the previous chapter we grouped plants by habitat into fairly distinct communities. Animals can be similarly divided based on the space they occupy in the Hudson. Looking at a cross-section of the river, organisms can be placed into three categories.

Living at the river bottom are the *benthos*, or *benthic* organisms: those that burrow in the sediments as do worms and clams; those, like amphipods and starfish, that creep and crawl over mud, rocks, rooted plants, and other objects found there; and those that can swim but usually stay on or near the bottom—the blue crab, for example.

Above the river's bottom is the *water column*. Of the animals found there, some are not able to propel themselves strongly enough to make headway against the current—jellyfish, for example. These are called *zooplankton* (as opposed to phytoplankton, the plant plankton described in the last chapter).

Also found in the water column are the *nektonic* creatures, free-swimming animals capable of traveling faster than the currents of the river. Most fishes are nektonic; one notable nektonic invertebrate—the squid—enters the estuary.

Note that these categories are based on how and where organisms live rather than on taxonomy. They include both vertebrates and invertebrates.

While the definitions of benthos and plankton are fairly clear, precise assignment of the taxonomic groups of invertebrates to one or the other category can be tricky. Most amphipods and water mites, for instance, are benthic creatures, yet there are a few planktonic species in each group. In addition, many benthic invertebrates do swim above the substrate, and are often swept up by the Hudson's currents and taken on an unplanned joyride in the water column as more or less "accidental" plankton. Thus placement of the various invertebrate groups in the zooplankton or benthos sections below indicates their occurrence in general rather than absolute fashion.

A Key Link in the Chain: Zooplankton

The profusion of phytoplankton and detritus found within the Hudson estuary supports an abundance of zooplankton. It is estimated that a coastal estuary provides such a rich habitat for zooplankton that a cubic meter of water may contain several million individuals. Forms of zooplankton include many species of protozoans, crustaceans, comb jellies, true jellyfish, and larval forms of fish, mollusks, and insects.

Many invertebrates are planktonic in their early life stages and become nektonic or benthic as they grow. Barnacles are a good example; their larvae ride the currents before cementing themselves to rocks and docks. As the young of such creatures hatch from eggs and take up the drifter's life, they create seasonal variation in the makeup of the Hudson's zooplankton community. Early summer, for instance, finds the river laden with freshly-hatched planktonic fish larvae.

There is also seasonal variation among organisms that are permanently part of the zooplankton. In general, zooplankton populations are at their minimums in winter and spring due to low temperatures that slow their growth and high flows that transport them out of the estuary rapidly. In summer and fall, various species peak at different times.

Salinity has a major influence on zooplankton distribution. Some species are found only in the freshwater stretches of the river, others in brackish water, and more only in the saltier areas. Some, tolerant of diverse conditions, are found through much of the estuary.

Zooplankton feed on phytoplankton, bacteria, detritus, and smaller zooplankton. Their numbers are not limited by phytoplankton, except perhaps in the case of copepods in the lower, more saline estuary. By the same token, grazing by zooplankton generally does not affect phytoplankton populations significantly. On the other

Representative Species of Comb Jellies

Leidy's Comb Jelly (*Mnemiopsis leidyi*) *left*, also called the sea walnut, is 1–4 inches long and has a slight brown or pinkish tint. The species is often abundant in summer in New York Harbor and is common as far north as Yonkers. The somewhat larger Beroe's comb jellies (*Beroe* species) *right* are also occasionally found in the lower estuary.

hand, zooplankton numbers in summer and fall may be regulated by creatures that eat them, including juvenile fish and plankton-feeding adults such as the bay anchovy, Atlantic silverside, and various herrings.

Comb Jellies

Among the most fascinating plankton in the saltier regions of the estuary are the prolific ctenophores, also called comb jellies. Like jellyfish, they are graceful when supported by water, and amorphous blobs when removed. However, comb jellies lack the stinging cells possessed by true jellyfish and are in a phylum all their own—Ctenophora.

Comb jellies are shaped like an egg with one end hollowed out to form a digestive cavity. The outside of the body has eight comb-like rows of cilia, tiny hairs that are in constant motion, propelling the animal slowly through the water. As these cilia move, an iridescent refraction of light can be seen. At night, an eerie green chemically-produced light emanates from these animals. Like insects to a streetlight, copepods and other creatures are attracted to this odd glow and consumed. When abundant, ctenophores can reduce populations of smaller zooplankton—they have been observed to eat five hundred copepods in one hour.

True Jellyfishes

True jellyfishes are members of the phylum Cnidaria. The familiar jellyfish, an umbrella with tentacles hanging below, is actually one of the two forms in which a single species may exist. This free-floating form is called a *medusa*, after the snake-haired monster of Greek mythology. The second form is attached to the bottom of the estuary; in this benthic form, known as a *polyp*, the creature resembles a plant. Successive generations often alternate between the two forms. The larger species are simply called jellyfish; small species are called *hydrozoans*,

Representative Species of Larger Jellyfishes

Lion's mane (*Cyanea capillata*) (*top*) is commonly called the red jelly because of the reddish orange color of its cap, which generally reaches a diameter of 8 inches. Young butterfish (*Peprilus triacanthus*) often live among its numerous tentacles, protected from predators. The fish are immune to the poison of the jellyfish and actually feed on their tentacles. Moon jelly (*Aurelia aurita*) or white jellyfish (*bottom*) is typically 4–6 inches across. The tentacles form a short fringe around the nearly flat bell. In spring when the moon jelly is sexually mature, the gonads appear as four distinct rings looking like craters on the moon. Reportedly, their sting is barely noticeable.

Representative Species of Hydromedusae

Clapper hydromedusa (*Sarsia tubulosa*) has a long stomach tube dangling below the umbrella-shaped body, resembling the clapper in a bell. The medusa is no more than one-half inch across.

Bougainvillia species are similar in appearance to *Sarsia tubulosa* but lack the long stomach tube. Their tentacles are located in four distinct clusters symmetrically arranged around the bottom of the medusa.

their planktonic forms *hydromedusae*, and their polyp forms *hydroids*.

Jellyfishes are opportunistic carnivores, using their numerous tentacles to entangle and capture any prey that happens by. The tentacles are armed with special stinging cells called *nematocysts*, coiled springs waiting to go into action. In some species, the nematocysts inject a powerful neurotoxin into the body of the prey, paralyzing the animal before it is eaten by the jellyfish. The species described here, primarily residents of marine environments, enter New York Harbor and the lowest reaches of the Hudson.

Planktonic Arthropods

The phylum Arthropoda contains more species (about 80 percent of all classified species) and more individuals than any other group of animals. Arthropods—including such beasts as spiders, insects, and crabs—have jointed legs and an exoskeleton, a hard shell made of chitin. As they grow, they must shed the old shell and grow a new one. It is during this molt that many arthropods are most vulnerable to predators. Of the five classes of arthro-

pods—crustaceans, horseshoe crabs, sea spiders, true spiders and their kin (arachnids), and insects—crustaceans dominate the Hudson's zooplankton community.

Copepods. The most numerous Hudson River crustaceans are the copepods. Copepods are tiny (rarely more than one sixteenth of an inch long) with bodies that are somewhat pear-shaped and distinctly segmented. The head bears a single eye and two antennae; the latter serve as sensory devices and also create a current that brings food to the mouth. Body segments behind the head bear mouthparts and swimming legs.

Two major groups of copepods are found in the Hudson, the calanoids and the cyclopoids. Most of the river's copepods are filter-feeding calanoids dependent on phytoplankton. Female calanoid copepods carry a single bundle of eggs, looking much like a bunch of grapes, at the base of the tail; they resemble tiny exclamation points darting through the water. Typically, the calanoids prefer saltier water, each species requiring a particular salinity level.

Cyclopoid copepods, named after the mythical one-eyed Cyclops monster, prefer fresh water. They have biting mouthparts and are more apt to be predatory or even cannibalistic. Female cyclopoids usually carry twin bundles of eggs, one bundle on either side of the tail.

Calanoid copepods are a significant food source for young fishes in the saltier reaches of the estuary. Larval striped bass, one of the Hudson River fish most important to people, are almost entirely dependent on copepods. In fresh water, cyclopoid copepods are an important food source for newly-hatched fish during a brief period in spring, a role assumed later in the year by the water fleas.

Water Fleas. Water fleas or cladocerans are often lumped together under the name "daph-

Representative Species of Copepods

Eurytemora affinis is a calanoid copepod abundant from March to May, before the river warms appreciably and where salinity is low (5–10 ppt). *Eurytemora* is an important food for many larval fishes, including striped bass and white perch.

Acartia tonsa is generally found in warmer water and at slightly higher salinities (10–20 ppt) than *Eurytemora*. Common downriver in summer, *Acartia* replaces *Eurytemora* as food for young-of-the-year fish.

Cyclops is the genus containing the typical cyclopoid copepods. Many hard-to-distinguish species are found in the river.

nia," though *Daphnia* is actually but one of many genera of cladocerans. These crustaceans have a bivalve shell that makes them look somewhat like swimming clams. A pair of large antennae is their chief means of locomotion. Water fleas do have small legs used to create a current carrying food to the mouth. Their large eyes distinguish them from their benthic relatives, the ostracods. Most are less than a tenth of an inch long.

Like the calanoid copepods in saltier water, cladocerans are of key importance to food webs in freshwater portions of the Hudson. The most abundant variety, *Bosmina*, attains its greatest numbers (calculated to be as many as 90 trillion animals weighing nearly 30 tons!) at just the time of year when larval fish populations are peaking, making it an important food source for these youngsters.

Larval Crustaceans. Several species of benthic crustaceans are planktonic in their early life stages. Significant among these are barnacles, lobsters, and crabs. They are primarily marine during their larval phases, though often found up into the Tappan Zee. Untold numbers of these creatures' eggs can hatch in a short period of time, during which they may dominate plankton samples. The adult benthic forms of these species will be discussed later.

Planktonic Insects. Insects are the most familiar of the arthropods, their six legs typically distinguishing them from crustaceans and other classes in the phylum. A relatively small percentage of the estimated one million species of insects are adapted for aquatic life, and most of these inhabit fresh water. Of these, only the larvae and pupae (a resting stage of development similar to the cocoon of moths) of a few phantom midges regularly appear as zooplankton, and even these spend more time in the sediments of the benthic

Representative Species of Water Fleas

Bosmina longirostris is abundant in fresh water, reaching peak densities between Hudson and Kingston, typically in June. This cladoceran also occurs in brackish water up to salinities of 8 ppt.

Diaphanosoma species are a bit larger than *Bosmina*. Its head is small compared to its body. *Diaphanosoma* is most common during August and September in fresh and low-salinity water, absent in winter and spring.

Moina species are found in saltier regions of the Hudson, most abundantly in the Tappan Zee in summer. It is absent from samples taken in other seasons.

Some Larval Crustaceans of the Plankton Community

Barnacles have two planktonic phases found in brackish and marine waters. The first phase—the nauplius—is triangular in shape, with distinct horns on the corners in the head region, a single eye, and three pairs of hairy legs. The second—the cypris—develops a bivalve shell somewhat obscuring the legs, though the eyespot is still visible.

Northern lobster (*Homarus americanus*) larvae are strange spiny things that only vaguely resemble their parents. By their fifth molt the young are about one inch long, look much more like a lobster, and settle into the benthic community.

Crab larvae are initially called zoeae. They look like a creature from outer space: one twenty-fifth of an inch long, transparent, adorned with odd spines, two large eyes, and several hairy little legs. After several molts, another larval form emerges—the megalops—which more closely resembles an adult crab.

Phantom Midge Larvae (*Chaoborus* species)
These larvae—nearly transparent, slender, and typically one-fourth inch long—move with a distinct jerking action. Eyes and mouthparts are visible in the head region. One pair of conspicuous air sacs is located just behind the head, another near the tail. The larvae are predatory, using their prehensile antennae to catch other tiny invertebrates. Adults resemble mosquitoes but do not bite or feed at all.

community than they do drifting in the water column. Larvae of their close relatives, the mosquitoes, drift on the currents but breathe air at the water's surface. Other insects become accidental plankton when currents sweep them up off the bottom.

Life Down Under: The Benthos

The benthic community in the Hudson is highly diverse, with representatives from nearly every invertebrate phylum. Ecologically, they fill a variety of niches. Some are stationary filter-feeders, others are active predators, able to travel with some facility over the river bottom. Many are detritivores, organisms eating dead organic material—in a fashion, the garbage collectors of the estuary.

Most benthic invertebrates found in fresh and slightly salty reaches of the Hudson are very small, exceptions being pearly mussels, crayfish, and the blue crab. In the more saline waters of New York Harbor a variety of larger species are found. Salinity is one of the factors influencing distribution and abundance of benthic animals. Others are the nature of the substrate and the presence or absence of rooted vegetation.

Unlike the Hudson's zooplankton, zebra mussels and other benthic organisms that filter suspended material from the water can and do regulate phytoplankton numbers. Not only do the mussel-caused reductions in algae have ramifications further up the food chain, they also create competition for food within the benthic community—another factor controlling the abundance and distribution of its invertebrates.

Benthic organisms are present in the river in all seasons. Most year-round resident fish depend on this food source, as do the young of many migratory species once they grow beyond the larval stage. The most abundant of these invertebrates, par-

ticularly the amphipods and midge larvae, play key roles in supporting fish populations in the Hudson.

A few benthic invertebrates have negative impacts on human infrastructure. Zebra mussel colonies can clog water intakes at industrial facilities and water treatment plants. In New York Harbor, two marine borers—the shipworm (not a worm but a bivalve with a pair of small chisel-like shells) and the gribble (an isopod)—burrow into wooden pilings that hold up piers, weakening them to the point of collapse.

Sponges

While sponges are most familiar in the saltwater settings of New York Harbor and Raritan and Sandy Hook Bays, they are found in the freshwater Hudson too. Assigned to the phylum Porifera, sponges are the simplest forms of multi-cellular animals, strange masses of tissue held rigid by tiny

---

Representative Species of Sponges

Red beard sponge (*Microciona prolifera*) comes in bright shades of red or orange and grows in a form looking suspiciously like thick, fleshy fingers. It occurs in relatively shallow waters, below the tide line, and has been found in salinities as low as 15 ppt. The redbeard sponge can grow to 8 inches high and 12 inches wide.

Boring sponge (*Cliona* species) is actually an interesting sponge; its name comes from its growth habit. This species frequents oyster beds, growing on shells in forms ranging from a light crust to a large mass completely engulfing the host. After entirely dissolving a shell, the boring sponge, sulfur-yellow in color, can live independently, growing more than 8 inches high.

Representative Species of Sea Anemones and Hydroids

Snail fur (*Hydractinia echinata*) polyps encrust snail shells occupied by hermit crabs. Out of the water, these hydroids look like an indistinct brown fuzz. Under water, their extended tentacles surround the shell in a soft, pinkish cloud.

Tubularian hydroids (*Tubularia* and *Ectopleura* species) are found in more saline areas of the estuary. They look much like plants with clear stalks and delicate pink blossoms, the "blossoms" being the tentacles. Prey is stung with nematocysts, paralyzed, and digested by the hydroid.

White or ghost anemone (*Diadumene leucolena*), our most commonly seen anemone, grows on rocks, docks, and the backs of a variety of hard-shelled animals. Out of water it is an amorphous white, pink, or olive blob no more than one-half inch in diameter. When its 60 tentacles emerge under water, the animal looks like a beautiful flower.

calcium-laden spines called *spicules*. Some scientists believe a sponge mass to be one organism—others, a colony consisting of many individual organisms.

Tiny pores on the surface of a sponge bring water into the animal's body, where it flows through a network of canals while food and oxygen are filtered out. Water and waste products pass out through larger pores on the sponge's surface.

Sea Anemones and Hydroids

Many jellyfish kin in the phylum Cnidaria are part of the estuary's benthic community where salinity is high. These include the sea anemones and hydroids—the polyp phases of the small jellyfish called hydrozoans. The former spend most of their lives in the benthic community and do not go through a medusa stage; the latter are, for the most part, temporary bottom dwellers. Like jellyfish, these benthic organisms all have tentacles—some sticky, some armed with nematocysts—used to trap prey. They can retract during low-tide periods of exposure to air to avoid dessication.

Segmented Worms

The segmented worms (phylum Annelida) are well-represented in the benthic community of the Hudson. Most significant are the bristle worms and earthworms, known to scientists respectively as *polychaete* and *oligochaete* worms.[2]

Bristle worms vary a great deal though they are most often distinctly segmented, have a head of sorts, and possess bristles or little legs helpful in movement. Polychaete

Representative Species of Segmented Worms

Red-gilled mud worm (*Marenzelleria viridis*), one of the estuary's most abundant invertebrates, has two distinct tentacles on the head, red gills, and prominent bristles along the body, which can be up to 4 inches long. This polychaete constructs a tube of detritus particles bound together with mucus and set vertically into the bottom. With only its head protruding, the worm filters detritus from passing water. It is eaten by crustaceans and fish.

Tubificid worms (family Tubificidae) are oligochaetes, which, like terrestrial earthworms, feed mostly on detritus. As their name suggests, many species dwell in tubes, their mouths down in the mud and their tails projecting out of the other end into the water.

worms are most abundant and diverse in salt water.

Almost all aquatic earthworms have bristles too, but they lack a distinct head segment. In the Hudson's freshwater benthic communities, oligochaete worms are numerically dominant. They are among the benthic invertebrates that play an important role in mixing the sediments of the river bottom and exchanging nutrients and toxic pollutants between water and sediment. Some of these worms, notably *Tubifex* and *Limnodrilus*, can survive indefinitely in waters with little or no dissolved oxygen. Their dominance in a given benthic community can be an indicator of organic pollution; the most concentrated populations occur in areas heavily polluted with sewage.

Another class of segmented worms, the leeches, is most common in freshwater reaches of the river. They lack bristles, are flattened from top to bottom, and possess a sucker at each end of the body. Though infamous as "bloodsuckers," many kinds are predators or scavengers rather than parasites.

Snails and Clams

Snails, whelks, mussels, clams, and oysters—all mollusks of the phylum Mollusca—are among the most familiar invertebrates of the Hudson's benthic community. Though the most well-known are creatures of brackish and salty water, ninety-two species have been reliably recorded from the fresh waters of the Hudson River drainage basin, and about fifty have been found in the river itself.

Two features found in mollusks and nowhere else in the animal kingdom are the *mantle* and the *radula*. The mantle is a special fold in the body wall that secretes the calcium carbonate shell so prominent among clams and snails. The radula, characteristic of snails but lacking in clams, is a tongue-like organ bearing rasp-like teeth. It is variously adapted depending on the feeding habits of particular mollusks. Most mollusks have a foot, a flexible muscular mass responsible for the creeping movement of snails and the burrowing of clams.

Gastropods. The snails and their kin are called *gastropods*. They typically have one spiral-shaped shell and an oozing foot that can be quite large. Some members of this group have an *operculum*, a leathery door that closes the opening of the shell once the foot has been retracted. Unlikely as it may seem for such slow-moving creatures, a number of gastropods—moon snails and whelks, for example—are predators, feeding on even slower mollusks such as clams.[3] Others feed on algae, rooted vegetation, and detritus.

Bivalves. Clams and other bivalves make up the largest group of mollusks in the Hudson estuary. As the name implies, each has two shells (valves) joined by strong muscles. The shells close tightly for protection and moisture retention when the animal is exposed to the air. With shells open, a bivalve takes in water, extracting oxygen for respiration and feeding on phytoplankton and detritus. Many species can also extrude a muscular foot used in locomotion and burrowing.

While the saltwater clams and oysters are the most familiar members of this group, freshwater clams and mussels have historically been diverse and abundant in the Hudson. Twenty-three species of pearly mussels have been recorded from the Hudson basin, along with another twenty-three species of fingernail clams.

Bivalves—zebra mussels in particular—are very efficient filter feeders. It is estimated that the Hudson's zebra mussels can filter a quantity of water equal to the entire volume of the freshwater portion of the estuary in about two days. Their ability to sweep phytoplankton and small zooplank-

Representative Species of Gastropods

Atlantic moon snail (*Neverita duplicata*) or shark eye has a smooth tan or gray shell up to 3 inches across. The enormous foot can be retracted and sealed into the shell. Moon snails are found in more marine sections of the estuary, primarily below low-tide level. Their egg masses, often discovered on beaches, are called sand collars as they resemble a starched shirt collar 5–6 inches in diameter.

Channeled whelk (*Busycotypus canaliculatus*) shells, up to 9 inches long, have distinct channels in their coils; inside they are yellowish to tan in color. Whelks are found in New York Harbor from the low tide line to a depth of about 50 feet. Their egg cases, cast up on beaches, look like a string of coins made of parchment. Each coin, about 1 inch in diameter, is a capsule containing from 20 to 100 eggs.

Atlantic slippersnail (*Crepidula fornicata*) occurs in the saltiest areas of the estuary. Its shell (up to 1.5 inches long) forms an oval cup, the half open underside suggesting a bedroom slipper. They typically live in stacks in which the bottom individual is female and those on top are male. As the stack gets taller, those close to the bottom eventually become female as well. Slipper shells feed on algae. They often hitchhike on the underside of horseshoe crab shells or on other mollusks.

Swamp or seaweed snails (*Hydrobia* species) are found in brackish water weed beds. These animals are no more than one-fourth inch long. The smooth shells are nearly translucent and yellowish brown in color.

Freshwater snails number over 45 species in the Hudson basin; many are common. *Valvata tricarinata* (left), about one-fourth inch in diameter, is abundant on tidal mudflats, where it feeds on algae and detritus. It has an external plumelike gill. The nonnative *Bithynia tentaculata* (right), about three-eighths inch long, prefers hard substrates in the intertidal zone, sometimes covering the undersides of rocks.

Representative Species of Bivalves

Blue mussel (*Mytilus edulis*) *top*, the common edible mussel, inhabits saltier regions of the lower estuary. It attaches to hard substrates: rocks, piers, scattered shells, or other mussels, forming colonies. The smooth shell—blue-black outside, violet inside—may be up to 4 inches long. The ribbed mussel (*Geukensia demissus*) *bottom*, a solitary dweller of brackish marshes, has rough ribs radiating outward from the narrow end of the shell.

Eastern oyster (*Crassostrea virginica*) shells, rarely up to 10 inches long, vary in appearance and shape. The bottom shell, usually more cuplike than the top, binds to a hard substrate: rock, broken shell, or another oyster. Empty shells from once flourishing populations are common from the Tappan Zee south. Live oyster numbers are increasing, but the reefs once important commercially and ecologically have yet to reappear.

Softshell clams (*Mya arenaria*), or steamers, have thin shells 3–4 inches long with an elongated oval shape. They live in stiff mud in the intertidal zone and under water to depths of 20 feet. Their long siphon draws in food and water and spits water when the clams are disturbed. Hardshell clams (*Mercenaria mercenaria*), the wampum clams once used as money by native peoples, have thick shells up to 4 inches wide and broadly oval in shape, with brilliant purple coloring inside.

Pearly mussels (family Unionidae) typically have an oval shell—variable in color outside, pearly inside—up to 6 inches long. Their larvae are parasites of fishes, to which they must attach within a day or two of release from the mother. They spend one to several weeks on a fish, metamorphose into juvenile mussels, and then fall free to settle on the bottom. Shad and herring serve as hosts for *Anodonta implicata*, one of the most common of this family in the Hudson.

Zebra mussel (*Dreissena polymorpha*) larvae are planktonic; they hitchhiked to North America in the ballast water of ships from Europe. This small (up to 2 inches) freshwater bivalve infested parts of the Great Lakes by the late 1980s, appeared at Catskill in 1991, and by 1993 had reached an estimated population of 550 billion in the Hudson.

ton from the water column has had serious repercussions among native bivalves and other animals sustained by this food source, and subsequently on creatures further along the Hudson's food webs.

Prior to the zebra mussel's arrival, pearly mussels reached densities of 125–200 individuals per square meter between the Troy Dam and Castleton. Though smaller, zebra mussels are more efficient filter feeders and present in enormous numbers: up to 30,000 per square meter cover some rocky areas of the river bottom near Poughkeepsie. In fall, 2005, shallows just below the Troy Dam were still densely littered with pearly mussel shells, but they were all empty. Literally being starved to death, the Hudson River populations of some species face extinction.

While they do not compete directly with zebra mussels for food, young-of-the-year American shad may depend on populations of tiny zooplankton that have been shrinking due to the mussels' effects on algae concentrations. Young shad headed for the ocean in fall appear to be smaller in size since the zebra mussel invasion, and as a result may find it harder to survive the rigors of life at sea.

The Real Creepy-Crawlies: Benthic Arthropods

Many benthic arthropods are found in the Hudson. In fresh water they are mostly insects and tiny crustaceans. Once the water turns salty, the diversity of insects decreases while that of crustaceans increases greatly. The three other classes of arthropods lacking or not numerous in the plankton community (arachnids, horseshoe crabs, and sea spiders; the latter omitted here) join insects and crustaceans among the benthos.

Water Mites. Water mites look much like tiny spiders the size of a pinhead, and like spiders are classified as *arachnids*.

They are red or brown in color, and use their eight legs to propel themselves in a rolling manner. Water mites consume their prey, often larger than themselves, by boring a hole in the animal's body and sucking out the liquids held inside. They are mostly restricted to freshwater habitats. Like other small benthic invertebrates, mites are occasionally swept off the bottom and suspended in the water column; there are also a few truly planktonic species.

Horseshoe Crabs. The world's five species of horseshoe crabs, more closely related to spiders than crabs, stand in a class all their own. Their body plan has survived virtually unchanged for over 350 million years; it features a helmet-like body and spiky tail. Though fearsome-looking, the tail is not a sword nor does it have a venomous sting; it enables the crab to right itself when flipped over by waves.

On the horseshoe crab's underside are five pairs of legs, the first adapted as claspers in the male and the last pair with splayed ends for digging. The mouth is set between the legs, the bases of which break up the animals' food, chiefly clams and worms. Behind the legs are five pairs of book gills, flat appendages that look like the

Atlantic Horseshoe Crab (*Limulus polyphemus*) This is the only horseshoe crab of North American waters and is present in New York Harbor. It breeds on some beaches there in May and June. These animals are fairly long-lived; they do not reach sexual maturity until age 10. Females, larger than males, reach a length of 2 feet, including the tail.

pages of a book. They flap back and forth to create a current for breathing and to propel the animal through the water. On the upper shell are two large, sophisticated compound eyes and tiny simple eyes.[4]

Ostracods. Ostracods are even more clam-like in appearance than their relatives the cladocerans. They are crustaceans, though their distinct bivalve shells suggest kinship with clams. Under magnification, the antennae used for locomotion are visible. Without magnification, ostracods resemble tiny animated seeds. For this reason they are sometimes called seed shrimp. While found in both freshwater and marine habitats, the freshwater species are the better known.

Isopods. Most aquatic isopods resemble their more familiar terrestrial relatives, the sowbugs and pillbugs. These crustaceans are generally flattened from top to bottom, and have seven pairs of legs. Isopods eat detritus as well as living plants and animals; a few are parasites of fish. In New York Harbor,

Representative Species of Isopods

Edotea triloba has the typical isopod shape and is present from New York Harbor to Haverstraw Bay.

Cyathura polita has an elongated body and its first pair of legs are clawlike. It is one of the Hudson's most abundant benthic species, present from the George Washington Bridge north.

the gribble tunnels just under the surface of submerged wood and eats fungus and other microorganisms that grow in the tunnels. Fish, ducks, and predatory invertebrates include isopods in their diets. While each species has particular salinity requirements, the group is represented throughout the estuary.

Amphipods. Amphipods, also called sideswimmers or scuds, are small, shrimp-like animals, typically no more than half an inch long, with bodies compressed from side to side. While they occasionally appear in the plankton community, amphipods are most abundant as benthic creatures throughout the Hudson. Healthy populations of some species in New York Harbor exceed 20,000 individuals per square meter.

In addition to their numerical importance, amphipods are a vital part of Hudson River food webs. These crustaceans feed on all kinds of plant and animal matter, including detritus, algae, tiny invertebrates, and dead animals. In turn, they are a major food source for the estuary's fish. Examination of fishes' stomach contents has shown that amphipods form a significant part of the diets of Atlantic sturgeon, Atlantic tomcod, white perch, and young striped bass from the Hudson.

Barnacles. Barnacles are benthic as adults, only vaguely resembling their planktonic larvae or their crustacean relatives. They are sessile, attached (essentially by their heads) to piers, rocks, boats, or any somewhat solid substrate. A shell is formed of six calcareous (containing calcium carbonate) plates. Two are overlapping end plates that open and close, allowing six jointed legs to extend beyond the shell, filtering food from the water.

A Representative Amphipod — *Gammarus*
Amphipods in this genus are extremely abundant and readily observed; one study determined that they seasonally constituted more than 30 percent of all animals in slightly salty (0.5–5.0 ppt) parts of the river.

Representative Species of Shrimplike Crustaceans

Crayfish (order Astacidae) are the only crusta-ceans found exclusively in fresh water. Crayfish resemble small lobsters, usually no more than 6 inches long. They frequent shoreline shallows and wetland areas of the estuary. Of the nine species in the Hudson, five are nonnative.

Northern lobster (*Homarus americanus*) is the saltwater cousin of the crayfish. Those found in New York Harbor are typically 8–12 inches long; giants caught offshore can reach a length of 3 feet, weighing in at 45 pounds.

Sand shrimp (*Crangon septemspinosa*) *left* and common grass or shore shrimp (*Palaemonetes pugio*) *right* frequent shallows from the Tappan Zee south. The former, up to 2.5 inches long, may be translucent or gray in color. Females bear egg masses on the underside of the tail. The smaller grass shrimp is nearly transparent. Both are favorite foods of many fish.

Barnacles flourish in saltier areas of the estuary and are found as far upriver as Newburgh Bay.

Shrimplike Crustaceans. Several members of the class Crustacea have a long body, distinct tail region, and often large pincers. These include the crayfishes, lobsters, and the most familiar of the shrimp. Together with the crabs, these crustaceans are grouped in the order Decapoda; counting the claws, all have ten pairs of legs.

Crayfish and lobsters are opportu-nistic feeders, scavenging the benthic re-gion for anything but the most putrid of fare, including members of their own spe-cies. The smaller shrimp are omnivorous, feeding on tiny invertebrates, plants, algae and detritus.

Crabs. The true crabs are crustaceans with a broad body, a tail folded underneath as a protective plate, and stout claws. Most are scavengers, but some (particularly the blue crab) are active predators, and the

fiddler crabs eat bacteria, algae, and plant detritus.

As with all arthropods, a crab's shell does not grow. As a crab gets larger, it periodically sheds its old exoskeleton, and a new one underneath swells and hardens. Soft-shelled crabs are freshly molted crabs whose shells have yet to harden, a process that takes several days in adult blue crabs.

A crab's gender can be determined by looking at its underside. Sexually mature females have a very broad plate that pro-tects the eggs they carry until hatching. Immature females have a narrower, more triangular plate. The male, regardless of maturity, has a narrow plate, shaped like a pencil.

Benthic Insects. Most insects of the Hudson's benthic community are larvae that develop into winged, air-breathing adults. Some go through a pupal stage as do caterpillars turning into moths or butterflies. Others, called nymphs, have a form similar to that

Representative Species of Crabs

Hermit crabs (*Pagurus* species) are among the smallest crabs residing in New York Harbor, and perhaps those that kids love best. They make their homes in abandoned snail shells, which when outgrown are discarded in favor of new, larger shells.

Red-jointed fiddler crab (*Uca minax*) is common in marshes north to Piermont, occasional in the Highlands . Their squarish shell can be up to 1.5 inches wide. Males sit near their burrows waving a distinctive outsized claw at passersby, courting female fiddler crabs.

Rock crab (*Cancer irroratus*) has a smooth shell up to 5 inches wide and pentagonal in shape. To the outside of each eye the shell is edged with nine toothlike projections. This crab is common in New York Harbor.

Spider crab (*Libinia emarginata*) has a round shell no more than 4 inches in diameter, but its spidery legs can reach a foot in length. Found in the harbor, these slow-moving scavengers are also called decorator crabs since they are often festooned with algae, hydroids, sponges, barnacles, and other living things that may help in camouflage.

Blue or blue-claw crab (*Callinectes sapidus*) is large and feisty, its shell up to 9 inches wide point to point, its strong blue claws up to a foot in length. Paddlelike rear legs make this crab an able swimmer. In summer, males travel well into fresh water, often reaching Albany. Females do not travel as far upriver; the eggs and larvae require high salinities to develop.

of the adult. They skip the pupal stage, simply leaving the water and undergoing one or more molts during which they take on adult characteristics.

Benthic insects are primarily found in freshwater sections of the Hudson. The worm-like larvae of little flies known as chironomid midges are particularly abundant and important. They are a major food of many fishes including young shortnose sturgeon and young American shad.

Representative Species of Benthic Insects

Mayfly nymphs (order Ephemeroptera) have external gills along the abdomen and three (sometimes two) long tails. They spend 1–4 years in the benthos, feeding primarily on algae and detritus and being eaten by larger insects and fish. After emerging from the water as adults, mayflies mate and die in a few hours or days.

Damselfly *left* and dragonfly nymphs *right* (order Odonata) are voracious predators most common in silty areas and among plants in quiet waters. They capture prey (insects, small crustaceans, even tiny fish) using a double-hinged lower lip armed with spines. Dragonfly nymphs tend to have stout abdomens; damselfly nymphs are more slender with three tail-like gills.

Caddis fly larvae (order Trichoptera) are known for their case-building habit, though not all species build cases. Those that do spin a silklike tube and weave pieces of vegetation, tiny twigs, or grains of sand into it. The larva lives in the case, head and legs emerging as it feeds or moves about. Caddis fly larvae diets vary according to species; carnivores, herbivores, and detritivores are all represented.

Midge (order Diptera) larvae of the family Chironomidae creep or loop over the substrate, feeding on algae, higher plants, and organic detritus. The adults are tiny delicate flies that often appear in such swarms that they are bothersome even though they don't bite.

Sea Stars

Members of the phylum Echinodermata—spiny skinned animals like starfish (more properly sea stars) and sea urchins—are restricted to marine habitats. Only one species, a sea star, is commonly found in the estuary, and it is only in New York Harbor.

Like other echinoderms, sea stars possess a water-vascular system linked to hundreds of tube feet that act like tiny suction cups. These animals feed on bivalves by attaching their tube feet and slowly and persistently pulling the shells apart. When its prey is open, the starfish turns its stomach inside out into the bivalve, and secretes enzymes and digestive juices that dissolve the animal's tissues. Because the sea star feeds voraciously on clams, mussels and oysters, it is seen as a pest by people who make their living harvesting shellfish.

Starfish have an amazing ability to regenerate lost tissue. Any portion of a sea star that contains part of the central disk can regenerate anything it is missing. In this fashion a sea star missing one arm will replace the missing piece, and the severed arm can grow four new ones.

Animals with Backbones— Sort of: The Tunicates

The phylum Chordata includes those animals that have a spinal cord or some form of central nervous system. There are two subphyla. Vertebra, the animals with backbones, includes the fish, amphibians, reptiles, birds, and mammals. These will be discussed in later chapters. Urochordata includes some unusual little animals called tunicates that have a primitive nerve cord, or notochord, in their tadpole-like larval stage. This anatomical feature is evidence that—of all the creatures discussed in this chapter—tunicates are the most closely related to us.

The sea squirts may be the most familiar tunicates: small sac-like animals

Common Sea Star (*Asterias forbesi*) Yellowish orange to deep purple in color, this sea star typically has five arms around its central disk. On the disk is a bright orange spot often thought to be an eye. In reality this sieve plate or madreporite filters the seawater that fills the animal's water-vascular system. The actual eyes are located at the end of each arm. This sea star is generally about 4–6 inches in diameter.

Representative Species of Tunicates

Sea grapes (*Molgula manhattensis*) look like peeled grapes. This sea squirt can reach a height of 1.5 inches, though most are under an inch. Two siphon tubes protrude from the body: one brings water, food, and oxygen in, the other expels wastes. The sea grape is tolerant of rather polluted water and lives in profusion in New York Harbor, often in great clusters.

Golden Star tunicate (*Botryllus schlosseri*) colonies resemble a blob of gelatin up to 4 inches long. The animals, only about one-sixteenth inch long, are arranged in starlike groupings of 5–20, each individual being one point of the star. Each has its own intake siphon but there is a communal discharge siphon at the star's center. The gelatinous mass may be golden yellow with deep purple stars speckled with gold or white, or this color pattern may be reversed.

with a tough, translucent outer coat—the tunic—and siphons that squirt water when the animal is disturbed. Most tunicates are saltwater animals; a few penetrate into brackish environments.

A Nektonic Invertebrate: The Squid

Squid are mollusks with internal shells. The distinct head contains two very sophisticated eyes, comparable to those of vertebrates. The squid's mouth has a pair of strong parrot-like beaks surrounded by eight arms and two tentacles, all with suction cups that secure prey including fish, crustaceans, and other squid.

The squid can move swiftly by expelling water from its body cavity in a sort of jet propulsion. It can also change color to blend in with its surroundings or eject a black inky substance to obscure the view of predators, affording the squid an easy getaway.

Of Taste Treats and Food Chains

Many bivalve mollusks are well-known taste treats. The abundant and delectable blue mussel shows up in marinara sauce at many an Italian restaurant, and in garlic sauce in Chinese eateries. The soft-shelled clam is steamed in heaping quantities at clambakes or often served as an appetizer. The hard clam is called many different names (quahog, cherrystone, littleneck, chowder clam) and used in as many ways.

Over 90 percent of commercial shellfish species (those harvested for profit rather than recreation) are dependent on estuaries at some point in their life cycles. However, harvests in the Hudson estuary are limited by sewage pollution. As filter feeders, bivalves draw in and concentrate the pathogens (disease-causing bacteria and viruses) present in sewage. Clams are harvested from portions of lower New York and Sandy Hook Bays, but prior to being marketed they must be treated with ultraviolet light to kill pathogens or moved to cleaner waters where they purge themselves of such organisms.

When it comes to oysters, one either loves them or hates them. Raw oysters on the half-shell appeal to some and repulse others. Evidently they appealed to the first human inhabitants along the Hudson; shell middens—the refuse heaps left after their repasts—are common at Croton Point and other upriver sites. There were perhaps 350 square miles of oyster beds in New York Harbor and upriver as far as Croton, yielding more than a million and a half bushels of oysters per year until 1839. At New York City's numerous oyster bars, patrons could

Long-finned Squid (*Loligo peali*) This is the only squid found within the Hudson estuary, entering New York Harbor. Its body can be up to 19 inches long, though most in the area are smaller, up to 12 inches.

In New York City, both oysters and oyster bars are less common than they used to be. But these succulent shellfish are among the many invertebrates that still earn high ranking on many lists of culinary delights.

eat their fill for a few cents. As late as 1907, 300 million oysters were harvested from waters around the city. But soon afterwards, complaints about foul taste and outbreaks of typhoid fever linked to contaminated shellfish ended the local harvest. Later, dredging, filling, and silting destroyed the remaining beds.

Seed oysters (nickel-sized young) were once gathered from Haverstraw Bay and the Tappan Zee and transferred to saltier waters for growth to harvesting size. Hurricane rainfall in 1955 caused a lengthy discharge of fresh water over these upriver beds, killing off the oysters.

While sewage pollution would likely prevent commercial harvest, efforts are underway to restore New York Harbor's oyster reefs as valuable habitat supporting a unique community of benthic life. It is also possible that the filter-feeding activity of large numbers of oysters could make the water clearer. Those interested in such restoration can take heart from successes in nearby Oyster Bay on Long Island Sound, where oysters and the fishery have been preserved through wise management, mari-

culture techniques, and observation of environmental laws.

Many crustaceans are very popular food items. Lobster rides high on lists of delicacies, and there are still a few lobstermen at work in New York Harbor. Unlike the classic lobster fishery utilizing a buoy for each pot, the harbor fishery uses a string of unmarked traps dropped in sequence from the boat. The trapline is retrieved with a grappling hook.

Crabs, of course, are a prized catch. The blue crab is the desirable species found in the Hudson; a literal translation of its scientific name, *Callinectes sapidus*, is "beautiful swimmer with a most agreeable flavor." While a small commercial fishery exists in the estuary as far north as Poughkeepsie, most of the catch is taken by recreational crabbers.[5] Freshly molted blue crabs are the soft-shelled crabs found on restaurant menus; commercial crabbers can recognize crabs ready to molt, and keep them in holding pens until they do. However, this is not a common practice on the Hudson.

People do not eat horseshoe crabs, and once considered them of little use except as bait. In 1977, limulus amoebocyte lysate, a substance found in the crab's blood, came into wide use. It triggers blood clotting in the presence of certain bacteria and contaminants, a reaction which is used to test the purity of intravenous drugs and, experimentally, in diagnosing some diseases. Other creatures, notably shorebirds migrating north in spring, gorge on horseshoe crab eggs to fuel their long flights.

We humans are not the only predators that find invertebrates delectable. They are food for many species of fish, waterfowl, and other animals. Though often overlooked given the splendor of the Hudson's fishes, the invertebrates are just as valuable in the grand mosaic of the ecosystem.

Chapter 5

The Hudson's Fishes

The Chapter in Brief

Over 200 species of fishes have been found in the Hudson River system, many in abundance. A highly productive critical zone in the estuary serves as a nursery for young fish. All fishes share certain adaptations for aquatic life; individual species have particular adaptations for specific habitats and activities. Fishes exploit the variety of habitats and salinity conditions existing within the Hudson and some migratory species travel throughout the system and beyond. They can be categorized according to preferred habitats, though their mobility makes such groupings somewhat imprecise. A number of the river's fishes support valuable recreational and commercial fisheries here and in coastal waters. PCB contamination has had negative impacts on the Hudson's fisheries.

"This River Is Rich in Fishes"

From our perch in the early twenty-first century, it is easy to lament or dismiss descriptions like this one from a seventeenth century writer, Adriaen Van der Donck, as one more faded picture from the paradisical "good old days." But in spite of the wear and tear of human abuse of the Hudson, that image from bygone days has not faded as much as one might think. The river still supports abundant and diverse populations of fishes.

As of 2005, experts put the number of fish species recorded in the Hudson River drainage basin at 212. Of these, perhaps 50 are common to abundant in the tidewater Hudson. At the other extreme are some 80 strays, wanderers from coastal waters that have been observed here less than five times apiece. The numbers of individual fishes in the river are also impressive. For example, researchers have estimated that the Hudson's yearly spawning runs of American shad in the late 1980s numbered three to four million fish. However, such seemingly vast populations can quickly decline; the shad run had dropped to an es-

timated 400,000 fish by 1996, mainly due to overfishing.

Estimating fish populations in an ecosystem as large and complex as the Hudson is an inexact science. By using standardized sampling methods year after year, fisheries scientists can track relative abundance, noting years when they catch many or few of a particular species and trying to correlate that data with trends in other factors such as fishing pressure, pollution, or ecological change. But determining the absolute number of fish at any given time is difficult. In addition, that number may change greatly from year to year or month to month. Note

Biologists from New York State's Department of Environmental Conservation net, measure, and release Hudson River striped bass during the fish's spawning run each spring. Using data from scale samples, scientists determine the age structure of the striper population, an indicator of its prospects for the near future.
(Photo by Cara Lee.)

the age qualifier in a recent estimate that Hudson River striped bass number about two million adult fish. The entire population may swell suddenly by tens of millions in late spring as bass eggs hatch, then drop rapidly through summer and fall as these young-of-the-year fish encounter predators and other hazards.

The Hudson River Nursery

The numbers of striped bass in the Hudson are grand; its 7-foot sturgeon are awesome. But a real understanding of its abundant fish life and one of the ecosystem's most important roles begins with little fish—the teeming offspring of the big grownups that catch our attention. A Hudson River angler once took a group of striped bass experts from all around the country out fishing for fun on the Hudson. They caught lots of stripers, almost all young fish less than a foot long. When the angler apologized for their small size, the scientists told him they were just as happy to be seeing all these little fish. At that time in many of the estuaries they studied, they only caught big, old fish—impressive, yes, but without the young ones, the prognosis for the future of stripers in those estuaries was poor.

The lower Hudson estuary is a particularly favorable nursery for fish. In fact, the portion of the estuary where the salinity ranges from 0.6 to 11 ppt is recognized as a critical zone vital to the survival of fish in their first year of life. The geographical location of this zone varies from season to

season and year to year due to changes in freshwater runoff. But in spring and summer, when recently hatched fish abound, the critical zone typically stretches through the Tappan Zee and Haverstraw Bay. The broad expanses of shallow water here allow a maximum input of the sunlight needed by phytoplankton, and relatively slow currents in these bays allow the tiny plants to build up in large concentrations.

These concentrations of phytoplankton support great numbers of zooplankton. Their abundance is critical to newly hatched fish, for it is these tiny invertebrates upon which the fish depend for food. In addition, the turbid waters of the Hudson help to hide young fish from their predators.

Relatively few fish species actually spawn in the brackish water of the critical zone. Of the Hudson fishes most abundant and important to humans, the majority are *anadromous*—spending their adult lives in salt water but returning to fresh water to lay eggs—or are marine spawners. Their young are weak swimmers; they hitchhike on the appropriate river currents to reach the critical zone. The young of many marine spawners move upriver on the incoming flow of dense salt water near the river bottom; the young of anadromous species travel downriver on the outgoing fresh water nearer the surface. Eventually these fish will swim out into the Atlantic. The portion of their lives spent in the estuary may be short, but it is critical to these species' success. Scientists estimate that 65 percent of

The *critical zone* is an area of low salinity (0.6–11.0 ppt) water important as a nursery for young fish. The young of species that spawn in fresh water—striped bass, for example—move down the Hudson to this zone; the young of marine spawners such as menhaden move upstream into this area.

0.6   11.0

commercially important finfish along our coast are dependent on estuaries, many during this early phase of their development.

In freshwater regions of the Hudson, marshes and vegetated shallows serve as nurseries for many resident fish species. These habitats provide some of the advantages of the brackish water critical zone: abundant plant growth supports large concentrations of the tiny invertebrates eaten by young fish, and vegetation provides cover from predators.

What Makes a Fish a Fish?

Ask a group of children what makes a fish a fish and some typical responses will be: "They breathe water"—a reference to their gills; "they have fins and scales"—most do; "they're slimy"—frequently true; and "they're cold-blooded"—which is to say they do not metabolically maintain a set body temperature. By the way, the word "fish" itself can be singular—referring to an individual, or plural—referring to these animals collectively. The plural form "fishes" refers to an assemblage of two or more different species.

Looking at these and other characteristics, most scientists recognize three classes of fishes. Members of the class Agnatha (lampreys and hagfishes) lack jaws.[1] Representatives of Chondrichthyes (the sharks, skates, and rays) have true jaws, cartilaginous bones, and plate gills.[2] The largest class, Actinopterygii (the ray-finned fishes) includes those species with true jaws, bony skeletons, and covered gills. Many of these also bear scales.

Fishes are the most primitive of vertebrates, first evident in fossil records dating back 425 million years. Their appearance preceded that of human's apelike ancestors by some 400 million years, other vertebrates by about 100 million years. The first fishes, members of the class Agnatha, lacked jaws as did their invertebrate predecessors. No bones are present in their remains, indicating they had a cartilaginous skeleton that decayed rather than being preserved as fossil. From these evolved the sharklike species of cartilaginous fishes, and then bony fishes, which gave rise to amphibians, from which sprang reptiles and eventually mammals and birds. Many organ systems and basic life functions common to the "higher animals" first evolved in fish. With this in mind, a study of fish is a look at our own heritage, distant though it may be.

Supplying the Breath of Life: Gills

Water contains much less oxygen by volume than does air (by about twenty-five times). The need for an efficient method of oxygen extraction is met by fish gills, which can remove at least twice as much oxygen from a given volume of water as land animals' lungs can extract from the same volume of air.[3]

These simplifed drawings of a sunfish's head show the main external and internal features of its gills.

operculum (gill cover)

gill filaments

gill rakers

In most species gills are made of several parts including an operculum or gill cover, gill filaments, and gill rakers. The operculum functions like a pump. It seals as the fish opens its mouth to take in water. The mouth then closes and the operculum opens, allowing the water to pass the gill filaments as it flows out.

Gill filaments act much like the human lung. They are feathery structures, lined with blood vessels very close to the surface of the tissue. As water passes across the filaments, oxygen is absorbed into the blood stream and pumped throughout the fish's body by the heart.

At the forward end of the gills are rows of toothlike appendages called gill rakers. In many species these strainers trap floating plant and animal material which is then swallowed as food. A menhaden will swim through rich plankton swarms with its mouth open, filtering close to seven gallons of water each minute. During that time, the fish can swallow several cubic centimeters of food, mainly diatoms and small crustaceans. Fishes that feed primarily by filtering plankton have more highly adapted, finer gill rakers than those with predatory feeding habits.

That Slimy Skin

The body of a fish is covered with two layers of skin, the outer called the *epidermis*, the inner simply the *dermis*. Scattered throughout the epidermis are openings of mucus glands, from which slippery body slime is secreted. This mucus has several functions. Most significantly, it acts as an antiseptic, killing bacteria and fungi, and thus protecting the animal from disease. The mucus sloughs off rapidly, so that parasitic plants and animals find it difficult to become established on the fish's body. It seems logical that the mucus would also act as a lubricant, reducing body friction and enabling fish to pass more quickly through the water, but in experiments with fish-shaped models, unslimed models fell through a column of water just as fast as slimed models.

Coloration

A given fish species may vary greatly in color from individual to individual; even an individual fish may change its color radically from time to time. Variable coloration can serve the purposes of camouflage and advertisement. Many fishes are colored and patterned to blend well with their surroundings. Most possess color-changing cells called *chromatophores*, located in the dermis beneath the scales. These cells give a fish the ability to match new backgrounds as it moves. Flounder are noted for their color-changing abilities. Studies have been done with flounder placed on black, white, and checked surfaces. On black, the fish become very dark. An opposite response takes

The gill rakers of the American shad are long, fine, and closely spaced, allowing the fish to filter its food, primarily zooplankton, from the water as it swims.

place on white. On the checks, the fish exhibits a pronounced mottling, variable with the size of checks.

Fish are typically dark above, gradually changing to light or silvery below. As a result, a fish tends to merge visually with the background of light in the water. Sunlight is absorbed and scattered as it passes into the water, creating a dark background. The dark back of a fish blends into this background as seen by a predator from above. The light underside matches light coming down from the water's surface, making the fish less visible to a predator below.

Some fishes have color variations that help them to attract mates. Brilliant colors are a form of advertisement, luring a prospective partner.

Scales

The skin of most fishes is covered with some sort of scales. They are arranged on the fish's body in an overlapping pattern quite like the shingles on a roof. This assists in streamlining the body, affording it easier passage through the water. The scales also act as a protective layer, covering the body

The chromatophores (color-changing cells) in fishes have a network of branches extending from a central body. These cells contain pigments that can be kept in the central body, reducing intensity of color, or dispersed throughout the cell and the branches, intensifying it. Each black dot on this flounder results from dispersal of the pigment melanin within each of a group of adjacent chromatophores.

of the animal like a suit of armor. They vary in size; eels have scales so small as to be nearly invisible, while large carp have scales over an inch in diameter.

Scales grow with the fish, often leaving rings to mark periods of growth. A number of rings are created in a single year, spaced closely during times of slow growth, typically winter, and further apart during periods of rapid growth. Assuming that each band of narrowly spaced rings represents one winter, researchers can estimate the age of a fish.[4]

When the typical fish's dark back and light underparts are illuminated by the sun — lighting its back and shadowing the belly — the fish takes on a uniform color which blends into the watery background. This phenomenon is called *obliterative countershading.*

Left: The patterns of growth rings on a fish's scales often allow scientists to determine the age of that fish. *Right:* Fish scales overlap each other to form a flexible, protective body covering, as can be seen on this carp.

A few fishes have no scales at all, the Hudson's catfish and lampreys among them. These tend to be bottom dwellers and secrete a lot of mucus, a necessity in the bacteria-rich environment they call home.

To Float or Not to Float

Many fishes have a swim bladder in their abdominal cavity. This unique organ is filled with air taken from the water's surface, or with gases passed through the blood stream.[5] The swim bladder acts as a buoyant apparatus, enabling a fish to remain suspended without constant muscular effort and thus to conserve energy for other needs. Many fish that reside on the bottom of the estuary, flounder for instance, lack this organ.

Anglers may see evidence of the swim bladder if they pull in a fish hooked at considerable depth. The fish's belly may be swollen due to expansion of the balloon-like organ as the fish nears the surface where there is less water pressure to restrict the size of the bladder. If a fish is brought up fast enough that its swim bladder cannot adjust, injury may result.

Swim bladders have auxiliary functions. They are used in some species as a sound producing mechanism. Special muscles attached to the bladder's wall vibrate, the bladder itself acting as a resonating chamber, to create audible sound. These sounds are used in defense, mating, and establishing territory. Sounds produced by the swim bladder tend to be very low in frequency. The oyster toadfish, found in New York Harbor and the lower estuary, is notable for the unusual sounds it makes in this way.

The Five Senses . . . Plus One

When we look at the Hudson River, we see its surface and shoreline. To understand fish we must visualize the environment they inhabit below the river's surface. As a result of turbidity, sunlight does not penetrate far down into the water, and the channel's bottom is pitch dark. The bottom is often muddy, occasionally rocky, and littered with dead trees, old pier pilings, wrecks, tires, refrigerators, garbage, and the like. A variety of submerged plants grow in the river's shallows. Many of these things have unique smells. The interactions of water movements, living things, and human activity will create a cacophony of sound. In order to survive, a fish must sort out input from this environment. To this end, they possess the five well-known senses. In addition, many fishes have an unusual sixth sense, an ability to feel turbulence and fluctuating water pressures in their environments.

Sight. Fish vision is similar to that of humans. For some fishes, there is the complication of feeding on prey that live above the water's surface. Refraction, the bending of light which takes place when light rays pass from one substance (air in this case) to another with very different qualities (water), displaces an object in view from its actual position and requires compensation. Fishes feeding below the surface do not have to compensate for refraction; light rays travel in a straight line through a single substance.

Fish eyes differ from ours in having no eyelids. Eyelids protect eyes but also serve the function of washing them clean and keeping them moist. Living in an aquatic environment precludes this need. The iris (the ring surrounding the pupil) of the fish eye does not expand and shrink to regulate the amount of light passing into the eye. Since even the clearest of water is far less brilliantly lit than air, the pupil remains fully open to let in as much light as possible.

Fish aren't able to see further than about 100 feet in clear water, and much less in turbid water like the Hudson's. They mostly see objects at quite close range. Those living in the water column or at the surface have more highly developed sight capabilities. Largemouth bass, for instance, depend mostly on their vision to find food. Bottom dwellers like the hogchoker, a little flatfish, often have small eyes. As a result of living in a light-deprived environment, the value of sight is lessened. White catfish in the Hudson are sometimes afflicted with a parasite that eventually destroys their eyes, yet the blinded fish are often fat and otherwise healthy. They are able to depend on other senses to find food and avoid predators.

Touch. Fishes have a well-developed sense of touch centered in very sensitive nerve organs scattered over the skin, most prominently in the head region. In some fishes, these organs are on whiskerlike barbels, the most commonly known feature of catfish. Fins are sometimes specialized to enhance the sense of touch; searobins, for example, have fingerlike feelers on their pectoral fins.

Not only do the barbels (whiskers) of Atlantic sturgeon serve as an organ of touch, they also contain taste buds which allow the fish to taste-test its food before sucking it in.
(Photo by Chris Bowser.)

Taste. The senses of touch and taste in fish are sometimes combined in multipurpose organs such as catfish barbels. In addition, taste sensations experienced by fish are highly variable, as are the locations of receptor cells or taste buds. A catfish's taste buds are concentrated on the barbels, but are also randomly placed throughout the fish's skin. Other fishes have taste buds located on the gill rakers. In yet others, taste buds have been located in pads on the roof of the mouth, on the paired fins, and around the lips.

Smell. The sense of smell in fish is highly developed, as much so as in terrestrial animals. On a fish's snout are two sets of openings called nares. Each set has an incurrent and an excurrent opening. Water passing between the two flows through a chamber filled with many special folds of tissue, increasing the surface area on which smells can be sensed. The water is processed by special chemical receptors that pass information on to the brain.

The sense of smell is primarily associated with feeding, specifically in locating and discriminating among food items. The feeding habits of bottom dwellers tend to depend on smell; it is highly developed in catfish, bullheads, and American eels. Fish also use smell to detect predators, differentiate between types of aquatic plants (which may be significant in choice of habitat and location of appropriate cover) and in the case of many migratory species, locate parent streams.[6]

Hearing. Many people think fish cannot hear due to the absence of any obvious ears. But anglers fishing small streams and ponds quickly learn the value of being quiet. Fish do hear; they have a sophisticated ear with no external opening. In some fishes, the ear structure is

Searobins, common in New York Harbor, have fingerlike feelers evolved from the rays of their pectoral fins.

connected to the swim bladder through a chain of bones. In this fashion, the swim bladder becomes a resonator, amplifying the sound produced by vibrations or sound waves traveling through the water. The sounds perceived by the ear tend to be those at higher frequencies, perhaps those made by other fish. Lower frequency sounds are picked up by fish's unique sixth sense.

Sense Number Six. Along the side of the body in most bony fishes is a distinct line—the lateral line—consisting of special nerve receptor cells. Each cell has hair-like extensions reaching out of the skin. These hairs are surrounded with a gelatinous substance.[7] Turbulence in the water causes the thin jelly-covered hairs to bend, a motion then perceived by the fish. This sensory system is extremely important to fish, helping as they travel in schools, maneuver to avoid obstacles, or respond to water currents. The sensitivity of the lateral line and the information it provides a fish about even the slightest motion in its environment is one reason fish move so gracefully.

Movement in Water

Using the information processed by all of these sensory organs, a fish works its fins in varying combinations to propel itself through the water. Most fishes have two sets of paired fins (pectoral and pelvic), and three median fins (dorsal, anal, and caudal) located on the midline of the back and of the belly. In many species, there are two dorsal fins arranged in line, and the Atlantic tomcod has three. Some, like catfish and bullheads, have an additional fin—the adipose fin—that serves no function in locomotion; rather, it is a fat store, used during times when the fish is not feeding much.

Fish can swim without their fins; the movement is mainly a result of side to side undulations of the body. The fins, however, make swimming on an even keel much easier and more efficient. The caudal or tail fin can act as a propeller, moving the fish forward. The dorsal and anal fins function as keels, keeping the fish's travels in a relatively straight line. The paired fins assist in steering and braking, and also stem the tendency to roll unmanageably in the water.

Some fish have fins supported by spiny rays that may also assist in defense. Most notorious are catfish and bullheads, which have a spiny ray in their dorsal and each pectoral fin that can lock into an erect position. From this arises the assumption that a catfish can sting. They do not sting, but a person who handles a catfish carelessly could be stuck by a spine. Bacteria on the spine can infect the wound, causing lingering pain.

Common Hudson River Fishes

Communities of fishes are not defined in as clear-cut a fashion as plant communities because fish are mobile. Nonetheless,

This drawing shows the fins on a white perch. The pectoral fins and pelvic fins are arranged in pairs. The perch has two dorsal fins, the leading one supported by strong spiny rays, the rear one by soft rays.

spiny dorsal

soft dorsal

caudal

anal

pectoral

pelvic (ventral)

they can be roughly grouped according to habitats they most commonly frequent. Some fishes are benthic residents, living on or near the bottom. Others are nektonic, swimming freely in open water or inhabiting shallow waters and wetlands where vegetation provides cover as well as habitat for prey. In many species, the adults tend to prefer open water while their young reside in protected areas near the river's shore and in its marshes.

Benthic Fishes

Fishes that live at the river bottom have distinct differences from the more free-swimming species. They tend to be comparatively slow-moving and are often solitary. A few are omnivorous, some scavenge the river bottom, and many feed on benthic invertebrates—habits that do not require a great deal of mobility.

Sturgeon. Sturgeon, of which there are two species in the Hudson, are very primitive fishes and in evolution fit somewhere between sharks and bony fishes. Though classified as bony fishes, their skeleton is almost wholly cartilaginous. They do have jaws and covered gills. Five rows of armor plates make sturgeon look like a cross between a shark and a stegosaurus.

These plates provide protection when the animal is small and vulnerable. As it grows the fish needs less protection due to its rather ominous presence and size.

Sturgeon are long-lived—to sixty years and more—and reach sexual maturity later in life than do most fishes. The Atlantic sturgeon is anadromous; males will not return to the Hudson to spawn until they are eight to twelve years old, females not until they are fifteen to twenty. Subsequently, the females return to spawn only every third year. If depleted by pollution or overfishing, sturgeon populations take a long time to recover.

There are four sensitive barbels immediately in front of a sturgeon's mouth. When they detect food, the mouth protrudes to form a vacuum-cleanerlike tube that sucks up the tasty morsel. Sturgeons feed on bottom-dwelling invertebrates and small fish.

Catfish and Bullheads. Catfish are a favorite catch of many Hudson River anglers interested in putting food on the table. Unfortunately, they are also among the species most heavily contaminated with toxic pollutants. Catfish have four pairs of whiskerlike barbels around their mouths, giving rise to their name. Their skin is

Representative Species of Sturgeons

Atlantic sturgeon (*Acipenser oxyrinchus*) is the largest fish of the Hudson estuary, where adults average 5–8 feet long (one captured in Canada was 14 feet long and weighed 800 pounds). Mature adults enter the river in April or May to spawn, chiefly between Hyde Park and Catskill. Young spend 2–6 years in the estuary before heading to sea.

Shortnose sturgeon (*Acipenser brevirostrum*) is not rare in the Hudson, though federally listed as an endangered species; the estimated 50,000 here might be more than are found in all the rest of its range. Ninety percent of these fish may winter in deep water near the Esopus Meadows, just south of Kingston. This sturgeon does not go to sea. Spawning takes place from Coeymans to Troy. As with many fishes, females grow larger than males, reaching 3.5 feet and 20–25 pounds.

Representative Species of Catfish and Bullheads

White catfish (*Ameiurus catus*) is gray above, white below, and has a forked tail. These catfish can grow to 22 inches, but typically are 12–14 inches long. They are found in fresh and brackish water, commonly down-river to Yonkers.

Brown bullhead (*Ameiurus nebulosus*) is olive-green to brown above, pale white or yellow below, with a rounded or square tail. The bullhead, generally 8–12 inches long, is usually found in fresh water.

scaleless and covered with large quantities of mucus. They have an adipose fin and sharp, serrated spines in the front of their dorsal and pectoral fins.

Flatfishes. Flounder, fluke, dab, plaice, sole . . . all are flatfishes, a group well represented in the Hudson estuary. With one exception our species are most com-

mon in the saltier waters of New York Harbor, occasionally moving upriver to the Tappan Zee. The exception is the ubiquitous hogchoker, which tolerates both fresh and salty water and is regularly found north to Albany. It is most common from Haverstraw Bay to Yonkers.

All flatfish are either right-eyed or left-eyed, depending on which side of their

Representative Species of Flatfishes

Summer flounder or fluke (*Paralichthys dentatus*) is the Hudson's largest left-eyed flatfish; big ones, 30 inches long or more, are often called doormats. The brown body is dotted with dark spots surrounded by white rings. Active predators with conspicuous teeth, fluke range from bottom to top in search of prey; fish form a major part of their diet. They are called summer flounder because, after spawning offshore, many enter the estuary during the warmer months, when they are eagerly sought by anglers.

Windowpane (*Scophthalmus aquosus*) is also left-eyed. The name windowpane comes from its thin body; its underside is nearly transparent. It also goes by the name sundial. This flatfish can be up to 18 inches long.

Winter flounder (*Pseudopleuronectes americanus*) are right-eyed, solid brown above, and rarely over 16–18 inches long. This flounder lacks visible teeth, but has prominent lips. Adults come inshore to spawn in late winter/early spring (hence their name) and move into deeper, cooler water in summer. Young-of-the-year and year-old fish are common in the lower estuary. When New York anglers say "flounder," they are usually referring to this species, a very popular catch.

Hogchoker (*Trinectes maculatus*), another right-eyed flatfish, is typically 3–4 inches long, solid or mottled brown, and nearly oval in shape, with a narrow tail and tiny, beadlike black eyes. The body is covered with small rough scales and thick, viscous slime. Its name reputedly comes from farmer's observations of pigs meeting their demise when fed this fish; its rough scales caused the hogchoker to stick in the animals' throats.

body the eyes are located. At birth, they look like "normal" fish larva, but within weeks the body flattens out and one eye migrates to join the other on what becomes the upward-facing side. This side is colored, typically in a brown or olive shade that blends in with the bottom. The downward-facing side is white.

Eels. Their snakelike shape and writhing behavior when reeled out of the river engender distaste among anglers, but eels are true fish. The American eel common in the Hudson is a *catadromous* fish: one that is born in salt water, spends the majority (anywhere from five to thirty years) of its life in fresh or brackish water, and returns to the sea where it spawns and dies. All American eels breed in the Sargasso Sea, a region of the Atlantic Ocean southeast of Bermuda. No one has caught adult eels in the Sargasso, but it is there that the smallest larvae have been found.

These larvae are transparent and shaped like willow leaves. In their first year they grow little but drift about one thousand miles on ocean currents to reach the Hudson. As they approach coastal areas they transform into small "glass eels." Moving into estuaries and inland, they gain pigment and are called *elvers*. Eels are very hardy, able to take in a large percentage of their oxygen needs through their skin. They can travel overland when conditions are wet. But in spite of their hardiness, American eel populations along the Atlantic Coast appear to be in decline, for reasons as yet unknown.

Nektonic Fishes

Of the Hudson's common nektonic fishes, those that inhabit the open water of the channel are mainly plankton feeders or predators that eat the plankton feeders.

American Eel (*Anguilla rostrata*) This eel, up to 3.5 feet long, is grayish green above, white below, becoming more yellow-brown with age, and metallic silver or bronze immediately prior to the spawning migration. Eels have distinct nares on the head and are on a par with dogs in their acute sense of smell. They feed on invertebrates, small fish, and carrion, and are generally most active at night.

Other Common Bottom Dwellers

Atlantic tomcod (*Microgadus tomcod*) has three dorsal fins. The body is rarely more than 12 inches long, olive-green to brown with darker mottling and a distinctly white belly. Sometimes called frostfish, tomcod enter fresh water to spawn in late fall and winter; the eggs hatch at a chilly 40 degrees, sometimes while ice covers the Hudson. Tomcod grow fast, feeding first on zooplankton and later on small benthic organisms. Nearly all mature in one year.

Lined seahorse (*Hippocampus erectus*), a fish people are surprised to see here, is quite common from the George Washington Bridge south. Seahorses cling to plants and other objects with prehensile tails and suck up small invertebrates with their tube snouts. They swim by fluttering their pectoral and dorsal fins. The male gives birth; the young hatch from eggs that a female deposits in his abdominal pouch.

Northern pipefish (*Syngnathus fuscus*) is a close relative of the seahorse, and similarly adapted. Its body looks very much like a twig or piece of grass. It is fairly common from Peekskill south into marine waters. An average pipefish is 6 inches long; a big one may reach 12 inches.

Tesselated darter (*Etheostoma olmstedi*) is an odd little fish (3–4 inches long) of freshwater habitats. Its name comes from its staccato, darting movements. It is a mottled brown color, has two large dorsal fins and a pair of very large pectoral fins. Darters feed mostly on insects.

Both travel in schools. Nektonic species of the shallows may eat plankton, benthic invertebrates, or other fish. All have swim bladders and are able swimmers, the open water species particularly so.

River Herring. Millions of herring swim in the Hudson. Writers of bygone years describe schools of young shad headed downriver in fall as ruffling the water like a breeze, though the air was calm. Most of the six herring species common in the Hudson are slender fish with a deep body, a single dorsal fin, a deeply forked tail, and a saw-toothed belly. They lack a lateral line but have the same sense organs located in canals in the head region. Most are olive green to blue above, bright silvery white on the sides, sometimes with one or more rows of dark spots behind the upper end of the gill opening.

Most herring travel in large schools and feed on plankton; in turn, they are a major prey of striped bass, osprey, and other predators. People also pursue herring for

food, bait, and sport. The American shad historically supported the Hudson's most important commercial fishery. However, its numbers are declining; the causes are unclear, but may include fishing pressure out in the ocean, the impacts of zebra mussels on food chains on which young shad depend, or increased predation by a growing population of striped bass.

Temperate Basses. Of the three species found in the Hudson, the most abundant are striped bass and white perch, familiar as sportfish, as environmental icons, and as the generic fish diagrammed in many biology texts and field guides. These fish have two dorsal fins; one has spiny rays, the other soft rays. They also have strong spines in the anal and pelvic fins.

Bluefish and Weakfish. Along with striped bass, bluefish and weakfish are the premier gamefishes of our region's coastal waters. The two are not related taxonomically, but are grouped together here because

Representative Species of River Herring

American shad (*Alosa sapidissima*) is the Hudson's largest river herring, reaching a length of 30 inches and a weight of more than 10 pounds. Adults appear in late March and spawn until early June, mostly between Hyde Park and Catskill. The young grow to 4.5 inches long before migrating to sea in fall. Maturing females return after 5–7 years, males after 4 years. Most Hudson shad survive the spawning migration, and may live 10 or 11 years, spawning each year after maturity.

Alewife (*Alosa pseudoharengus*) and blueback herring (*Alosa aestivalis*) look much alike, and both resemble shad in looks and anadromous habit. However, they seldom grow more than one foot long. Both migrate up the Hudson in spring—bluebacks later than alewives—and spawn in freshwater shallows and tributaries, where they are avidly pursued by people with all manner of nets. The catch is typically pickled for food or used as bait for striped bass and blue crab.

Menhaden (*Brevoortia tyrannus*), also called mossbunker or simply bunker, are usually less than a foot long. Their silvery sides may have a golden or brassy cast. This coastal fish spawns offshore in late spring, after which both adults and juveniles enter the estuary, moving upriver as far as Newburgh Bay, the young sometimes farther. They are the major bait used by commercial crabbers from Poughkeepsie to the Tappan Zee.

Representative Species of Temperate Basses

Striped bass (*Morone saxatilis*), sleek and silver with dark horizontal stripes, commonly reach a weight of 30 pounds and a length of 3 feet; a 125 pounder was caught in North Carolina in 1891. The species is anadromous, entering the river in April to spawn, chiefly between the Highlands and Catskill. Young remain for at least two years, many wintering among the piers on Manhattan's West Side. Adult bass feed primarily on fish and crustaceans.

White perch (*Morone americana*) rarely exceeds 10 inches in length and is a uniform silver color, slightly darker above, with no striping. The body is deeper than that of the striped bass, the back having a distinct arch. This fish, common throughout the river, is most abundant in brackish water. There is some movement upstream and into tributaries during spawning in May and June. Young perch feed primarily on small invertebrates, older ones mostly on small fish.

of similarities in life histories and habits. Both are fierce predators; their young, born in marine waters, enter the Hudson in their first summer to feed on its abundant small fish.

Sunfishes. The sunfish family includes the familiar "sunnies" and the larger black bass so popular with anglers; twelve members of this group have been recorded in the Hudson and its tributaries.

Many of the former are distinctively colorful as adults, though their young look quite a bit alike. The operculum of many species has an earlike flap, often with a dark spot on it. Sunfishes are spiny-rayed fishes; the spiny and soft dorsal fins are usually continuous. Most inhabit slow moving or standing fresh water, often favoring weedy shallows.

Sunfishes have interesting breeding habits. Males build nests in shallow water,

Bluefish(*Pomatomus saltatrix*)
Bluefish are shiny silver with a green or blue cast on the back and a black spot at the base of the pectoral fin. Young-of-the-year "snapper" bluefish range north to New Hamburg, feeding voraciously and reaching a length of 10 inches while in the river. Schools of adult "blues," some up to 15 pounds, occasionally enter the estuary and make the water churn and boil as they attack menhaden and other prey.

Weakfish (*Cynoscion regalis*)
Weakfish are long and slender, their body gray above, silvery below, with a yellowish cast to their pelvic and pectoral fins. Weakfish are less dramatic in their predatory behavior than bluefish, and they don't penetrate as far north, juveniles having been found upriver to Indian Point.

Representative Species of Sunfishes

Pumpkinseed (*Lepomis gibbosus*), the Hudson's most common sunfish, is very colorful: green with dark mottling, a yellow breast, blue on the side of the head and lower jaw, and a red spot on the black opercular flap. A pumpkinseed more than 6 inches long is a big one. Other sunfish common here include the redbreast sunfish (*Lepomis auritus*) and bluegill (*Lepomis macrochirus*). Both grow a bit larger than the pumpkinseed and lack the red spot on the opercular flap.

Largemouth bass (*Micropterus salmoides*) supports a major recreational fishery—including fishing tournaments—on the Hudson. It is the largest of the sunfishes, the New York record being close to 11 pounds. The body is greenish bronze in color with a dark horizontal band along its side. Largemouths, common residents of the river's shallows, are voracious feeders, known to eat almost anything that moves. Smallmouth bass (*Micropterus dolomieu*) have only slightly smaller mouths and generally prefer cooler, clearer, and rockier areas of the Hudson.

Black crappie (*Pomoxis nigromaculatus*) has the deep, compressed (from side to side) body of a sunny but grow to greater size (commonly to 12 inches) and have a larger mouth. The fish is greenish above, silvery on the sides, and covered with dark spots and mottlings which give it its alternative name, calico bass.

often so close together as to look colonial. In some species there is an intricate courtship ritual, in others the male waits in the nest to be discovered by an interested female. Courting males become more intensely colored. After mating, the male will guard the nest until the eggs hatch and may herd the young around for a short time.

Minnows. In many people's minds, minnow is a generic term for any small fish. Indeed, many minnows are small, but size is

Representative Species of Minnows

Common carp (*Cyprinus carpio*), imported from Eurasia in the 1800s, are usually yellow to metallic gold in color, with two pairs of barbels on the upper lip. They can be seen spawning in weedy shallows in early summer, a female attended by several males. The group moves together, thrashing wildly in water that barely covers them. Carp are omnivorous, feeding mostly on benthic life. They can tolerate polluted water with low oxygen levels.

Goldfish (*Carassius auratus*) resemble carp but are smaller, to a foot long, and lack barbels. Their coloration varies from olive-green to orange to red, often with black or white spots. They are also omnivorous. Goldfish are less tolerant of polluted conditions than are carp.

Golden shiner (*Notemigonus crysoleucas*) has a compressed, deep body, typically 4–6 inches long. Its lateral line dips low on the side. They are golden in color and have yellow or orange fins. These shiners prefer areas that are heavily vegetated while avoiding those with a lot of silt. They feed mostly on small invertebrates.

Spottail shiner (*Notropis hudsonius*) is a small, slender fish, typically 2–3 inches long. The body is olive colored above, white below. It has a distinct spot at the base of its tail. Spottail shiners feed on zooplankton and benthic organisms. The species name *hudsonius* refers to the Hudson River, in which this minnow was discovered and first described by DeWitt Clinton.

Representative Species of Killifish

Banded killifish (*Fundulus diaphanus*) inhabits fresh water and slightly brackish reaches of the river. It is olive green above and silvery on the sides, with numerous vertical bars. Compared to the mummichog, this killifish is more slender and its tail more squared off.

Striped killifish (*Fundulus majalis*) is common in the shallows around the Statue of Liberty and similar wetland areas in saltier parts of the estuary. It is pale olive or brown in color with dark stripes, vertical in the male and horizontal in the female.

Mummichog (*Fundulus heteroclitus*) is stouter than the other killies here. Males are dark green above, their sides indistinctly striped with silver and dotted with white or yellow spots. The belly and lower fins of breeding males become intensely yellow. Females are paler, olive drab in color, sometimes with dark vertical bars. This species ranges widely in the estuary; it is found with banded killifish in fresh water and striped in salt.

not the scientifically determining factor: the carp, often two feet long and twenty pounds in weight, is classified as a minnow. Typically, minnows have soft rays in their fins, and occasionally a hard, serrated ray at the front of the dorsal and anal fin. Their jaws are toothless. Some have barbels. Minnows have prominent scales, roughly round in shape, which detach easily. Many species live in the shallow, vegetated habitats of the Hudson.

Killifish. Killifish fall into the generic "minnows" category, but are easily distinguished from true minnows by their

rounded or squared-off tail fins; the true minnows have forked tails. "Killies" are seldom more than four to six inches long. Their mouths are aimed upward and well-adapted for feeding at the surface, but these fish also scout the bottom for their meals of small invertebrates. Killifish are abundant in the weedy shallows of the Hudson estuary, where—along with the true minnows—they are an important food source for larger predators.

Fish and Fisheries
The Hudson's fish populations have provided the river with a long history as a

Other Common Nektonic Species

Bay anchovy (*Anchoa mitchilli*)—not the fare served up with pizza or Caesar salads—is a small, slender fish, nearly transparent, with one dorsal fin and a distinct silver band along its side. The mouth is large, extending well past the eye. This anchovy feeds mostly on plankton and detritus. Abundant in the brackish portion of the Hudson, this fish is an important link in the estuary's food chains.

Atlantic silverside (*Menidia menidia*) is the most familiar of the Hudson's three silversides. These fishes are small, light in color or nearly transparent, and flash a bright silver stripe down the side. A very small spiny dorsal fin in front of the larger soft-rayed dorsal separates silversides from anchovies. This species is a common summer resident in the brackish water of the lower Hudson.

Fourspine stickleback (*Apeltes quadracus*) has four spines in front of its dorsal fin. Its length seldom exceeds 2.5 inches. Males develop bright red pelvic fins during courtship and breeding, when they establish and defend a territory, build a nest of plant material, and attend the eggs laid by a female. This species prefers thick vegetation, where it feeds on tiny invertebrates. This stickleback is found widely in the estuary and its tributaries.

While today's shad fishers use outboard motors and monofilament netting, the fishery essentially exists in the same low-technology, labor-intensive form it has had for centuries.
(Photo by Chris Bowser.)

pantry and a playground: those who fish and sell their catch for a living have pursued shad, sturgeon, striped bass, herring, eels, and other species; recreational anglers have focused on striped bass, black bass, shad, catfish, and other smaller panfishes.

A shad fishery has existed on the Hudson for as long as humans have inhabited the valley. The native people living here called the shad "porcupine fish turned outside in" because of its many bones. In spite of that unpleasantness, many still consider shad to be a seasonal delight of spring; its scientific name means "savory herring," or "herring most delicious." Some liken smoked shad to a religious experience. Shad roe—the pair of large egg sacs in a female ready to spawn—is considered a delicacy.

Gill nets are commonly used to catch shad; their nearly invisible nylon meshes are sized to allow a shad's head to push through, but not its body. As the fish tries to back out, its gill covers tangle in the mesh. In the Tappan Zee and Haverstraw Bay, gill nets are suspended between floats at the surface and heavy weights at the bottom. These nets are checked around slack water, when the current is about to change direction. In deeper areas from the Highlands north, gill nets are hung from floats and allowed to drift with the current for several hours.

Even in good years shad fishing was not a way to get rich, and in the early twenty-first century it scarcely pays to go out. Shad stocks are declining, the market is uncertain, and fishing time and gear are lost as increasing numbers of striped bass clog up the gill nets; by law, the bass cannot be kept. Only a handful of fishermen, few of them young, still carry on the tradition. Fishing lore and skills are disappearing; indeed, the stake net shad fishery along the Hudson's New Jersey shore ended about when the last century did.

Early accounts of the river tell of natives spearing sturgeon by torchlight. As Europeans came to dominate the valley, sturgeon were so abundant and useful that they were referred to as "Albany beef." Overfishing and pollution were likely causes of a decline in the catch after the 1800s. In the 1980s and early 1990s the Atlantic sturgeon—its eggs valuable as caviar and its smoked meat fetching a pretty price—again came under heavy fishing pressure in the Hudson and in coastal waters off New Jersey. Fisheries managers, concerned about the lack of young Atlantic sturgeon in the Hudson, put a moratorium on all sturgeon fishing here in 1996. After the turn of the millennium, researchers began to find young fish again, but given the many years that sturgeon require to reach maturity, it will be decades before the population can once more provide Hudson River caviar to gourmet markets.

Many economically valuable coastal species—bluefish and menhaden, for example—spend the early parts of their lives in the Hudson nursery, though while here they are too small to be of great interest to humans. The bluefish is one of the most important recreational species on the coast; anglers spend millions of dollars on bait, tackle, fuel, charter boats, motel rooms, and food during their trips to catch this species. Bluefish also are pursued by commercial fishing interests. Menhaden do not appear on dinner tables, but they are an important source of fish meal and oil and of animal feeds. By volume of catch and its dollar value, menhaden are a major commercial species on the East Coast.

Perhaps the best example of the contributions the estuary makes to the ecological, recreational, and economic resources of coastal waters is the striped bass. A substantial portion of the stripers migrating along the Atlantic coast come from the Hudson. For much of the twentieth century, most of these fish were from the Chesapeake Bay, but in the 1970s the bay's population crashed, and the fairly stable Hudson population became the mainstay of coastal runs. To protect the Chesapeake stock and arrest the overall decline in bass numbers, an interstate management plan set new coastwide fishing regulations, including raising the size at which bass were "keepers" and reducing commercial catches. This led to a resurgence of striped bass on the East Coast in the late 1980s and 1990s. While the Hudson's striper stock was not in bad shape to begin with, it too benefited. April and May on the Hudson now see a frenzy of anglers looking for big bass; fish weighing 56 pounds have been caught here.

The Hudson once hosted commercial fisheries for striped bass and American eel.

Eels are considered to be a delicacy in some Asian and European cultures, and striped bass are very popular food fish. But in 1976, New York State closed the Hudson's commercial fisheries for these species, and advised the public to eat neither. The reason: contamination by toxic polychlorinated biphenyls—PCBs.

Is It Safe to Eat the Fish?

Revelation of the PCB problem was a cruel blow, coming at a time when sewage treatment efforts were gearing up and public hopes for river cleanup were high. PCBs

Toxic PCBs are stored in the bodies of animals that ingest them. The dragonfly nymph feeding on water fleas accumulates small doses of PCBs from its prey. The sunfish that eats the dragonfly nymph thus gets a stronger dose; as the fish eats more nymphs, its PCB burden reaches higher levels. A largemouth bass at the top of this food chain, accumulating the concentrated doses in the sunfish it eats, builds up even greater concentrations of PCBs which may pose a threat to humans who eat bass.

are a suspected human carcinogen. Their stability and tendency to bioaccumulate in fatty tissue results in a phenomenon known as *biological concentration:* in moving up a food chain, one finds increasing levels of toxic contaminants. A predator near the top of a food chain, striped bass for example, can have as much as one million times the PCBs found in its watery environment.

Thirty years after New York announced that Hudson River fish were contaminated, PCBs remain a problem. As of 2005, New York State's Department of Health advises that women of child-bearing age and children under age fifteen eat no fish from the Hudson estuary, including New York Harbor, given special concerns about exposing fetuses, infants, and children to PCBs. Other individuals should restrict consumption based on location and species of fish. By law, only catch and release fishing is allowed from the Troy Dam to Hudson Falls, and the health department recommends against eating most fish caught between Troy and the Rip Van Winkle Bridge in Catskill. Below that bridge, advisories generally recommend no more than one meal per month.[8]

While covered by these advisories, American shad is sold commercially since its PCB levels fall below the federal limit of two parts per million in fish intended for human consumption. Being in the river only briefly limits its exposure to contaminants, and the fish eats little or nothing on its spawning run. When eating, the shad dines low on the food chain, consuming plankton.

While striped bass have historically been pursued for sport and food in the Hudson, the coastal fisheries for this species have been much more extensive. The Hudson's PCBs, traveling with the migrating bass, have had negative consequences for these fisheries in the past. Before the resurgence of the Chesapeake population, the largest percentage of stripers caught off Long Island's shores came from the Hudson. In the mid-1980s, worries about PCB contamination led to limitations on the commercial fishery there, where bass had been the mainstay of fishing families for generations.

As with so many other environmental problems, PCB contamination of striped bass reminds us of the interconnectedness of systems or geographic areas that we usually consider to be discreet entities. Many people tend to view the river as a closed system with a clear boundary, but, as described in earlier chapters, the watershed fuels life in the river through contributions of detritus, and the resources of the estuary support organisms in coastal waters beyond the Hudson. In the next chapter, we will explore the ways in which the reptiles, amphibians, birds and mammals of the river cross the boundary between water and air and depend on the Hudson's resources.

Chapter 6

The Chapter in Brief
As classes of animals, the amphibians, reptiles, birds, and mammals evolved to inhabit terrestrial environments, yet many species exploit and depend upon aquatic habitats like those found along the Hudson. Amphibians are uncommon in the estuary for reasons including tidal fluctuation, pollution, and predation. Reptile diversity in the river's wetlands is fairly low, a few turtles and snakes being the most common representatives of the class. Birds, however, are abundant and diverse: waterfowl, shorebirds, herons, gulls, raptors, and many other families use these habitats extensively. Their visibility and the high degree of human interest in birds makes them important indicators of environmental problems. Muskrats and a few other mammals are common residents of tidal wetlands; many other species opportunistically roam such habitats in search of food.

The Hudson's Birds and Beasts

Living on the Edge

To most humans, crossing the boundary between the watery world of the Hudson and the realm of air and dry land is a big deal. We post lifeguards, or at least make sure we are with companions, before entering the water. We may hesitate a bit, worried about the dangers of pollution. Toes or fingers go in first, testing the temperature; then there is a last delay for couple of deep breaths before we finally take the plunge.

For many of the Hudson's amphibians, reptiles, birds, and mammals, moving between water and air is a matter of course—an act performed as easily as we walk through doors to enter or leave a building. Many of them live on the edge—ducks floating on the river's surface, for example, or muskrats slipping in and out of the water as they forage busily in a marsh. Except for the amphibians, they do not breathe underwater, but are quite at home there. These animals depend on the Hudson for food and shelter just as the fish and invertebrates do, and are likewise exposed to the river's pollutants.

Many terrestrial animals make use of the Hudson's habitats, particularly its marshes and tidal swamps, on an occasional basis. On late summer evenings, for instance, tremendous flocks of migrating swallows swirl into the marshes to roost. This chapter, however, will focus on those animals and birds that call such habitats home, substantially depending on them for food, shelter, and breeding sites.

Amphibians

Amphibians lead double lives. Almost all of our amphibians hatch from eggs laid in water and live for a time as aquatic larvae—frog tadpoles being familiar examples. They then metamorphose—change form—into air-breathing terrestrial creatures.

Even as adults, amphibians require moist conditions for survival. Though most have lungs, they also "breathe" through their skin. Oxygen passes directly into tiny blood vessels concentrated under the skin. For this to happen efficiently, their skin must be moist.

Amphibians found in the Hudson Valley include frogs, toads, and salamanders. During a walk through woods bordering the river's marshes, or along streams flowing into the river, one might find good numbers of any of these animals. It might be reasonable to assume that the Hudson's wetlands would provide fine habitats for such water-dependent creatures, but in actuality, few are found there in any numbers. Five factors may account for this scarcity.

1. Amphibians are chiefly shallow-water creatures, and the shallows of the Hudson are subject to tides. The regular cycles of exposure and flooding in the intertidal zone may pose difficulties for adult amphibians, and certainly are problematic for their eggs, which must stay wet.
2. Though sometimes found in slightly brackish water, amphibians avoid salt water, and are absent from the lower portions of the Hudson estuary.
3. Intertidal waters are subjected to high temperatures in summer and ice scour in winter, conditions which threaten any animals that cannot leave or burrow deep in the mud.
4. Many predators—large fish, herons, and snapping turtles, for instance—prowl these areas and may limit amphibian populations.
5. Some amphibians are very sensitive to pollution, a problem in the Hudson.

The most likely place to find amphibians in Hudson River wetlands is in supratidal pools, rarely flooded by high tides. Usually found around a wetland's edge, these pools are less subject to the stresses listed above.

Frogs and Toads

Protuberant eyes, long hind legs, and a hopping style of locomotion characterize these familiar amphibians. Even when the animals are not visible, their calls are distinctive enough to allow a naturalist to distinguish them by ear.

The green frog is the most common amphibian of the river's tidal wetlands, though given the paucity of amphibians, that is not to say it is abundant. This frog breeds here in limited numbers. Bullfrogs appear more rarely. Two treefrogs—the gray treefrog and spring peeper—and the northern leopard frog occasionally are heard in these habitats but it is doubtful that they breed here. The American toad has been observed breeding in the Iona Island marsh, but this does not seem to be a common occurrence in the Hudson.

Salamanders

Salamanders are often confused with lizards; both have long, relatively slender bodies with distinct heads, four legs of roughly equal size, and long tails. However, salamanders lack the scaly skin and clawed toes of lizards, which are reptiles. In the Hudson Valley, salamanders are very common, lizards rare.

Though salamanders can often be found within a few frog leaps of the river, they are uncommon in the Hudson's wetlands. An aquatic salamander—the mudpuppy—is found in a few locations in the freshwater Hudson. One or two other salamanders common in tributary streams occasionally appear in river wetlands near the mouths of these streams.

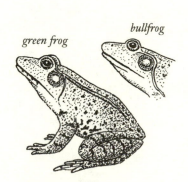

bullfrog

green frog

Representative Species of Frogs and Toads

Green frog (*Rana clamitans*) *below* is usually greenest around the face and browner on the back and toward the rear, where there is often darker mottling. Large individuals may be 3.5 inches long (excluding the legs). Green frogs differ from the similar bullfrog (*Rana catesbeiana*) *above* in having two ridges of skin extending rearward along the back, one from each eye. On the bullfrog, these ridges do not extend along the back but instead curve downward around the animal's ear.

Mudpuppy (*Necturus maculosus*)
This large (up to a foot long) salamander sports gills in plumes on each side of its neck. A benthic animal, it is occasionally caught by anglers fishing in tidal fresh water.

Reptiles

In evolution, amphibians link the fishes to the reptiles. All are vertebrates, and all are cold-blooded. The fishes, which lead completely aquatic lives, gave rise to amphibians adapted to air and land. The amphibians, still dependent on moist conditions and on water for their eggs and larval stages, gave rise to the reptiles, which severed those ties to the ancestral watery home. Reptiles have evolved well-developed lungs, for the most part eliminating the need for skin breathing with its attendant requirement for moisture.[1] Their embryos develop in an egg surrounded by protective membranes and a shell. These maintain fluid conditions around the reptile embryo, preventing it from drying out; thus the egg does not have to be laid in water.

While holding onto these evolutionary adaptations for terrestrial life, some reptiles nonetheless inhabit watery environments. As is the case with amphibians, many reptiles common in wetland habitats elsewhere in the Hudson Valley are much less so in the river's tidal wetlands. However, a few turtles and snakes can be seen regularly.

Turtles

Among river valleys worldwide, the Hudson Valley stands out for its diversity of turtles: twelve species have been found here. Those most commonly found in the river lead almost completely aquatic lives, venturing onto dry land only to lay their eggs or when forced away from their watery homes by drought or other extreme conditions. Some, the painted turtle for example, sunbathe on rocks or floating logs. Others, including the most common turtle of the river's tidal wetlands, the snapping turtle, seldom bask out of the water but can be seen swimming near the surface or lying half-buried in the mud flats left by a retreating tide. On calm, warm days, pools in river marshes are stippled here and there by just the tips of the noses of snapping turtles getting a breath of air.

Snakes

Start discussing snakes of aquatic habitats and quickly someone will describe the water moccasin they saw while out fishing here in the Hudson Valley. Large nonpoisonous water snakes, dark and thick-bodied, may react in threatening fashion if sur-

Representative Species of Turtles

Snapping turtle (*Chelydra serpentina*) is found even in the brackish Piermont Marsh; substantial populations live in some of the river's freshwater marshes. The big head and long tail are distinctive. The largest of the region's turtles, one Hudson specimen weighed 44 pounds. While snappers occasionally dine on ducklings, their reputation as fearsome carnivores is greatly overstated; most of their food is plant matter, carrion, and small or slow-moving fishes.

Painted turtle (*Chrysemys picta*) is small (shell up to 6 inches long) and ornately patterned — the head with bright yellow stripes and spots, the shell's edge with red lines. These turtles are widespread in the river's freshwater marshes, but in low numbers. They eat plants and small invertebrates.

Diamondback terrapin (*Malaclemys terrapin*) prefers brackish tidal wetlands. There is a small population in the Piermont Marsh, and it may range up to Iona Island. This turtle is considered common in tidal wetlands at New Jersey's Liberty State Park. In most individuals the plates of the top shell are patterned with concentric rings or ridges.

Northern Water Snake (*Nerodia sipedon***)**
This able swimmer and diver preys mostly on fish. It basks on logs, branches, and rocks, quickly slipping into the water when approached. The rock riprap of railroad causeways is a favored habitat within the river's tidal wetlands. Older individuals, 3–4 feet long, are heavyset and drably dark; younger ones are more slender with brown crossbands and blotches on a lighter background.

prised or cornered, but the venomous water moccasin, more properly called the cottonmouth, comes no nearer the Hudson than the state of Virginia.[2]

Two snakes are widespread but apparently not especially common anywhere in the Hudson's tidal wetlands. The well-known garter snake with its yellow stripes is nearly ubiquitous in the Hudson Valley. Fish are included in its diet, and the search for such prey may bring it into the river's wetlands. More truly aquatic is the northern water snake.

Birds

Be it the dog days of summer or a below zero morning in February, there is one class of creatures almost always in evidence on the Hudson: the birds—at least a few gulls, maybe a flock of migrating waterfowl, or perhaps an osprey wheeling overhead in its hunt for fish. Among the Hudson's vertebrates, birds are second only to fish in overall numbers; they rival fish in their diversity.

There are many reasons for this abundance. Like other creatures of the estuary, birds benefit from its productivity, finding large supplies of food here. The Hudson Valley serves as a flyway, a route followed by birds as they migrate north in spring and south in fall. During these travels, many species settle on the river and its wetlands to rest and feed.

As a class, birds exploit all of the habitats available in the Hudson ecosystem, and are active in all seasons. Their warm-blooded nature and feathery insulation allow some species to survive even the coldest months, when sparrows flit through frozen marshes hunting seeds, and ducks dodge ice cakes on the river's surface and dive beneath them to catch fish and invertebrates. Each species has particular adaptations of anatomy and behavior which suit the re-

quirements of its diet and life in the chosen habitat.

The Hudson's birds are too numerous to allow description here of all the varieties one might see. Only a few common species from the families of birds that use the river are included. The descriptions are organized in four major groups based on habits and habitats, but keep in mind that birds cannot read and will not always place themselves in such neat pigeonholes. Also remember that their presence follows seasonal patterns; these will be noted in the species descriptions.

Swimming Birds

The most familiar swimming birds are waterfowl—ducks, geese, and swans—but gulls, cormorants, coots, and an occasional loon or grebe can also be seen on the Hudson's surface. Many are social, associating with one another in flocks ranging from loose collections of a few birds to huge rafts—groups of hundreds.

Most of these birds have webbed feet which serve as efficient paddles. Some are excellent divers; they can reach the bottom to find fish and benthic invertebrates. Others feed in the shallow water of the river's wetlands by tipping up: pointing their tails skyward and submerging the front half of their bodies. Except for cormorants, these birds can oil their outer feathers to waterproof them. The underlying downy plumage stays dry, retaining its insulating ability and keeping the birds warm even in frigid winter weather.

Duck hunting has a long history on the Hudson. In fall, duck-hunting blinds sprout on the river's flats and in its marshes. These are rafts or platforms covered with cattail or reed to hide hunters within. Occupied blinds are usually surrounded with waterfowl decoys. A few gunners employ a method of hunting called creeping: lying low in a camouflaged boat and very patiently paddling or drifting towards their quarry.

Geese and Swans. The largest of the water-fowl, geese and swans have especially long necks which enable them to reach sub-merged aquatic plants in deeper water than smaller ducks. Geese also graze on land, and will leave their aquatic habitats to find fresh young plant shoots in lawns and fields. Geese and swans have expanded their nesting range in New York in recent decades, and pose problems for wildlife managers. Canada geese in particular can negatively impact water quality with their droppings, which are also a nuisance in parks and other grassy areas favored by the birds.

Surface-feeding Ducks. These ducks are birds of shallow wetlands. They rarely dive, but more often tip up to reach underwater vegetation and invertebrate animals. They also feed by dabbling—scooping up water and food items and, like draining pasta in a colander, allowing the water to dribble out through comblike structures on the sides of their bills. Surface-feeding ducks take flight by leaping directly into the air.

These ducks are numerous in spring and fall, when a great variety drop in on

Representative Species of Geese and Swans

Canada goose (*Branta canadensis*) *right* is the familiar honker with its long black neck and white cheek patch. It nests along the Hudson, and is commonly seen in large flocks during migration and in winter. The some-what similar but smaller brant (*Branta berni-cla*) *left* migrates through the Hudson Valley and winters on saltier portions of the estuary. Large flocks can be seen in early spring near the Statue of Liberty.

Mute swan (*Cygnus olor*), the biggest bird on the Hudson, is present all year, though winter ice often pushes it downriver. Adults are pure white with a graceful curved neck and an orange bill. The species is not native; it was brought from Europe in the late 1800s for its beauty. Large flocks can damage beds of submerged aquatic vegetation; they con-sume large amounts and uproot more than they eat.

the Hudson during migration. They are less common in winter, when many of the shallows on which they depend are locked up in ice. Only the large, hardy mallard and black ducks winter in any numbers. Ducks are not all that common in the summer breeding season either. Fluctuating water levels in the river's tidal marshes limit avail-able nest sites. The species described here occasionally breed in association with these wetlands, but mostly nest on land and then raise their hatchlings on the marshes.

Representative Species of Surface-Feeding Ducks

Mallard (*Anas platyrhynchos*) males have a green head, white ring around the neck, and dark brown chest. As with most ducks, the females are much duller in color but share with the males a blue patch in the inner portion of the wing.

Black duck (*Anas rubripes*) is a very dark mottled brown in color. When it flies, the silvery white undersides of the wings contrast sharply with the dark body.

Wood duck (*Aix sponsa*) nests in cavities in large trees and sometimes feeds in forests adjacent to wetlands. They commonly use large nesting boxes put out in and around marshes. The male is generally acknowledged to be the most beauti-ful of North American ducks, colored in brilliant and varied hues.

Representative Species of Diving Ducks

Greater scaup (*Aythya marila*) and lesser scaup (*Aythya affinis*) males have a dark (black at a distance) head, chest, and tail; the body is light gray to white. The two species look so similar that, unless conditions are ideal, many birders and hunters do not distinguish between them. Both occur in large rafts and feed on mollusks and other invertebrates.

Bufflehead (*Bucephala albeola*) *left* males are little ducks with white sides and a big patch of white towards the rear of the head. They appear regularly in migration and winter (though not in big flocks), often with the larger common goldeneye (*Bucephala clangula*) *right*, also black with white sides and white on the head—a small oval between the bill and the eye. These species eat benthic invertebrates and plants.

Canvasback (*Aythya valisineria*) eats more plants than other diving ducks; as suggested by its scientific name, *Vallisneria* (wild celery) is a favorite food. The male has a white body, black chest, and a reddish head with a distinctive sloping profile.

Common merganser (*Mergus merganser*) *left*, a fish-eating duck, frequents fresh and slightly brackish waters. Small groups are often seen swimming among ice floes. The long white body, dark head (glossy green in good light), and long red bill identify the male. On saltier water around New York Harbor, the red-breasted merganser (*Mergus serrator*) *right* takes the place of the common.

Diving Ducks. When traveling the railroad along the Hudson's shore, one can quickly separate the diving ducks from the surface feeders. Frightened by the onrushing train, the former take to the air only after getting a running start over the river's surface, while the latter can spring up into the air.[3] Generally found on the open Hudson, these ducks are adapted for swimming underwater. Compared to surface-feeding waterfowl, their legs are placed further back on their bodies, making them better propellers.

These ducks often are seen in huge rafts during spring and fall migrations, and many winter on the lower Hudson, staying south of the ice cover or using openings in the ice to enter their underwater feeding

grounds. They rarely, if ever, breed along the tidewater Hudson, but mergansers and a few other species do nest in the Adirondacks and Catskills.

From a distance, the males of most of the diving ducks are patterned in black and white; the arrangement and shape of the white areas is very helpful in identification. Females are generally brown, with less obvious identification clues.

Cormorants. If it swims like a duck and quacks like a duck, it must be a duck. Cormorants swim like ducks but do not quack, and they are not related to ducks. They lack the ability to waterproof their plumage, so after spending time diving underwater in pursuit of fish these birds must climb out on a rock, log, or buoy and dry out, striking a distinctive erect pose with wings spread. Swimming, they ride low in the water, their long, snaky necks characteristically holding the head and bill tilted upward.

Coots. Though they swim and dive in ducklike fashion, coots belong to the family of

Double-crested Cormorant (*Phalacrocorax auritus*)
This large, dark bird can be seen on both fresh and salt water. Upriver it is a common migrant, and a few pairs nest on navigation light towers. There are large nesting colonies in New York Harbor. It is less common in winter.

American Coot (*Fulica americana*)
Among ducks, the coot is set apart by its evenly slate-gray body, black head, and white chickenlike bill. Not known to nest on the Hudson, it is a common migrant (most numerous in fall), and an occasional winterer. Coots eat plants and small invertebrates.

birds called rails. They lack webbed feet, but each toe has wide lobes of skin which serve as workable paddles. Coots bob their head back and forth in pigeonlike fashion as they swim.

Wading Birds

These birds haunt the river's margins, following the tide in and out over the shore-line, tidal flats, and marshes. Shorebirds, herons, and rails are not adapted for swimming; instead, they have long legs which allow them to wade out into the water.

Since their preferred habitat is covered with ice in the winter, at least in the Hudson's more northerly reaches, wading birds use the Hudson mainly in summer and during spring and fall migration. A few individuals may try to make it through the winter in more sheltered sites along the lower river.

Shorebirds. A typical image of shorebirds is a flock of little brown birds scurrying along a surf-pounded beach, darting after a retreating wave to glean delicacies from the wet sand in front of the next breaker. But a far greater number of these birds can be seen on mudflats or in shallow pools left in marshes by the falling tide.

Representative Species of Shorebirds

killdeer

semipalmated

Killdeer (*Charadrius vociferus*) *left*, a noisy shorebird of the group known as plovers, often forages along the Hudson. It nests in open spaces including railroad rights of way, athletic fields, and flat roofs of large buildings. Robin-sized, the killdeer is brown above, white below, with two black bands across its chest. During migration, the smaller semipalmated plover (*Charadrius semipalmatus*) *right*, appears along the river. It has a single black band across its chest.

Spotted sandpiper (*Actitis macularia*) breeds along the river. In summer it indeed has black spots scattered across its white underparts, but before seeing those, you might notice that this small sandpiper constantly bobs its rear end up and down—a behavior called teetering. It takes to the air in a distinctive manner, holding its wings stiffly bowed and flying with shallow, quivering wingbeats.

Least sandpiper (*Calidris minutilla*) is the smallest of a group of look-alike shorebirds called "peeps" by birdwatchers. Most are sparrow-sized and sparrow-colored. Flocks of least sandpipers are common along the Hudson in migration, particularly in marshes and freshwater habitats. The similar semipalmated sandpiper (*Calidris pusilla*) prefers more open flats and is more common near the coast.

Greater yellowlegs (*Tringa melanoleuca*) is pigeon-sized, grayish brown above, white below, with a white rump and tail and long, bright yellow legs. It is common in migration along the estuary. Yes, there is a lesser yellowlegs (*Tringa flavipes*), also seen occasionally during migration.

Representative Species of Herons, Egrets, and Bitterns

great egret

snowy egret

Snowy egret (*Egretta thula*) *right* is most common in the lower estuary but wanders upriver, particularly in late summer. Somewhat larger than a crow, this all-white heron has a black bill, black legs, and golden-yellow feet. The larger great egret (*Casmerodius albus*) *left* has a yellow bill and black legs and feet.

Least bittern (*Ixobrychus exilis*) is the smallest (the size of a pigeon) and least apparent of the Hudson's herons, though it regularly breeds in tidal marshes, hanging its nest in cattails and other emergent vegetation above the reach of the tides. The large buff-colored patch in each wing identifies this heron.

Green heron (*Butorides virescens*) has a dark green back, but it often appears black unless seen in good light or at close range. This crow-sized heron is widely distributed along the Hudson, nesting in tidal swamps and woodlands adjacent to tidal marshes.

Great blue heron (*Ardea herodias*) is the largest wading bird found along the Hudson, 4 feet tall with a 6–7 foot wingspread. The body and wings are as much gray as blue; the head is lighter, almost white. Breeding colonies are scattered throughout the valley, but none is currently known to exist right along the river.

In such habitats along the Hudson one might find an array of sandpipers, plovers, yellowlegs, and other shorebirds during migration, especially in the fall. Their number and diversity peaks around the Hudson's mouth, where shorebirds traveling down the river meet a larger contingent moving along the Atlantic coast. The breeding grounds for most shorebirds lie far to the north. Few nest in the Hudson Valley, and of these, even fewer nest along the river itself.

Shorebirds feed mainly on invertebrates—worms, crustaceans, insects, and mollusks. Many have long bills for probing in water and mud.

Herons, Egrets, and Bitterns. Some of the Hudson's showiest and most impressive birds, recognizable even from an Amtrak train speeding along the Hudson at 80 miles per hour, are the herons and their relatives. They have long, daggerlike bills adapted for catching fish and other small animals. Most people are familiar with the unmoving but alert posture of herons waiting for such prey. A few species, the snowy egret among them, more

actively pursue their quarry, dancing about in shallow water to stir up food.

The estuary's most impressive concentration of these birds occurs in New York Harbor. In the late 1970s and early 1980s, herons and egrets began nesting on islands once used by people but later abandoned and overgrown with shrubs and trees. In 1991, New York City established the Harbor Herons Wildlife Refuge to protect these nesting sites.

At first, the largest breeding colonies were on islands in the Arthur Kill and Kill van Kull, the waterways which separate Staten Island from New Jersey. Somewhat incongruously, the industrial development surrounding these islands created a no-man's-land where the birds found the isolation they require for nesting. However, oil spills there in 1990 severely impacted breeding success, and the birds moved to other islands in or near the East River, in Lower New York Harbor, and in Jamaica Bay.

As of 2004, over 1,700 nests of eight species of herons, egrets, and ibises were counted on seven islands. Black crowned night herons were the most common nesting species; glossy ibis, snowy egrets, and great egrets were also present in large numbers.

Rails. The expression "thin as a rail" refers not to railroad tracks or to fencing but to birds of this family, which compress themselves from side to side in order to slip through the dense growth of plant stems in marshes. Rails have very long toes, the better to distribute their weight over the uncertain support provided by soft mud and mats of vegetation. If you see one, it might remind you of a small chicken, but catching sight of them is difficult due to their secretiveness and the thick vegetation of their marsh habitats.

Perching Birds
of Wetland Habitats

Thrushes, blackbirds, wrens, finches, sparrows, flycatchers, swallows, jays—these

Virginia Rail (*Rallus limicola*)
This most common member of the rail family along the Hudson (except for the ducklike coot) nests in marshes. A long bill allows it to pick invertebrates from shallow water, mud, and marsh vegetation. A rich reddish-brown color covers its breast and is streaked through the feathers of its upperparts. The clapper rail (*Rallus longirostris*) is larger, grayer, and restricted to the saltier marshes around New York Harbor.

and most of the familiar birds of our yards, woodlands, and fields all belong to the largest order of birds, the perching birds. Very few of these have actually become adapted to an aquatic life, so you will not see them out on open water or bare tidal flats. But

Representative Perching Birds of Wetland Habitats

American goldfinch

yellow warbler

Marsh wren (*Cistothorus palustris*) populations are greatest in dense stands of cattail, where their bubbly trills are more evident than the birds themselves. Wait patiently to sight this tiny brown bird, stubby tail cocked over its back, clinging to a cattail stem. Marsh wren nests are a woven ball of cattail leaves the size and shape of a coconut, hanging on cattail stems a few feet over the water.

Red-winged blackbird (*Agelaius phoeniceus*) males are unmistakable, though the red wing patches are often hidden unless the bird is singing. The females resemble large striped sparrows. Of the marshes' migrant perching birds, the male redwings are the first to return in spring.

Swamp sparrow (*Melospiza georgiana*) is common but often overlooked given its retiring nature and relatively dull color. One cannot miss its song, however—a rattling series of chips reminiscent of a sewing machine in action. A reddish brown cap and unstreaked breast distinguish adult swamp sparrows.

Yellow warbler (*Dendroica petechia*) *left* is not restricted to marsh habitats but is abundant there, particularly at the edges. It nests in shrubs or small trees scattered around the marsh on higher ground. This tiny bird is all yellow; males have a few reddish streaks on their breasts. Another small yellow bird common in marshes is the American goldfinch (*Carduelis tristis*) *right*; its wings and tail are black. It nests in shrubs and in purple loosestrife.

in the high marsh and tidal swamps of the Hudson, perching birds are abundant. Most feed on insects and other small invertebrates; the blackbirds, finches, and sparrows also eat large quantities of seeds.

Of the many perching birds that you might see in these habitats, most are visitors in search of food and shelter. Fewer actually live the larger part of their lives there. The species described here do breed in the Hudson's marshes and swamps. Excepting the goldfinch, a year-round resident, they are migratory, with only the rare straggler hanging around into the winter. The red-winged blackbird, marsh wren, and swamp sparrow are the most abundant summer birds of the river's freshwater marshes, and are also common in brackish marshes.

Wide-ranging River Birds

The birds grouped here can not be assigned to one particular river habitat; they may be seen over, or in, different ones. Most typically hunt over open water, be it the channel or shallow water covering flats or submerged vegetation.

Gulls. "Sea" gulls are familiar to everyone, even people who live far from the sea. Virtually every shopping mall near the Hudson has its complement of gulls patrolling for garbage. Their catholic tastes have allowed gulls to prosper in direct response to the increasing amounts of wastes tossed out by humans. Garbage dumps and sewage outfalls have been considered hotspots by birdwatchers interested in finding rare gulls.

Representative Species of Gulls

Herring gull (*Larus argentatus*) is the "standard" gull, found along the river in all seasons. It is about 2 feet long with a wingspread of 4–5 feet. The smaller ring-billed gull (*Larus delawarensis*) has a dark ring around its bill and yellowish or greenish legs (herring gulls' are pinkish). Ring-billed gulls chiefly nest outside the Hudson's watershed, but are common migrants and summer stragglers. In winter, upriver observers see more ring-billed than herring gulls.

Great black-backed gull (*Larus marinus*) is larger than the herring gull and has a very dark gray (almost black) back and upper wing surface. It regularly wanders upriver, but is most common in New York Harbor.

Laughing gull (*Larus atricilla*), common around the harbor, is smaller than the herring gull and readily distinguished in summer by its black head and darker back. Unlike other species described here, this gull is rare in winter. Upriver it is usually seen only in migration, and is uncommon even then.

Gulls are strong fliers; they also have webbed feet and can swim well. Their bills are hooked and powerful; in addition to scavenging, the larger species will prey on other birds and small mammals as well as more typical gull fare: fish, mollusks, crustaceans, and human food scraps. Most adult gulls are gray on their backs and wings and white below. Young birds, however, go through two to four years of brownish plumages before gaining the adult coloration.

Gulls can be seen in all seasons along the Hudson. Herring, great black-backed, and laughing gulls nest in scattered colonies around New York Harbor, but not along the Hudson itself. Those seen in summer upriver are young birds, nonbreeding adults, or stragglers from breeding grounds elsewhere.

Kingfishers. Kingfishers plunge headlong into the water to catch small fish with their strong, daggerlike bills. They may fish from a perch or hover over a likely spot. Since their style of fishing requires shallow, ice-free water, only a few hardy individuals hang around the Hudson in winter. Of eighty-six species of kingfishers found worldwide, only one occurs on the Hudson or in most of the U.S. for that matter.

Raptors. Raptors are the birds of prey: eagles, hawks, falcons, and owls. All have hooked beaks for tearing the flesh of their prey, which is captured with taloned feet. While a variety of species may hunt along the river and over its marshes, the bald eagle and osprey depend on water, for fish is their preferred food.

Numbers of both these species declined through the 1950s and 1960s. Use of the pesticide DDT, identified as a major culprit in this decline, was banned in the U.S. in 1972. Osprey populations in the Northeast have steadily recovered since then.

Belted Kingfisher
(*Ceryle alcyon*)
Our kingfisher is shaggy-headed, pigeon-sized, and slate blue in color, with a distinct white collar. Its harsh rattling cry is a familiar sound along the Hudson. Kingfishers nest in burrows excavated into embankments.

Bald Eagle (*Haliaeetus leucocephalus*)
Adults are huge and easily identifiable; eagles less than four years old lack the white head and tail. They feed on fish, usually dead or dying, snatched from water's surface. In winter 2005, when much of the Hudson and other nearby water bodies were ice-covered, as many as one hundred eagles per day were seen along open water between Peekskill and Croton. In 2004, eleven pairs nested along the river, fledging thirteen young eagles.

Osprey (*Pandion haliaetus*)
Ospreys soar or hover over the river till prey is sighted, then plunge in feet first to catch fish, most often goldfish, catfish, and herring. They are smaller than eagles, brown above, and white below. The "fish hawk" is a common migrant here. A few stragglers are seen in summer, but the species is not known to nest along the tidewater Hudson. Ospreys do breed in the Adirondacks, on Long Island, and at a few sites around New York Harbor.

Eagle restoration required more effort. It had virtually disappeared as a breeding bird in New York State, so young eagles were brought from other parts of the country, placed in artificial nests in suitable habitat, and fed until they could fly and hunt on their own. It was hoped that the birds would return to these sites to nest once they reached adulthood. As the eagle is less tolerant of human intrusion than the osprey, restoration also required protection of nesting habitat.

The first inklings of possible success came in 1992, when a pair of bald eagles set up a nesting territory along the Hudson. But eagles often require some time to master the skills necessary for successful breeding. It was not until 1997 that the announcement of the first baby eagle born on the Hudson in one hundred years appeared on the front page of the *New York Times*. Since that year, the number of nesting pairs along the river has slowly but steadily increased. The Hudson has also become a major wintering habitat for bald eagles from Canada and the northeastern U.S.

The Miner's Canary

In the days before sophisticated electronic detection equipment, coal miners took canaries underground to warn them of low oxygen levels in deep shafts. The birds would succumb as oxygen levels dropped, warning miners of the hazard to their lives.

Even with today's sophisticated analytical instruments, birds still warn us of environmental problems. Birds' visibility and the number of people interested in them makes fluctuations in their populations more apparent than might be the case with other creatures—an example being the bald eagle story above. Another well-studied example is the peregrine falcon, which vanished as a breeding species in the Hudson Valley and throughout the eastern U.S. due

mainly to poisoning by chlorinated hydrocarbons, most notably DDT.

Predatory birds—raptors like the peregrine as well as cormorants, gulls, and herons—are at the end of long food chains which concentrate toxic chemicals. In the 1960s, ring-billed gulls in a Long Island salt marsh were found to have levels of DDT a million times higher than levels in the water. Similar concentrations in raptors interfered with their calcium metabolism, resulting in thinner eggshells (which broke during incubation) and other reproductive problems.

Until the mid–twentieth century, the speedy peregrine falcon commanded the air over the river from long established eyries between the Highlands and New York City. The birds survived egg collectors, nest-robbing by falconers, the ill will of people who shot at them out of hatred for predators, and the disturbances of road construction along the Palisades. As of the early 1940s, eight pairs nested at the historic sites, but with increasing pesticide use following World War II, their breeding success declined. After 1951, when two peregrine chicks hatched on the Palisades opposite Yonkers, thirty-seven years elapsed before another successful nesting occurred on the Hudson in 1988—three young raised on a tower of the Tappan Zee Bridge, a modern stand-in for the cliffs once preferred for eyries. By 2000, nesting pairs occupied almost all of the Hudson's bridges, and the skyscrapers and bridges of New York City had become a mecca for the expanding peregrine population. By 2004, twenty-three breeding pairs were found in New York City and the Hudson Valley south of Albany.

One must hope that research and appropriate action will have similar positive results in halting other recent population declines—those among waterfowl and some songbirds, for instance. Destruction of wetlands and acid rain are among the suspected reasons for the decline of waterfowl; the cutting of forests both here in the U.S. and in the tropics might be a factor in the dwindling numbers of some migrant songbirds.

Of course, the miners were not all that concerned with the death of their canaries per se; they were worried about their own welfare. We should be concerned about both; maintaining the abundance and diversity of native species in the Hudson and other ecosystems, and protecting ourselves from the deleterious effects of toxic pollutants, acid rain, and habitat destruction in the forests and elsewhere. We should appreciate the Hudson's birdlife both for itself and for the warnings it might provide.[4]

Mammals

Like the reptiles from which they evolved, mammals are primarily terrestrial creatures, some of which have become adapted for watery environments. And given the opportunistic natures of many mammals, even

those not especially adapted for life in water have learned to take advantage of resources offered by the Hudson and its wetlands—white-tailed deer, for example, which relish some marsh plants. A 1978 study of natural areas along the river in Columbia and Dutchess Counties listed thirty-five mammals as occurring there; twenty-two are known to use tidal wetland habitats. However, only a handful of these reside and reproduce in such environments.

Mice and Mouse-like Mammals

To most people, the tiny furry animal that scurries away from underfoot is a mouse. To the naturalist, it could be any of a number of small mammals: perhaps one of the rodents—mammals with strong front teeth used to gnaw food (primarily seeds and plants, with the occasional smaller creature tossed in)—or one of the insectivores, voracious little bundles of carnivorous energy. These tiny animals are important links in the food chain, eaten by larger mammals, hawks, herons, and many other predators.

Representative Mouselike Mammals

White-footed mouse (*Peromyscus leucopus*) is brown above, white below, with large ears, big eyes, and a tail almost equal to the body in length. This 7-inch long rodent is generally a woodland creature, found along the edges of marshes, but it does inhabit tidal swamps and brushy sections of marsh, commonly occurring in purple loosestrife. On occasion it will nest in duck blinds out in marshes.

Meadow vole (*Microtus pennsylvanicus*) is the so-called meadow mouse. It has smaller eyes and ears and a shorter tail than the white-footed mouse. Only small numbers of this animal use freshwater tidal wetlands; however, it is abundant in the Spartina meadows of brackish and saltwater marshes.

Norway rat (*Rattus norvegicus*), perhaps the most familiar of the Hudson's rodents, is larger than a mouse and has a long tail only sparsely covered by hair. Common in both urban and rural settings, rats frequent old docks, duck blinds, and rock riprap. They can swim when the occasion calls for it. This rodent is not native to the U.S.; it arrived here on ships from the Old World.

Short-tailed shrew (*Blarina brevicauda*), about 5 inches long at most, is an insectivore. A leaden gray in color, this energetic mammal has no visible ears and tiny eyes. It mostly eats insects and other tiny invertebrates; larger prey creatures may be disabled by the shrew's poisonous saliva.

Muskrat (*Ondatra zibethica*)
Muskrats may reach a length of about 2 feet, including a long, naked tail that is flattened from side to side, perhaps for use as a rudder. They are excellent swimmers and divers.

Muskrats

Muskrats are common inhabitants of the Hudson's marshes, both brackish and fresh. These rodents build houses out of plant stems and mud; though these structures project above the water, the entrances are below the surface. They also live in burrows excavated into the river's shore. Muskrats are active all year around, their thick brown fur providing warmth in winter and making them a favorite quarry of trappers. They feed chiefly on plants; cattails are particularly favored. The larger beaver is not common in tidal habitats.

Large Predatory Mammals

Dogs, cats, foxes, and raccoons are among the familiar predatory mammals that include the Hudson's tidal wetlands on their hunting rounds. However, they are not dependent on such habitats. Otter and mink do depend on wetland habitats such as those found along the Hudson. These members of the weasel family generally stick close to water, denning along the shoreline, and feeding largely on fish. These animals and the other large wild carnivores, often most active at night, are elusive and seldom seen. Clues to their presence are scat—fecal droppings, the shape, size, and contents of which often distinguish the species which left them behind—or tracks in wet sand or mud along the river's shore.

Marine Mammals—Whales, Dolphins, and Seals

The whales and dolphins have become so thoroughly adapted for life in water that many people consider them to be fish. But like all other mammals, they are warm-blooded, breathe air, have at least a little hair, and produce milk to feed their young.

A whaling industry was based on the Hudson for some fifty years starting in the late 1700s. The main port was the city of Hudson, which in 1785 had twenty-five sailing vessels out on the oceans. In the early 1830s, another peak period for the river's whalers, four companies in Hudson, Poughkeepsie, and Newburgh sailed about thirty ships.

The whalers' catch came from the high seas, not the river. Large whales are very unusual visitors in the Hudson. Historians tell of two which made it past Albany to Cohoes in 1647, one of which beached itself and died. Practical settlers rendered the remains to produce a great deal of oil, yet enough was left in the rotting carcass to coat the surface of the river for three weeks. There are other records of whales off New York City, including a humpback whale that made a brief tour up the Hudson in 1988.

Harbor porpoises were regular summer visitors through the mid-1800s, following the salt front north as far as Peekskill. They are rare visitors today. In autumn, 1936, common dolphins swam upriver; individu-

River Otter (*Lutra canadensis*)
This large predator (adults 3–4 feet long), unlike its relative the mink, has webbed feet and a furry tail which tapers to a point. Otters range widely; their home territories may be 15 miles in extent. Sighting one along the Hudson is thus a very lucky occurrence, especially since their numbers have apparently declined, perhaps due to PCB poisoning.

Mink (*Mustela vison*)
Smaller than otters (usually less than 2 feet long), mink are covered in rich brown fur of value to the fashion industry. Few are found along the Hudson these days, however. Mink are known to be very sensitive to PCBs; it is suspected that PCB pollution has led to a decline in their populations there.

Harbor Seal (*Phoca vitulina*) Most often observed
in winter and spring (when it sometimes eats shad
caught in nets), this seal might be seen at any time of
year—perhaps hauled out of the river lying prone or
with head and back flippers elevated to give its body
a bananalike shape, or in the water with just its head
poking above the river's surface. Adults are roughly
5 feet long.

als were found dead in Albany and in Highland (across from Poughkeepsie).

Seal sightings have become more numerous in the Hudson in recent years. Swelling seal populations in the North Atlantic have brought more to nearby ocean waters, especially in winter and early spring. The animals stray into the estuary or follow runs of fish upriver. The species most often observed is the harbor seal, but a few juvenile harp seals were seen in New York Harbor and north as far as Verplanck early in 2005.

Seals often haul out on ice floes, rocks, beaches, docks, or boats. Their awkward-

ness out of water can create an impression of illness even when they are healthy. Young harp seals can seem tame. However, well-intentioned efforts to befriend or rescue such animals can endanger both seals and people. It is unwise to disturb these animals; if a seal does need help, contact environmental conservation officers or an officially designated marine mammal rescue group.[5]

The Most Commonly Seen Mammal

Of all the mammals found along the Hudson, none is more commonly seen than the human being. Like the white-tailed deer, raccoon, and other animals, we humans do not make our permanent residences in the Hudson or its wetlands, but we do capture food from the river, travel on its waters, and find recreational pleasure and aesthetic inspiration there. However, our power to alter the physical nature and the ecological functioning of the Hudson far exceeds that of the creatures discussed so far. The next few chapters will survey our interactions with the river, first in historical narrative, and then in terms of impacts on the Hudson ecosystem.

Chapter 7

Exploration, Colonization, and Revolution

The Chapter in Brief
Belief in a northwest passage to the Indies shaped the European conception of the New World and lured explorers to the Americas. Rivers were central to early exploration and settlement and became the basis for community building and trade. Native peoples, with a ten-thousand-year history and an ancient culture, were quickly displaced following the European invasion. The Hudson, so central to the growth of colonial New York, was also a strategic key to the Revolution, and as a result was memorialized as our first national river.

The World Turned Upside Down

The history of the Hudson River is often said to begin with its discovery by Henry Hudson in 1609. This Eurocentric view of events has neglected the ancient history of the native peoples who lived along the Hudson and in the valley for ten thousand years and first named the river "Muh-heakantuck" sometime in the Woodland period (1500 B.C. to A.D. 1600).[1] The loss of this name is symptomatic of the loss of the region's native history. Even in those instances where native names have survived, such as Esopus, Neperhan, Nyack, Os-sining, Pocantico, Poughkeepsie, Tappan, Wappinger, and Weehawken, we tend not to identify them with the pre-European story of the river.

The Euro-American history of the Hudson is but a moment in the great sweep of geological and native time in the Hudson Valley. While literacy and technology have convinced many that what happened before the European invasion was prologue, recalling the native Muhheakantuck should serve as a counter to this ethnocentric view of our history in general and of the Hudson River in particular. If European explorers laid claim to the lands of the New World by the act of naming, then we must recognize the prior claim of native peoples inherent in Muhheakantuck and examine the disposition of that claim by the Europeans.

The difficulty in reconstructing the native history of the Hudson River is tied to the nature of the surviving record, much of it found in archaeological sites and oral traditions. The early record begins with the discovery and classification of projectile points found in Orange County, dated from about 10,600 B.C., and shell heaps at Haverstraw Bay and Croton Point, dated from 6000 B.C. The historical record is more abundant as we move to the period from 1500 B.C. to the European invasion in the seventeenth century.

Shatamuc

In the Late Woodland period the native population along the Hudson consisted of tribes or bands of the Algonquin or Lenape nation, an Eastern linguistic group including the Munsee, who settled along the

The 1650 Janssonius-Visscher map of New Netherlands included names and locations of river-based native tribes. The depiction of the Hudson and its tributaries is generalized. The map includes an outline of New Amsterdam's seventeenth-century skyline.
(Courtesy of Clearwater.)

Hudson south of Albany, and the Mahicans, speaking a different dialect, to the north. Often referred to as the River Indians, the Mahicans called the Hudson "Shata-muc." The Munsee speakers formed bands known as Highlanders or Wappingers, and were further identified by their locale—Wappinger (Dutchess and Putnam), Kich-tawank (Northern Westchester), Sin-sink (Ossining), Wiechquaeskeck (Tarrytown–Dobbs Ferry) and Rechgawank (Yonkers, the Bronx, and Manhattan).

Population estimates for the valley are hard to come by, ranging anywhere from six thousand to twelve thousand natives in the seventeenth century. Settlements—those at Wicker's Creek in Dobbs Ferry or on Cro-ton Point, for example—were often located along the Hudson or its tributaries, insuring ease of transportation, abundant food, and fertile land, and establishing a settlement pattern duplicated by the Europeans.

From Manhattan to Albany, on the eastern and western shores of the river, native groups of a few hundred members burned, cleared, and planted the land. They built clusters of wigwams, sometimes protected by a palisaded wall. Food consumption and diet followed a seasonal pattern. Fall was the principal hunting time; game included deer, bear, wolf, raccoon, weasel, and other small animals along with turkeys, passenger pigeons, and other birds. Spring and summer were the time for fishing the Hudson and its tributaries, filled with shad, striped bass, sturgeon, eels, and oysters. Fish were caught with stone-weighted seines, weirs, nets set on poles, hooks, and even bow and arrow. Fish and shellfish were sun-dried on racks, their discarded bones and shells providing archaeological clues for future historians. Fishing and river transportation depended on the dugout canoe, hollowed-out from the trunk of a tulip tree with the aid of scrapers.

Daily meals, boiled in conical clay pots or baked in corn husks, consisted of corn-meal mush and fish or meat. The evolution of cooking utensils offers additional clues to the natives' way of life. Illness was fought with the curative powers of the sweat bath and the spiritual skills of the *shaman* who used local herbs and indigenous plants.

Native Algonquin bands were led by a chief or *sachem*, who served as mediator and religious leader. Family organization, birth and death rituals, political structure, and a symbiotic relationship with nature were all informed by a rich mythological tradition. Manitous, the lesser gods or spirits, dwelt in the earth, water, and sky, with the great god Manitou who, according to their mythology, confined rebellious spirits in the Highlands until the Hudson broke through this ancient "prison." There can be little doubt that at the time of European exploration native peoples had created a rich and substantial cultural life.

Bone harpoons, made from antlers or leg bones of deer or moose, were used to take large fish such as sturgeon. After being split lengthwise, the bone was ground into the appropriate shape.

Without salt, smoking and drying were the principal means of preserving fish for food. Fish were cut into chunks; crabs were roasted in their shells.

The river valley has a long native history predating Hudson's arrival, one which links a way of life to the river and its natural resources. Its reconstruction remains a

Natives felled trees by using dried moss and wood chips to fire the trunk area close to the roots. Limbs were burned off, the bark stripped, and the raised log burned and chipped into shape to make a dugout canoe.

This print, titled *Sa Ga Yeath Qua Pieth Tow, King of the Maquas,* was redrawn by John Simon from a 1710 print by John Verelst. The latter, titled *Etoh oh Koam, King of the River Nation,* is the only known detailed depiction of a Mahican chief.
(Print Collection, Miriam and Ira D. Wallach Division of Art, Prints and Photographs, The New York Public Library, Astor, Lenox and Tilden Foundations.)

challenge to all who seek a full understanding of the life of the river.[2]

Exploration and Settlement or Invasion?

To understand the transformation of the native peoples after 1609 we need to examine the impact of their seventeenth-century contacts with Europeans. The journals of Hudson's 1609 voyage document the transformation from their first response, when Europeans were greeted with friendly curiosity, to one of suspicion and hostility. Revisionist historians use the term invasion to describe the first phase of European exploration and settlement of the New World. Invasion, they argue, is the proper

term to describe the rapid displacement of the natives from the river valley and the destruction of their culture by technology and European civilization. But the term is most appropriate when applied to the traumatic introduction of European diseases such as measles, smallpox, and typhus, to which the natives had no immunity. According to a 1640 statement attributed by the Dutch to river natives, disease reduced the native population to one tenth of its original size. Venereal disease, spread by promiscuous fishermen and fur traders, also contributed to the rapid decline.

Trade with the native peoples not only introduced European technology but profoundly changed the equilibrium between the Munsee, the Mahicans, and the natural world. Trapping for profit, which drove natives to maximize their yield, brought destructive pressures on the beaver population and altered village and family work habits. Interdependence slowly gave way to exploitation, and the ensuing tribal rivalries over territorial claims led to war and further population loss.

Native civilization, which had been slowly evolving for ten thousand years in the valley and along the Hudson, came to a sudden and quick end within the first century of European settlement. The river natives who survived the encounter migrated westward in small bands, first to New Jersey, and eventually as far as Oklahoma where they were absorbed into larger regional groups.

The Northwest Passage

At the center of European *cartography* of the New World was the enduring idea of a northwest water passage to India. When specific geographic information was in short supply map makers did not hesitate to embellish their work with an imagined

Arrival of Henry Hudson, September 4, 1609 (Asher B. Durand). Natives met the Half Moon in the Tappan Zee on September 13–14, 1609. Local natives had prior knowledge of Europeans, but their expectations about the encounter are only partially known. (Collection of The New-York Historical Society.)

Northwest Passage. This idea, so fixed in the minds of European explorers, shaped their views of the New World and drove many to obsessive, unsuccessful, and even tragic explorations.[3]

The belief in a westward-leading water route focused the energy and planning of the explorers of the 1600–1700s and their underwriters on the rivers of the New World. Dreams and expectations, indeed the future itself, were tied to America's rivers, which not only served as avenues of exploration but also contained the promise of a new history.

European expansion took place in an atmosphere of fierce economic and religious rivalry. It is not surprising that the rivalry would extend to exploration and colonization. The Hudson of the seventeenth and eighteenth centuries is integral not only to American colonial history but is a key element in Europe's global history as well.

Knocking at the Door

Europe's adventurous spirit ignited a passion for exploration that was so powerful it created a generation of men eager to journey to the New World. In 1524 the Italian Giovanni da Verrazano, under the sponsorship of King Francis I of France, crossed the Atlantic in search of the westward passage, sailed up the northeast coast, and entered New York Bay. Verrazano recorded the first impressions of the harbor and the native peoples and described the lower Hudson as the "River of the Steep Hills" and the "Grand River."

Estevan Gomez, a Portuguese in the employ of the Spanish, followed Verrazano in 1525 and may have explored the lower

The Stadthuys of New York in 1679, Corner of Pearl St. and Coentijs Slip (G. Hayward & Co., issued 1867). The commercial nature and architectural fashion of New Amsterdam is visible in this print of the seventeenth-century waterfront. Sloops are tied up at a wharf constructed with landfill, a practice which the Dutch initiated in New York. The large building is the Stadt Huys, the administration center for the company governing the colony. *(Eno Collection, Miriam and Ira D. Wallach Division of Art, Prints and Photographs, The New York Public Library, Astor, Lenox and Tilden Foundations.)*

Hudson. Spanish maps recognize this as fact by naming the Hudson "Rio de Gomez," and "Rio de Guamas." The French followed the Spanish and, based on evidence of their trading with the natives, may have ascended the Hudson. But none of these claims stuck.

Henry Hudson

At the beginning of the seventeenth century, the Dutch, locked in a struggle with Spain and Portugal and eager to compete with their English rivals, established the East India Company, which financed the Englishman Henry Hudson's third trip to the New World. The *yaagt*, or pursuit ship *Halve Maen*, (*Half Moon* in English)—84 feet long, 20 feet wide, and displacing 112 tons—sailed on April 16, 1609, with an Anglo-Dutch crew of eighteen men. Hudson, bolstered by maps from the Virginia explorer Captain John Smith, remained convinced that he was destined to discover the Northwest Passage.

Ice forced Hudson to revise his charted northern course and on the 14th of May

turn southward, still confident that the passage to the East would be found at forty degrees latitude. The *Halve Maen* arrived in New York Harbor on September 4, 1609, and remained there for nine days, exploring the Upper Bay and trading with the natives. Hudson then began a slow, methodical northward exploration of the river which, based on initial indications of breadth, depth, and salinity, recorded in the journal of Robert Juet, the *Halve Maen*'s mate, seemed promising.

On September 11, they passed through the Narrows and anchored off the upper west side of Manhattan. From this point Hudson moved northward, continuing to measure the river's salinity and depth. On the 13th of September he reached the site of present-day Yonkers, on the 14th the Highlands and West Point, on the 16th what is now Hudson, and on the 17th he anchored off Castleton. The crew explored farther northward and confirmed what Hudson had begun to suspect: that this river was not the Northwest Passage but an estuary with a freshwater source. A continent, not an ocean; lay before him.

Juet's log records the first European response to the river and the valley landscape. He observed that the land was "pleasant, high and bold" and the Hudson "as fine a river as can be found." Hudson and his crew were intoxicated with the river's smell—the perfumes of grasses, wildflowers, and trees, so sweet "that we stood still."

This sensual and *aesthetic* response did not blind Juet to the economic possibilities: "The land is the finest for cultivation that I have ever in my life set foot upon," a place to appreciate and to develop, a garden of the new world, one which could be profitably cultivated. The European's dual response at the moment of discovery foreshadowed the later history of the Hudson River as a source of both aesthetic enrichment and economic opportunity.

In September 1609 the Hudson River and valley were rich in natural resources: forests of oak, chestnut, and hickory, and game and fish so abundant that newcomers could "imagine that animals of the country will be destroyed in time, but this is an unnecessary anxiety." The river seemed like a limitless resource. Even Manhattan Island, cut with bays, coves, marshes, and streams, had ample fresh water and plentiful trout.

Hudson had several encounters with the native population, and following one exchange he concluded that "they were a very good people." However, the curiosity, gift-giving, and trading quickly deteriorated into petty thievery and mutual suspicion, culminating in open hostility and loss of life. These first exchanges with the natives left the Europeans doubting their preconceived notions about the nobility and innocence of the "savage."

While Hudson's return journey to Holland was interrupted when he was removed from the *Halve Maen* by the English at

Establishing Hudson Valley farms like this one, complete with windmill, Dutch farmers cultivated corn, oats, and wheat. However, the more lucrative beaver trade slowed down Dutch agricultural development here.

Dartmouth in October 1609, the Dutch would quickly seize the initiative and lay claim to the river and the valley. Though Hudson had not discovered the Northwest Passage, he had come upon the "Manhatees" as he styled it, a river to the north and to the American wilderness.

Of Beavers and Bouweries

The Dutch wasted no time in capitalizing on Hudson's discovery. In 1610 Amsterdam merchants sent a ship out to "the Groote Rivier" to trade with the natives for beaver pelts, soon to become the river's cash crop. This first response reflected the Dutch commercial view of the Hudson as the source of a valuable commodity and a highway for trade.

The Dutch organized the West India Company in 1621 to monopolize the river trade. To solidify their economic connections, in 1624 they dispatched thirty families of Walloons who set sail for the "River of the Prince Mauritius," an official designation chosen to honor the Dutch military hero, Maurice of Orange.[4] While Walloon communities in Manhattan and Fort

Orange (the site of present-day Albany) provided the seed for the establishment of permanent towns, the Dutch failed to expand the number and size of their agricultural settlements necessary to sustain their territorial claims. They also failed to attract sufficient numbers of colonists, and those who came moved inland, secure from the threats of hostile natives and their French allies. Their long-term inability to build a population base in New Netherland would limit Dutch colonization of the valley and by midcentury undermine their control of the river.

Determined to attract colonists to New Netherland, the Dutch employed innovative land schemes like the patroon system, offering a sixteen-mile land grant along one shore (or eight on both sides) of the Hudson and awarding quasi feudal powers to the grantee provided he establish a colony of fifty people. Two patroonships were begun on the Hudson; one at Rensselaerwyck took hold. The centrality of rivers—the Connecticut, Delaware, and Hudson—to such land schemes underscored their importance to the development of New World colonies.

It was understandable that the first Dutch towns and the adjacent farms or *bouweries*, including New Amsterdam, Beverwyck, and Esopus, would be located along the river, where economic function joined with transportation and communication. The Dutch bouweries produced corn, peas, oats, and wheat, and to satisfy the Dutch taste for beer, hops were cultivated as well. The standard Dutch fertilizer was oyster shells, discarded in great heaps along the Hudson's banks. Their diet depended heavily on the river's oysters, perch, sturgeon, bass, smelt, shad, alewives, eels, and tomcod.

The fur trade relied on ships not only to transport furs to Europe but also to sup-ply traders with the necessary items for barter. Vessels from Holland anchored in New Amsterdam harbor, loaded with cloth and clothes, implements, blankets, liquor and liquor glasses, candles, and even cattle to trade for pelts brought downriver by fly boats soon to return upriver loaded with imported goods to trade for more pelts.

Trade between Holland and New Netherland quickly established the protected harbor at New Amsterdam as the fulcrum of an international exchange linking Europe with the New World and became the commercial center of the Dutch colonial enterprise in the region. These early exchanges fixed the Dutch view of the Hudson as a highway for trade. The seventeenth-century Hudson was as closely linked to the European market as to the interior of colonial America. For transplanted Europeans it represented not only the promise of a new future but the link to a known past.

Hudson River Sloops

River trade was dependent on Dutch boats and seamanship. One of the lasting contributions of the Dutch was the Hudson River sloop, which came to dominate river trade for two centuries. Sloops measured 65 to 75 feet in length, in a few cases 90 feet. They had a single mast with a mainsail, a jib, and often a topsail. At first the Dutch used leeboards but these soon were replaced by a centerboard or keel. They were steered by a long tiller. The ample holds and deck space could accommodate up to a hundred tons of cargo. Their shallow draft enabled them to reach into tributaries of varying depths, linking the Hudson to the valley's interior settlements.

The sloops' dependence on winds and tides made river travel unpredictable. A trip from New Amsterdam to Fort Orange could take twenty-four hours under optimum conditions, or extend to several days. Though good seamanship reduced the time of the journey, passengers and crew were forced to wait on the river and the uncertainties of nature. Dutch sloop captains, with their skill and knowledge of the Hudson's topography, survived the English takeover and Dutch remained the language of the river well into the nineteenth century. Seventeenth-century sloop crews included Africans who, according to some observers, communicated in Dutch. African Americans would play key roles in the maritime activities of the Hudson well into the nineteenth century, captaining vessels and maintaining shipping companies.

Sloop captains measured the Hudson from the Palisades to Albany by the reach, a stretch of river between two bends.[5] Distance measured in reaches rather than miles reminds us of the river's significance in the conceptualization of space. Expanding river trade and passenger traffic encouraged the development of shipbuilding in Manhattan and upriver in locations like Nyack, famous for its brightly marked sloops.

The sloop *Clearwater* reminds us of the Dutch sloops that were the workhorses of Hudson River trade well into the nineteenth century. Sloop captains were close observers of the river, dependent as they were on personal knowledge to safely navigate its waters.
(Photo by Charles Porter. Sloop schematic courtesy of Clearwater.)

The Dutch Imprint

Historical assessment of the Dutch colonial experience in the valley has been complicated by Washington Irving's caricature of the Dutch in *Diedrich Knickerbocker's History of New York* (1809). These folk characters, whom Irving filled with fear of the New World and the superstitions of the Old, would overshadow the historical Dutch who were practical, profit-seeking farmers and traders, fully open to the sensual pleasures of the river and the valley. Irving's distorted view of the Dutch did contribute a sense of mystery—an important element in the construction of the romantic Hudson—to the common early nineteenth-century view of the river as a commercial waterway.

The Dutch vision of the Hudson established the river as an economic artery connecting the American hinterland to Europe, with New Amsterdam at the center of New World trade. Though they failed to attract a sufficient number of Dutch settlers to create an enduring community, they welcomed other groups to New Netherland, creating a polyglot population that has marked the subsequent history of the river and the valley.

English Claims

In August 1664 an English fleet under Colonel Richard Nicolls anchored off the Battery, raised the English flag, and ousted the Dutch governor, Peter Stuyvesant. With this surprisingly bloodless victory the English established their hegemony over New Netherland and the Hudson River using claims that went back as early as 1619 when they challenged the Dutch right to trade on the "Great River."

The English argued that their territorial rights were based on the dominion of the monarch of the discoverer and not of his employer. Thus the river, which they renamed Hudson in 1664, constituted the historical basis of their claim to all of New Netherland. The Dutch term "North River," used to indicate the northern boundary of Dutch territory, was now meaningless.[6]

The European battle for empire, which for fifty years had contested trading rights to the Hudson, ended with the English flag-raising at the Battery, inaugurating the ceremonial role of the Hudson. Again in 1783, the Americans marked their newly won independence with another river celebration at the tip of Manhattan, deepening the ritual significance of the Hudson.

New Names, New Settlers

The renaming of the river in 1664 was followed by rapid Anglicization of Dutch culture—New Amsterdam became New York and Beverwyck became Albany. Dutch survivals along the river included Hoboken and Harlem, Spuyten Duyvil and Peekskill, Kinderhook, Catskill, Watervliet, Yonkers, and Fishkill. Pockets of Dutch culture persisted on the farms and in the schools and churches, and spoken Dutch language could be heard into the nineteenth century.

Land holdings were retitled as part of the English manorial system.[7] Four permanent river manors were established: one at the former Dutch patroonship of Rensselaerwyck, a second grant to Robert Livingston, a third to Frederic Philipse, and a fourth to Stephanus Van Cortlandt. These

Hudson Valley manors were primarily located on the east side of the river and peopled with tenant farmers. The manors would be dismantled after the Revolution and the land sold to tenant farmers or returning Continental soldiers.
(From Atlas of American History, edited by James Truslow Adams.)

English manors once again emphasize the importance of the river to colonial geography and patterns of land distribution.

The English had modest success in attracting settlers to the river valley, though, like the Dutch, their century-long struggle with native resistance made new settlements vulnerable. The valley population continued to diversify as the original Dutch, Huguenots, and English settlers mingled with Germans, Danes, Flemish, and—after 1730—New Englanders migrating westward. Like those who came before, the new arrivals left their mark in the names of river communities—the Germans in Rhinebeck and New Hamburg, the Yankees in Highland Falls and Cornwall.

The Yankees entering the valley at the end of the eighteenth century brought with them vestiges of their Puritan attitude toward nature, which they saw as a dangerous threat to the advance of Christianity. These emigrating New Englanders, consisting of yeomen farmers, traders, and small entrepreneurs, were indifferent to the aesthetic and pleasurable aspects of nature. They hoped to civilize the river and valley and domesticate the landscape in the name of progress. Ironically it may not be the Dutch, in spite of Irving's efforts to the contrary, who brought fear of nature to the Hudson, but rather their Yankee cousins.

Predators of Another Sort

Trade continued to dominate the economic life of the colonial Hudson in the eighteenth century. The strategic roles of New York and Albany as trading centers were strengthened under the English in spite of the dangers of piracy. New York City's harbor served as a safe haven for pirates who were often treated as celebrities. At one point late in the seventeenth century, nine pirate ships were anchored in the harbor, all protected by English colonial officials who shared in the profits. Pirated cargoes made their way to river markets via New York merchants whose vessels off loaded contraband goods outside the port.

Pirates, not content to remain in the harbor, ventured upriver, according to *Albany Record* of 1696, to "waylay vessels on their way to Albany, speeding out from covers and from behind islands and again returning to the rocky shores, or ascending the mountains along the river to conceal their plunder." The situation became so desperate that the Earl of Bellomont , the provincial Governor from 1698 to 1702, with the support of Robert Livingston, formed a company, procured the thirty-

A South Prospect of the Flourishing City of New York, by T. Bakewell, a 1746 view from Brooklyn, depicts a busy New York Harbor, the Manhattan skyline, and a newly constructed wharf on the Brooklyn side of the East River. (Collection of The New-York Historical Society.)

six-gun ship *Adventure*, and hired Captain William Kidd to break up the pirate trade. A reversal of fortune found Kidd, at sea with a mutinous crew, turning to piracy to survive. Upon his return to New York Kidd was arrested and sent to England, where he was tried and hung as a pirate. The Hudson's pirate history illustrates how open and contested were the seas and rivers of the world in the battle for new trade and more profits.

The Enslaved Africans

The African population, brought to the valley as slaves by the Dutch, increased under the English. By 1750 the ratio of blacks to whites was one to nine; in New York City it was one to four. Many worked the ships of the river, serving as crews for sloops and as cargo handlers for larger transatlantic vessels. But throughout the Hudson Valley, Africans worked as slaves on farms and in domestic service, and as soldiers battling the French and the native peoples. They were concentrated not only in New York City but also in Newburgh, Poughkeepsie, Hudson-Claverack, and Albany. It is difficult to ascertain the exact mix of free blacks and slaves in these communities during the early days of settlement, but it is believed that the number of free African Americans increased after the Revolution.[8]

By the middle of the eighteenth century the Hudson Valley constituted one of the major regional societies on the continent, "distinct in peoples, economies, and cultural landscapes."[9] The region would be increasingly shaped by internal dynamics as it matured and became more conscious of its distinctive identity. The confrontation between this inchoate sense of identity and England's attempted imperial reorganization following the French and Indian War led to political tensions and hastened the coming of revolution.

Revolt along the Hudson

One of the central objectives of the British revolutionary war plan of 1776 was to seize, hold, and use the Hudson as a wedge to separate New England from the Middle Atlantic and Southern colonies. The British recognized the Hudson's strategic value as the keystone to the unification of the colonies and as a central artery for intracolonial trade. George Washington and his commanders understood this and chose to stand and fight and to commit part of the Continental Army to the Hudson's defense.

The British plan of attack required that they gain control of New York City and Albany and establish military posts along the Hudson. General William Howe would secure Manhattan and then move up the river toward Albany to meet a second British Army coming from the north under the command of General John Burgoyne.

In anticipation of this line of attack Washington assembled an army of twenty-five thousand men to defend the city. Hulks were sunk in the harbor and *chevaux-de-frise* placed on the East River. Additional forts were established along the river: Fort Washington near Manhattan's northern tip and Fort Lee across the Hudson, posts at Stony Point and Verplanck's Point overlooking Haverstraw Bay, Fort Independence near Peekskill, Forts Clinton and Montgomery in the Highlands at Popolopen Creek, and further north Fort Arnold, Fort Putnam, Constitution Island, and West Point. Their placement was determined by the course of the river. Those in the Highlands offered particular advantages where the difficulties of navigating a narrow and irregular river channel combined with the advantages of high ground, making these ideal locations for cannon placements. Topography determined much of the revolutionary map of the Hudson River.

Battling for the River

In July 1776, General Howe sent several warships, including the *Rose* and *Phoenix*, up the Hudson. Favored by a flood tide and a strong breeze, the vessels moved quickly and suffered little damage from the American batteries at Forts Washington and Lee. From anchorages in the Tappan Zee, where the river's width provided safety from shore based cannon, the British warships harassed local residents for several weeks until they were engaged by five American ships, including the *Lady Washington*. This, the only major naval battle of the Hudson, proved indecisive; both sides withdrew and the British eventually dropped downriver.

In fall of 1776, after defeats in Brooklyn and White Plains, the Americans retreated across the Hudson to New Jersey, leaving Fort Washington as their only remaining defense in Manhattan and southern Westchester. The British landed troops at Dobbs Ferry, advanced rapidly on Fort Washington, and on November 16 captured the fort and over two thousand American soldiers. A few days later, a British force ferried across the Hudson from Yonkers and seized Fort Lee.

Having secured Manhattan Island for the Crown the British were able to initiate their two-pronged strategy—north from the city and south from Canada—and thereby seize control of the valley. Americans hoped the defenses at Forts Clinton, Montgomery, and Constitution Island, and a chain and boom stretched across the Hudson from Anthony's Nose to Bear Mountain would check the British advance up the Hudson. In October 1777, a British fleet sailed upriver and feigned an attack on Peekskill, drawing the Continentals' attention and diverting reinforcements while two thousand British soldiers landed at Stony Point in an early morning fog. Marching inland around Dunderberg Mountain, they

The many forts in the Highlands remind us of the strategic value of this section of the river. The topography of the terrain offered decided advantages to the defending Continentals.
(*From* Atlas of American History, *edited by James Truslow Adams.*)

The patriots' defensive structures included chains on log booms and chevaux-de-frise placed across the river from Fort Montgomery to Anthony's Nose and from West Point to Fort Constitution. Links of the chain are on display in the West Point Museum.

attacked Forts Montgomery and Clinton from the rear, surprising the Americans and capturing these posts.

This victory enabled the British to dismantle the chain and sail northward, taking control of the Hudson and wreaking havoc along its shores. They burned all river vessels they encountered, cannonaded homes of Whigs, and set houses afire. The provincial capital of Kingston was a major casualty: put to the torch, only one of 116 dwelllings was left standing.

To the north, the second battle of Saratoga took place in September and October 1777. The Americans under General Hora-

tio Gates held Bemis Heights; General John Burgoyne hoped to drive them off and back toward the river. The Continentals prevailed and forced the British to surrender, offsetting the advantages gained by the English victories in the Highlands. Burgoyne's defeat at Saratoga halted their advance from Canada and prevented them from completing their Hudson River strategy.

When the British withdrew to New York later that autumn, Washington decided to strengthen the fortifications at West Point and surrounding areas north of the city. A second Fort Clinton was constructed at West Point, and a second chain was planned for the narrow section with its sharp bend between West Point and Constitution Island.

The Gibraltar of the Hudson

In the summer of 1778 Washington again visited the Hudson, inspected the fortifications at West Point, and established headquarters in White Plains. Through the following winter he shadowed British moves and feints up the Hudson. In 1779 he remained tied to the river with headquarters at New Windsor and West Point, anxiously watching the British take Stony Point and Fort Lafayette on Verplanck's Point in the spring. That victory gave them control of King's Ferry, a critical river crossing, and set in motion plans for Anthony Wayne's successful recapture of Stony Point.

The British, checked south of the Highlands through the summer of 1780, decided on a bold stroke to capture West Point, gain control of the Hudson, and divide the Americans. The scheme involved General Benedict Arnold, at the time the disgruntled commanding officer at the Point, who was prepared to surrender the "Gibraltar of the Hudson" for $50,000 in gold. Major John Andre, his British co-conspirator, came up the Hudson on the HMS *Vulture*, disembarked, and secretly met with Arnold on the western side of the Hudson between Stony Point and Haverstraw. At this meeting the details for the capture of West Point were worked out. Andre, armed with plans and notes on its defenses and a pass from Arnold, returned to the *Vulture*, only to find it had been chased downriver by patriot shelling from Teller's Point. Forced to cross the river and return to British lines by land, Andre was captured at Tarrytown on September 23, 1780.

Arnold's plot was now exposed and he rushed to the Hudson, boarded his barge, and rowed downriver to meet the *Vulture* and eventually to escape to England. The Arnold conspiracy highlighted the importance of the Hudson to the conduct of the war and the key role of West Point in defense of the river. Washington called attention to West Point's significance by visiting it frequently from his winter quarters at New Windsor.

In the summer of 1781 Washington met French troops and officers at Dobbs Ferry and planned to attack New York City with the help of the French fleet. However, Admiral De Grasse put in at Yorktown, Virginia, instead of New York Harbor; consequently, the final battle of the Revolution took place on the York and not on the Hudson River.

Washington spent the closing months (March 1782 to August 1783) of the Revolution headquartered at the Hasbrouck House in Newburgh, struggling to hold his army together on the western banks of the Hudson. He made two journeys downriver: to Verplanck's Point to honor Comte de Rochambeau's French troops, and to Dobbs Ferry to arrange with Sir Guy Carleton for the evacuation of British troops. On the latter occasion, British warships in the Hudson honored Washington with a seventeen-gun salute in the "first complimentary salute fired in honor of an officer of the American Army and indeed in honor of the New Nation."

America's River

The war came to a formal conclusion with the evacuation of British troops from the Bowery, Washington's entrance into the city, and the raising of the American flag at the Battery. The Hudson, which was the strategic key to the Revolution, the site of naval and land battles, and home for much of the duration of the war to Washington

George Washington stayed at the Dutch Colonial style Hasbrouck House in Newburgh from April 1782 to August 1783. Here he wrote the "crown letter" rejecting the offer of monarchy, and here he bid farewell to his army. Purchased in 1850 by New York, it was the state's first preservation effort.

and the Continental Army, provided the new nation with a series of historical associations essential to the forging of a national identity. From the Battery to West Point, the Hudson River and valley were memorialized; one river traveler noted that "almost the name of every place" reminded him of "that glorious struggle for independence."

In the search for symbols of identity, the young republic nationalized the Hudson, making it America's river inspired with the hope that a citizen of the new republic would "feel the prouder of his native land" while sailing up the river. For the first half of the nineteenth century, the Hudson—marked by Revolutionary shrines and battle markers—embodied our national identity and recalled the struggle for independence. In their search for free-

dom in the first half of the nineteenth century African Americans, left behind by the revolution, reaffirmed this historical association when they incorporated the Hudson into the Underground Railroad and provided runaway slaves with a direct north-south route to western New York and the safety of Canada.

The Hudson, which had served not only as an avenue for exploration and a waterway for commerce, now became a source of national inspiration and democratic aspiration. It became America's River. A roll call of the roster of nineteenth-century steamers and twentieth-century bridges and numerous memorials testifies to the persistence of the Hudson's Revolutionary associations and our desire to keep them before us.

Chapter 8

The Romantic River

The Chapter in Brief
In search of a national identity, Americans turned to the landscape where they found God's blessing manifest in the land. The celebration of nature by painters and writers transformed the Hudson River and its valley into a sublime and picturesque landscape, dotted with the great estates of the wealthy, into a source of pride for the young nation. The Hudson was America's river.

"A Spot of Earth with Soul"

Americans emerged from the Revolutionary War free and independent, yet uncertain about their national identity and no longer able to use the unifying catalyst of an external enemy around which diverse groups could rally. Now they would get a second chance.

After the conclusion of the War of 1812, Americans—having secured the original Revolutionary victory—turned to the consolidation of nationality by cultivating a consciousness of shared values and common history. They not only found examples of these values in their Revolutionary history but also increasingly looked to the landscape which they experienced in a deep and meaningful way. It was rich not only in historical associations but in transcendent and moral possibilities—as Nathaniel Parker Willis wrote, "a spot of earth with soul."

By the second quarter of the nineteenth century the young nation believed its destiny was made manifest in the gift of the land, a sign that its history was providential. Through discovery of God's presence in nature, Americans sought to verify our destiny and legitimate the belief that we were a chosen people. The search began for particular places in the landscape where the spiritual and the historical were united.

The Revolution provided the Hudson River with abundant historical associations, and it remained for the Romantic painters and writers of the nineteenth century to educate the public about the Hudson River as a source of spiritual nourishment. N. P. Willis looking out from Idlewild, his home in Cornwall, described the Hudson as the "grand aisle" in the "cathedral" of nature, with his beloved Highlands serving as the "gallery."

Discovering the American Landscape

The English-born engraver Thomas Cole's first trip up the Hudson in 1825 and his visit to the Catskills inspired the painting *Lake with Dead Trees* (1825). One of the first paintings of the Catskills, this canvas depicts a mountain lake rimmed with barren trees. Other landscape paintings followed and their sale in New York City established Cole's reputation and launched American landscape painting. We acknowledge Cole

Thomas Cole's *The Clove, Catskills,* c. 1827, contains some of the main elements in the painting vocabulary of the Hudson River School: a blasted tree and picturesque rock formations in the foreground, tension between dark and light portions of the middle ground, and a distant horizon filled with sky, clouds, and light. Looking out from the clove one can see the Hudson and the Berkshires.
(Courtesy of the New Britain Museum of American Art, Charles F. Smith Fund. Photo by E. Irving Blomstrann.)

as the founding father of what would later be known as the Hudson River School.

Cole's paintings celebrated the *sublime*—the awe and reverence inspired by nature—which he imagined as a religious, moral, and national force. He found the sublime in the picturesque valley of the Hudson where the purity and transparency of water and sky constituted for Cole the "soul of all scenery." By Christianizing the sublime and endowing it with the moral virtue Cole offered the young America a kind of democratic aesthetic that was accessible to all.

In large canvasses filled with detailed nature scenes that displayed his engraving skills to the fullest, Cole began to document the American landscape and its representative example, the Hudson River. His work, imbued with a strong sense of place, filled the young nation with pride and optimism and found in New York City's merchant class a ready audience with the leisure to appreciate his talent and the capital to purchase his works. The city, linked to the Hudson commercially, now found an aesthetic harvest was also to be had. The city's newly wealthy, always eager to demonstrate their cultural sophistication and to identify with the new nationalism, found Cole's work congenial to these aspirations.

Cole, who wrote a great deal about his attitude toward nature and thought of himself as a painter-poet, believed the Hudson's landscape was superior to Europe's. His personal success and the rising popularity of the Hudson River School however made him apprehensive. From his home in Catskill, overlooking the mountains, he observed the inevitable movement of civilization into the wilderness at a speed that impelled Cole to document the landscape he now believed threatened. He expressed his fears in *The Course of Empire* (1836), five large canvasses which traced the transformation of an allegorical landscape from the savage stage through the pinnacle of civilization to its ultimate desolation.

Later painters attempted to reconcile this early Romantic passion for wilderness with the growing recognition of the transforming power of human intervention and technology by celebrating the domesticated landscape where one could see the reworking of the land, ostensibly to enhance the experience of nature. The river and valley became the focal point for a new equilibrium—one which balanced civilization and nature in a middle ground poised between the original wilderness and artificial cities.

Disciples

After Cole's death, leadership of the landscape painters passed to Asher Durand, who had memorialized Cole in *Kindred Spirits* (1849), a work which depicts Cole and the poet William Cullen Bryant sharing a moment of contemplation in the Catskills. Durand studied and learned from nature and, like Cole, he believed art must capture the work of God expressed in nature. A second and third generation of painters, including John Kensett, Sanford Gifford, Frederic Church, and Jasper Cropsey, modified the work of the founder and in some instances

Asher Brown Durand's *Kindred Spirits* (1849) was commissioned by a New York patron to commemorate William Cullen Bryant's friendship with Thomas Cole, who had died unexpectedly in February of 1848. The painting represents an idealized view of the Kaaterskill Clove. *(Oil on canvas, 44" × 36." Reproduced with permission from Crystal Bridges — Museum of American Art.)*

pushed toward luminism, the celebration of American light.[1]

Discussions of the Hudson River School run the risk of neglecting some lesser-known landscape painters, one of them William Guy Wall, whose *Hudson River Portfolio* (1821) traced the path of the Hudson from Little Falls, Luzerne, to Governor's Island, New York, and is recognized as the first aesthetic tribute to river scenery. Plates from this work were used for a moving panorama at the Bowery Theater in 1828. The size and breadth of some of the works by Cole and other Hudson River

William Wade's 1845 *Panorama*, 12 feet long, is a detailed engraving showing farms, estates, villages, and commercial and industrial activities on the Hudson's east and west shorelines. The work is part of the panorama tradition of nineteenth-century landscape painting, which had a theatrical quality about it. This tradition was extended to photography in the late nineteenth and early twentieth centuries.

School painters constituted a kind of "landscape theater"—panoramic paintings which attempted to embrace the fullness of the imperium and inspire new forms extending the appreciation of the beauty of the Hudson to new audiences. Willam Wade's 1845 *Panorama of the Hudson*, a twelve foot pocket folding map of the river illustrating both sides of the Hudson from the Battery to Albany, helped instruct steamboat travelers about the history and aesthetics of the river.

While the lure of the West and the popularity of the camera led to the late-nineteenth-century decline of the Hudson River School, its artists had succeeded in sanctifying the Hudson as a place where God was manifest. Their work deepened the nationalization of the Hudson, and by midcentury reaffirmed its standing as America's river.

Kindred Spirits

Kindred Spirits, Durand's 1849 painting of Cole and Bryant, recognized the link between the Romantic artists and writers who shared a common interest in the exploration of nature and the American wilderness as sources of national identity. But their work had been anticipated by Washington Irving, who between 1819 and 1820 published *The Sketchbook of Geoffrey Crayon Gent*, which described the Hudson as "that bright and holy influence of nature upon us." The scenery he depicted included the Hudson and the Kaatskill Mountains which had been imprinted earlier on his youthful imagination. Irving created a folk history for the river, the valley, and New York City, using characters derived from German tales and setting them in the local landscape. His work imbued the American landscape with a poetic association and inspired painters to come to the Hudson and join with Rip, who—looking down from the Catskill Mountain House—saw "the lordly Hudson, far, far below him moving on its silent but majestic course."

Irving's Knickerbocker friends James Kirke Paulding and William Cullen Bryant also contributed to the nationalizing of the regional landscape. In his 1828 work *Mirror for Travelers*, Paulding described the Hudson as "this magnificent river, which taking in all of its combinations of magnitude and beauty, is scarcely equaled in the new, and not even approached in the old [world]." Bryant echoed these sentiments in his travel accounts in the *Evening Post* where he complained that so many Americans went to visit Wales or Scotland instead of the western shore of the Hudson, which was "as worthy of a pilgrimage across the Atlantic as the Alps themselves."

Some writers shared Thomas Cole's concerns about the tension between civilization and nature, few as clearly as James Fenimore Cooper in his *Leatherstocking Tales* (1823–1841). In these works Cooper maps the American wilderness, notes the incursions of humankind, and mourns the loss of the virgin forest. He describes in detail the

Sunnyside by the Hudson (artist unknown) depicts Washington Irving's "snuggery" set alongside two transportation innovations, the steamboat and the railroad. Some thought these new elements added to the picturesque quality of the landscape, as they seem to in this painting.
(Historic Hudson Valley, Tarrytown, New York.)

regional landscape which he felt contained scenes distinctly American because of the very fact that they embraced both civilization and the forest. *Home As Found* (1838), *Satanstoe* (1845), *The Spy* (1821), and his short story "The Water Witch" provide examples of Cooper's embrace of the topography of the valley and the river.

These nationally recognized American writers tended to eclipse the work of Nathaniel Parker Willis, a valley journalist and editor. Late in his career Willis built his country house Idlewild near Cornwall, where he explored local history and wrote a series of popular essays for the *Home Journal* published later as *Out of Doors at Idlewild; or the Shaping of a Home on the Banks of the Hudson* (1855). Willis's Romantic sensibility extended to local place names; he changed Butter Hill to Storm King and Murderer's Creek to Moodna Creek.

The writers who peopled the landscape with romantic characters and celebrated the river's grandeur shared with the artists the sense of the Hudson as a marker of American identity and the soul of the young nation.

The Velvet Edge

Many Hudson River painters and writers sought to awaken the romantic imagination through direct encounters with nature. Steamboat excursions up the Hudson to the Highlands and the Catskills in the 1840s and 1850s became romantic rituals. But for some this occasional encounter was not sufficient to sustain their work. They needed to live in close proximity to the river.

Beginning with Cole, who occupied a farmhouse at Cedar Grove in Catskill, and moving across the Hudson to Frederic Church's Olana near Hudson (1870), and downriver to Jasper Cropsey's studio Ever Rest (1885) in Hastings, we have a pattern that was shared by many of the generations of the Hudson River School. River living also attracted wealthy urbanites who, in search of country seats, initiated a suburban migration of New Yorkers to the Hudson Valley, following the lead of the Romantic artists and writers.

The most extraordinary example is Washington Irving's Sunnyside, a Dutch farmhouse transformed into a Romantic stone mansion so remarkable that it inspired the landscape aesthetic of Andrew Jackson Downing and the architectural ideas of Alexander Jackson Davis.[2] Sunnyside, with its eclectic architectural style, located "with that glorious river before me . . . which has ever been to me a river of delight," was another attempt by Irving to historicize the Hudson. The cottage grounds are one of the best examples of Romantic landscape practice.

Nathaniel Parker Willis's estate Idlewild, with a commanding view of Newburgh Bay, became widely known as a Romantic retreat and intellectual salon where one could enjoy nature, the river, and good conversation. Living in the country became the fashion. A. J. Downing encouraged this

A. J. Downing recommended the bracketed cottage model because its projecting roof, supported by "brackets," produced "the kind of beauty called picturesque." The sketch appears in his 1850 work, *The Architecture of Country Houses,* the style book that inspired thousands of homes in the eastern United States.

This photograph of the Catskill Mountain House shows the viewing area at the edge of the escarpment.

pattern with the publication of *Cottage Residences* in 1842. This guide for country living appealed to New York businessmen, flush with success and imitative of English gentry, seeking to escape the city.

Country Living

The term "country living" defined the new domesticated landscape and distinguished it from the cult of wilderness that had dominated earlier Romantic thinking. The Hudson River fulfilled the ideals of the emerging middle ground by balancing the natural and the human.

By the second half of the nineteenth century, the valley was in the grip of a frenzy of estate building. The riverscape was outlined with a "velvet edge" of manicured lawns and gardens and neo-Gothic cottages extending from Weehawken to Albany. A river journey could now be marked not by reaches but by great river estates: Wave Hill in Riverdale, Glenview in Yonkers, Lyndhurst in Tarrytown, Castle Rock in the Highlands, the Vanderbilt Mansion in Hyde Park, the Mills Mansion in Staatsburg, Edgewater in Barrytown,

and Montgomery Place in Annandale. New Yorkers who likened the Hudson to the Rhine appropriately built European-style castles, including Fonthill in Riverdale, Ericstan in Tarrytown, Castle Rock in Garrison, and Bannerman's Castle on Pollepel Island.

The Mountain House

For those who found the cost of a river estate beyond their means, the mountain house or river hotel—situated on high ground with a panoramic view of the river—offered New Yorkers refreshing doses of mountain air. The premier nineteenth-century example was the Catskill Mountain House, opened in 1824. Several variations quickly appeared along the Hudson, from the Fort Lee Hotel and the Palisades Mountain House in New Jersey to Cozzen's Hotel at Buttermilk Falls in the Highlands.

The emergence of a middle class with a sufficient wealth and leisure contributed to the increase in steamboat travel and river excursions, providing connections to not only to the Hudson and mountain houses,

Cozzens' Hotel (*below*) at Buttermilk Falls, located in the village of Highland Falls, was built on an escarpment 180 feet above the river. This representative nineteenth-century mountain house offered a panoramic view of the Hudson and abundant clean air for its three hundred patrons.

but to the new amusement parks (some built by the steamboat companies) on the New Jersey Palisades and at Hastings, Indian Point, Iona Island, and Kingston Point. The influx of the public seeking to escape from the miasmic city populated the Hudson with a series of recreation destinations that comprised the foundation for a therapeutic river, one which could heal both the body and the spirit.

The work of the painters, writers, and estate builders contributed to the development of a Hudson River aesthetic which linked river, land, and home into the definitional components of the sublime and picturesque. Unlike the raw wilderness of the American West, where many of the painters would soon migrate, the Hudson River valley was now established as the national example of Americans' ability to improve on nature and live in harmony with it.

Chapter 9

Industrialization and the Transformation of the Landscape

The Chapter in Brief

Until the opening of the Erie Canal, the Hudson Valley was the breadbasket of the United States. The presence of New York as a commercial center, entry port, and growing city at the Hudson's mouth influenced the economic development of industries such as brickmaking, iron making, lumbering, and quarrying. Completion of the Erie Canal enlarged the market area served by the Hudson and lifted the valley's economy out of its provincial status. Industrialization of the valley required a transportation revolution including the steamship and railroad. The process reshaped the landscape and led artists and writers to develop new and broader definitions of the sublime.

A Republic of Small Farmers

The nineteenth century was not only an age that celebrated nature and the American landscape, but also one that witnessed the beginnings of industrialization of the United States, which in time would radically alter the river and the valley.

The prerequisite for the industrialization of the Hudson was a prosperous commercial and agricultural history that provided capital and food essential for growth. Axe-wielding settlers, who had cleared most of the valley's original forest cover for agriculture by the time of the Revolution, used the Hudson to connect farmers to the city and foster the development of commercial agriculture. River landings became points of exchange where sloop captains who served as farmers' agents bartered produce for finished goods. The production of wheat, barley, and rye on choice soils was so successful that the region became known as the "Bread Basket of the Nation." Agriculture flourished in the valley and along the river until the second quarter of the nineteenth century.

Industrial Development: The First Stage

Early in the eighteenth century, industrial development was inhibited by undercapitalization, few local markets, and limited transportation. The valley's nineteenth-century industrial growth was ultimately driven by the needs of an expanding New York City at the river's mouth, which was emerging as the nation's commercial center.

Among the earliest of these industries was lumbering, which provided materials for home construction and shipbuilding, fuel for steam engines, and pulp for paper production. Lumbering stimulated the expansion of mills, dependent on water power and frequently located on tributaries of the Hudson. Milling included not only sawmills but also gristmills and paper mills.

Bricks and Quarries

Quarrying in the Palisades and the Highlands began as early as 1736 and accelerated in the nineteenth century with the increase in New York City's building needs, especially home and road construction. In the

117

Catskills, quarry operations produced slabs of bluestone used as paving blocks for city streets and sidewalks.

Brickmaking started in Haverstraw in 1815 and expanded rapidly, employing at its peak twenty-four hundred workers, making Haverstraw the brickmaking capital of the valley. Local forests supplied the wood needed to fire the kilns; clay deposits and anthracite coal dust provided the basic ingredients. The industry's energy needs consumed the cedar which formerly stood in great abundance along the western shore of the river. Broken and misformed brick castoffs—clinkers—still litter the Hudson's banks in Haverstraw, Verplanck, Kingston, Fishkill, and other river communities.[1]

The success of quarrying and brickmaking provided impetus for the growth of shipbuilding. Between 1815 and 1828, Nyack shipyards turned out a sloop a year, making the town the shipbuilding center

of the Hudson. Nyack was succeeded by Newburgh and Rondout, where steamboat production dominated later in the century and continued through World War II.

Upriver industrial activity included ironmaking in the Highlands, cement production at the foot of the Catskills, and tanning along Catskill Creek. Ironmakers cleared large tracts of forest to manufacture charcoal, constructed forges and furnaces, and played an important role in arming the Union forces during the Civil War. Nineteenth-century iron production in the valley was concentrated in the Cold Spring area.

Beds of limestone found near the river proved suitable for cement making, but the river itself was the key factor in establishing the industry. Powdered cement, made by burning chunks of limestone in kilns, was a bulk cargo most easily and cheaply shipped by water. Even today, up-

The brickworks of John Derbyshire, one of the largest brick producers of the late 1800s, were set in a treeless landscape at Haverstraw. Clay unloaded from barges along the southern dock was stockpiled adjacent to the works; schooners tied up at the long wharf to the east transported finished bricks to New York.

A standard ice house was made of wood and measured 200 feet by 150 feet with a storage capacity of 20,000 to 30,000 tons. Most were located on the Hudson's western shore and set broadside to the river. For insulation, the space between their double outer walls was packed with sawdust.

river cement factories ship their product downriver in barges.

Leather and Ice

Tanning, the process of converting animal skins into leather, required tannic acid from hemlock trees, which were found in the Catskills along with abundant supplies of fresh water essential to the operation. Untanned hides, some from South America, were transported up the Hudson by steamer, and finished hides reshipped to New York City for export.

One of the best examples of the influence of New York City on industrial development along the Hudson is ice harvesting. In 1826, ice blocks were cut from Rockland Lake and shipped downriver to be stored in city ice houses. The newly incorporated Knickerbocker Ice Company built an inclined railway from the landing to the lake, ran a fleet of thirteen steamboats, and eventually employed up to three thousand men. Upriver, ice was cut from the Hudson and stored in ice houses from Marlboro to Troy. One firm, the Mutual Benefit Ice Company, had ice houses in West Park, Port Ewen, Staatsburg, and Barrytown; its storage capacity of sixty thousand tons was essential to meet the needs of a major urban market.

Industrial Development: The Second Stage

Industrial growth in the early antebellum era provided the precedent for a second stage of industrial development in the late nineteenth and early twentieth centuries, including automobile assembly plants, cable wire production, cement manufacturing, electrical power production, oil and sugar refineries, and paper making.[2]

Many of these industries attracted immigrant workers to river towns, where they provided cheap labor and the core of a heterogeneous population. They tended to concentrate in the towns' older sections, close to the river, near industrial facilities and the railroad, while old-stock residents and new suburbanites moved up the hill, thereby creating the town/hill split that still characterizes the geography of many river villages.

The legacy of the industrial transformation of the Hudson valley landscape was quickly visible in the scarring created by activities such as quarrying, the kind of legacy that heightened concerns about the preservation of the natural beauty of the landscape. But not all observers shared these concerns; Nathaniel Parker Willis and Benson Lossing, the historian and the engraver, believed that mills and factories added to the picturesque.

"A Monster Moving on the River Defying Wind and Tide, and Breathing Flames and Smoke"

The Dutch sloop, because it depended on nature, often found its passengers and cargo held captive by the Hudson's winds and tides, introducing uncertainty and irregularity to commercial and passenger travel. Industrialization and modernization of the valley's economy required a transportation system that could reach distant markets and carry goods in a predictable and timely manner. Innovative technology helped overcome the primary obstacles of winds and tides.

In May of 1804 James Renwick and his Columbia College classmates observed a crowd moving quickly toward the Battery to watch "Jack Stevens going over to Hoboken in a queer sort of boat." When they arrived they saw that a boat "with no visible means of propulsion" was speedily under way. What Renwick and his friends had observed was the first known successful application of steam to twin screw propellers and river travel in North America.

Robert Fulton is thus neither the inventor of the steamboat nor the first to build one on the Hudson; this honor belongs to New Jerseyan John Stevens of Hoboken. What distinguished Robert Fulton from Stevens and others was his commercial and entrepreneurial savvy and the backing of Robert Livingston of Clermont, who provided the capital to underwrite Fulton and the legal expertise to monopolize steam travel on the Hudson.

The Clermont *making a landing at Cornwall on the Hudson, 1810* (E. L. Henry). The interlocking nature of the transportation system was documented every day at river landings large and small. Here turnpike, coach, inn, dock, and the *Clermont* all meet with the exchange of goods, passengers, and gossip.
(I. N. Phelps Stokes Collection, Miriam and Ira D. Wallach Division of Art, Prints and Photographs, The New York Public Library, Astor, Lenox and Tilden Foundations.)

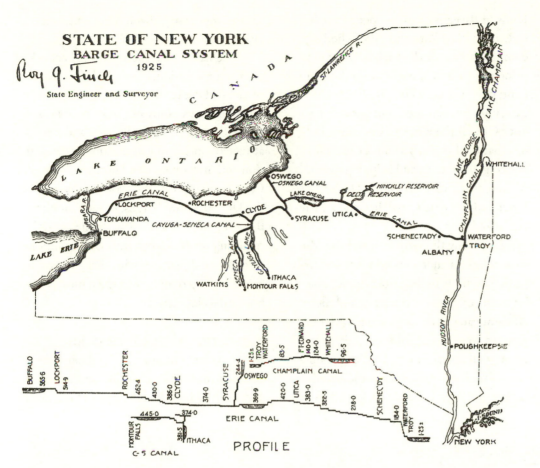

STATE OF NEW YORK
BARGE CANAL SYSTEM
1925

Roy G. Finch
State Engineer and Surveyor

On August 17, 1807, off the west side of Manhattan near the old state prison and in front of a large crowd, Robert Fulton left the dock aboard his *North River* (later dubbed the *Clermont*), a 130 feet long vessel with a beam of 16 feet and open paddle wheels. Making his way up the Hudson, he arrived at the Livingston estate, a distance of 100 miles, in twenty-four hours. The next day Fulton continued to Albany, completing a journey of 150 miles in thirty-six hours. He fully appreciated the significance of steamboat travel to the life of the river and the economy of the region. The steamboat age had begun.

The full impact of this new technology was delayed by the legislative monopoly Fulton and Livingston had secured to protect their invention; it enabled them to fix prices and eliminate competition. This chokehold on steamboat travel on the Hudson slowed the transportation revolution until 1824 when the monopoly was broken by the U.S. Supreme Court decision in *Gibbons v. Ogden*.[3] Very quickly competition increased, rates fell, and river traffic expanded.

The Erie Canal

River transportation, while relatively inexpensive, was limited by the provincial economies of the river towns. Completion of the Erie Canal in 1825 provided a major avenue for economic expansion, linking New York City with the Great Lakes and the Midwest via the canal and the

Hudson River. The canal opened the hinterland to New York and established a commercial network which became the principal economic corridor on the continent; one year after completion it was carrying nineteen thousand boats. New York City, at the nexus of interstate and international trade, became a center for banking, insurance, and shipping, while Albany, at the juncture of the Hudson River and the Erie Canal, became a thriving inland port.

Drawn by the fertile soils of the Midwest, wheat farmers moved west, accompanied by flour milling operations. The low costs of wheat production and more efficient canal/river shipping allowed midwestern wheat to be sold more cheaply and undercut the Hudson Valley producers. New York lost its primacy as the breadbasket of the nation and was forced to

shift to more specialized dairy and fruit farming.

The Erie Canal extended the network of river transportation, created a larger market, broadened the resource base, and elevated the region's economy out of its provincial status. Savings in shipping costs and time attracted more traffic and stimulated expansion and investment that launched New York City's emergence as the economic engine of the United States. Barges, in such number that they were described as "barge towns" requiring services from river communities, were towed downriver with cargo to South Street, a daily reminder of the nation's economic development.[4]

Keeping to a Schedule
By 1850 over a hundred steamboats were carrying more than a million passengers and arriving on schedule. Speed became an

Entering the Lock (E. L. Henry). Canal boats had colorful and evocative names including *The Chief Engineer, The Seneca Chief, The Young Lion of the West,* and *Noah's Ark.* Boats were named for love, pride, patriotism, and even the exotic — the *Breath of Cashmere,* for example.
(Collection of the Albany Institute of History and Art.)

The celebration of technology was always tinged with apprehension about human ability to control the machine. The *Henry Clay* disaster served as a reminder that the machine could quickly become the monster in irresponsible hands.

American virtue and was thought to be indispensable to an efficient society. The passion of steamboat captains, crews, and owners to be the fastest boat on the river was so consuming that they often endangered the lives of their passengers. The most infamous of the steamboat races pitted the *Armenia* against the *Henry Clay* in July of 1852 and ended with the *Clay* in flames and a shocking loss of life, including that of Andre Jackson Downing, the noted landscape architect.

The steamboat conquered time with its promise to arrive and depart at a given hour. One of the most significant documents in the history of transportation may be the schedule—the commitment to regularity and predictability so necessary to the

Hudson River Day Line,
NEW YORK & ALBANY DAY BOATS.

General Offices, Desbrosses St. Pier, New York.

DIMENSIONS OF STEAMERS.

	"New York."	"Albany."
Length over all	341 feet.	325 feet.
Breadth " "	74 "	75 "
Breadth of Hull	40 "	40 "
Tonnage	1,850 tons.	1,415 tons.
Horse Power	3,850	3,200
Stroke of Piston	12 feet.	12 feet.
Diameter of Cylinder	75 in.	73 in.

DAY LINE TIME TABLE, 1899.
DAILY EXCEPT SUNDAY.

GOING NORTH.	A. M.	GOING SOUTH.	A. M.
Brooklyn by Annex, 8.00		**Albany, - - -**	**8.30**
New York:		Hudson, - -	10.40
Desbrosses St.,	8.40	Catskill, - -	11.00
22d St., N. R.,	9.00		P. M.
Yonkers, -	9.45	Kingston Point,	12.25
West Point, -	11.50	Poughkeepsie,	1.20
	P. M.	Newburgh, - -	2.15
Newburgh, -	12.25	West Point, -	2.50
Poughkeepsie, -	1.15	Yonkers, - -	4.30
Kingston Point,	2.10	New York:	
Catskill, - - -	3.25	22d St., N. R.,	5.30
Hudson, - -	3.40	Desbrosses St.,	6.00
Albany, - - -	6.10	Brooklyn by Annex, 6.20	

Interior of the steamer Drew. *"River palace" aptly describes the* Drew *with its luxurious interior. The cost of early steamboat travel may have compelled designers to embellish the interiors to offer passengers a "travel experience" — something more than a speedy connection between two points. While falling rates, which helped democratize travel, made such luxury unnecessary, a similar pattern of interior design appeared in railroad cars as well.*
(Collection of The New-York Historical Society.)

development of a capitalist order. Schedules for steamboat travel made their appearance on the Hudson as early as September 1807, long before they appeared on any other American river.

Hudson River painters and lithographers have provided us with a rich visual record of the steamboat's progress. The best of these are the works of the Bard brothers, James and John, who captured the efficient beauty of the machine. They celebrated the "technological sublime" in the Hudson River steamboats and saw in them an optimism and confidence that nature and technology could coexist.[5] The deep and abiding faith of nineteenth-century Americans in the inevitability of progress impelled technology to search beyond the steamboat in an attempt to overcome the obstacles of space and river-bound travel.

Railroads: The Great Machine

Land travel along the Hudson had remained a primitive affair over the Albany Post Road. Competing stage lines merged in 1835 and provided regular passenger service between New York and Albany. Winter ice and snow required the use of sled runners, clearly restricting mobility for four months of the year.

NORTH RIVER · 1807-1808

Robert Fulton and Robert R. Livingston

1807: 142 × 14 × 4 feet ◖ 79 T ◖ 43,280 × 4,267 × 1,219 m

1808: 149 × 17.92 × 7 feet ◖ 182 T ◖ 45,414 × 5,462 × 2,134 m

The elaboration of steamboat design is clear in comparing a diagram of Fulton's *North River* (*bottom*) with the *Drew* and the *St. John* (*top*), depicted passing in the Highlands by Currier and Ives. The extension of the deck out over the narrow hull increased passenger capacity. Triple decking also underscored the designers' intention to provide a visual travel experience. The decorated paddle box was one of the distinguishing characteristics of each vessel.

(Collection of The New-York Historical Society.)

Syracuse (James Bard). The art of the Bard brothers, James and John, stylized the steamboat as a fast, sleek, and modern-looking vessel — a nineteenth-century prefiguring of the streamlined style we identify with twentieth-century design. Their representations have become icons, defining our image of the Hudson River steamboats. (Collection of the Albany Institute of History and Art, Gift of William Gorham Rice.)

In 1831, when the Mohawk and Hudson Railroad reached Albany, and in 1841 when the Erie Railroad connected to the Hudson at Piermont, stage travel had been declining and the steamboat had its first real competition. The Hudson River Railroad was completed in 1851, hugging the eastern shore from New York City to the town of Greenbush, across the river from Albany. The first railroad trip from New York to Greenbush in October 1851 took four hours. Fulton's steamboat had taken thirty-six hours to make the same journey—recall that sloops needed several days.[6]

Travel, now freed from the physical limits of the river, stimulated commercial development, population growth, and the suburbanization of many river towns. The railroad not only linked the river valley more closely to the city, but also established a corridor of industrial development along the right-of-way. It accelerated the expansion and integration of markets and the economic revolution begun by the steamboat and the Erie Canal.

The railroad made its presence felt with bold and powerful signs. No one could miss the size, sound, and smoke of this new engine of progress, which promised to complete the conquest of the wilderness and the domination of nature. Residents of river towns and estates felt its transforming power close at hand. The Hudson's shoreline was now bounded by a steel highway that regularized the water's edge and, with electrification, barred residents from the river.

First Railroad Train on the Mohawk and Hudson Road (E. L. Henry). *Scientific American* reported in April 1851 that "one of the grandest sights is a locomotive with its huge train dashing along in full flight . . . when a large train is rushing along at the rate of 30 miles per hour, [it] affords a sight both sublime and terrific."
(Collection of the Albany Institute of History and Art, Gift of Friends of the Institute.)

By the mid-1800s the new railroad lines had been linked to established steamboat landings, creating a travel network in which passengers were likely to move from one means of transportation to another in the course of a single journey. Steamers from New York took vacationers to the landing at Catskill; from there they were conveyed by stagecoach and railroad to the Mountain House.

The first bridge to span the Hudson below Albany was the railroad bridge at Poughkeepsie, completed in 1888. Bridges are only one reminder of how engineers were central, though too often neglected, figures in the river's history. In the 1800s they played key roles in exploiting the valley for transportation and water supply. John B. Jervis, for example, had major responsibilities in building the Delaware and Hudson Canal, the Croton Aqueduct, and the Hudson River railroad.
(Courtesy Adriance Memorial Library, Poughkeepsie, New York.)

The Machine Enters the Garden

Nineteenth-century responses to the railroad were ambivalent. Lovers of the Hudson like Thomas Cole welcomed the advance of civilization that the railroad represented while they despaired over the accompanying destruction of nature. Cole lamented scenes of beauty made desolate in the name of improvement. The Hudson River, which the Romantic painters and artists viewed as a special creation of God, was—in the hands of railroad builders and land developers—quickly becoming the work of civilization.

The railroad's power to break through the boundaries of time and space and re-shape the riverscape far more than the steamboat intensified the tension between civilization and nature. How were these forces to be balanced to ensure the beauty of the Hudson River and the valley?[7]

The railroad, in choosing the Hudson's shoreline for its right of way, followed the topography of the river and the route of least resistance and lowest cost. This decision, based on economics rather than aesthetics, established the precedent for later riverside automobile highway building, thus doubling the barriers to river access.

Driving to the Country

Apologists for the twentieth-century highway, like the railroad's nineteenth-century defenders, argued that it used engineering to make the river and valley accessible to more people and thereby heighten public appreciation of nature. Advertisements for both the railroad and the automobile shared a common vocabulary and imagery that emphasized the healthful virtues of the region's countryside and the great outdoors, now within reach of many more city dwellers.

The shift to the automobile and truck as principal means of transportation signaled a profound change in the economic growth pattern of river communities. Industries no longer dependent on the Hudson or the railroad eventually began to turn away from the river toward other sections of the country. River-based industrial facilities were abandoned and withered into vacant, ghostly monuments to an old order. Many of these old industrial sites have become contested ground as communities plan for their return to the river's edge.[8]

Over and Under

Engineers were stymied by the difficulty of burrowing underneath the Hudson River until 1904, when the first tunnel was completed linking Hoboken in New Jersey and Morton Street in New York City. In 1924 the Bear Mountain Bridge, the first vehicular spanning of the Hudson below Albany, was opened. More bridges and tunnels followed, and the Hudson no longer stood as a natural boundary between states and counties, urban and rural.

The transformation of river communities formerly separated by the Hudson and now linked by a bridge or tunnel was rapid. Inevitably the newly accessible communities in the lower valley grew in population and became twentieth-century suburbs. A modern example of this is the surge of growth in Rockland County following the completion of the Tappan Zee Bridge in 1955. The 1950 pre-bridge census showed a population of 89,000; by 1970 the figure

had jumped to 230,000. The river had historically contained population dispersal; now engineers had broken through this barrier.

Bridges and tunnels, unlike the old ferries and steamers, insulated the public from the direct physical experience of the river's

African-Americans played a role in the construction of major Hudson River public works projects including the West Shore Railroad. In this kind of unskilled labor they shared a common experience with Irish and Italian immigrants who found similar work in the building of the two Croton aqueducts.

smells, sounds, and even its spray. Today commuters move across the Hudson in engineered spaces that are enclosed and unnatural. Modern society's mastery over nature has detached us from a first-hand experience of the river and may have altered our physical and emotional relationship to the Hudson. The restoration of ferry service and an increase in the number of excursion boats promises to bring people back into more intimate contact with the river and widen public understanding and support.

The nineteenth century witnessed both the establishment of the Romantic conception of the Hudson as an example of the sublime in nature and the transportation and industrial revolutions that reconfigured the riverscape in the quest for

---

CROSSING THE RIVER

Bridges and Tunnels Located Between Albany and New York City

1. Parker F. Dunn Memorial Bridge *(1969)*
2. Castleton Thruway Bridge *(1959)*
3. Castleton Railroad Bridge *(1923)*
4. Rip Van Winkle Bridge *(1935)*
5. Kingston-Rhinecliff Bridge *(1957)*
6. Poughkeepsie Railroad Bridge *(1888 - no longer in use)*
7. Mid-Hudson Bridge *(1930)*
8. Newburgh-Beacon Bridge *(1963 - 2nd span completed 1980)*
9. Bear Mountain Bridge *(1924)*
10. Tappan Zee Bridge *(1955)*
11. George Washington Bridge *(1931 - lower deck opened 1962)*
12. Lincoln Tunnel *(1937 - first of 3 tubes)*
13. Pennsylvania Railroad Tunnel *(1906 - now Amtrak)*
14. Holland Tunnel *(1927)*
15. Hudson & Manhattan Railroad Tunnel *(1904 - now PATH uptown tube)*
16. Hudson & Manhattan Railroad Tunnel *(1909 - now PATH downtown tube)*
17. Verrazano Narrows Bridge *(1964)*

---

progress. By the end of the century, a basic historical and cultural paradigm was in place in which the forces of nature and civilization pushed and pulled against each other in a relentless battle over the future of the Hudson.

The Bear Mountain Bridge seems to be the perfect example of the technological sublime in which the work of the engineer is fully absorbed into and compatible with the work of nature. Such a view is typical of America's basic faith, rooted in the nineteenth century, in harmony between civilization and nature. *(Photo by Charles Porter.)*

Chapter 10

Conservation and Environmentalism

The Chapter in Brief

By the end of the nineteenth century, America faced a crisis in the struggle between the forces of progress and preservation. River defenders argued that the benefits of industrialization needed to be balanced with needs for long-term economic growth and land preservation. Fears over depletion of the resource base and the natural environment led state governments to intervene to preserve the Adirondack Forest and the Palisades. This was the beginning of the conservation movement, an effort to protect the beauty of the landscape and effectively manage natural resources. The battle over Storm King, a struggle that engaged a power company, the federal government, and citizen action groups, not only involved issues of scenic beauty and use of natural resources but also issues of health and habitat, the concerns of the new environmental movement of the 1960s and 1970s.

Woodsman, Spare the Axe

The end of a century has always been a time for cultural self-scrutiny and predictions about either impending collapse or a new age of progress. At the close of the nineteenth century, Americans swung between extremes of fear and exhilaration fueled by recognition that the frontier was closing, its character-forming power dwindling, with a concomitant loss of America's youthful vigor and natural resources.

The signs of crisis were heard in the outcries over the destruction of the wilderness and the desecration of the landscape. Natural resources, once thought of as inexhaustible, now seemed threatened by aggressive businessmen driven only by immediate profits. The pattern of depletion and destruction was visible along the Hudson River, where intensive lumbering in the Adirondacks and quarrying of the Palisades posed a threat to its watershed and its geological beauty.

In 1870 Verplanck Colvin complained about the environmental problems caused by the "chopping and burning off of vast tracts of forests" in the Adirondacks. The state legislature responded with a series of studies of the various uses of the Adirondacks and in 1885, after several reports and investigations, established the Forest Preserve in the Adirondacks and the Catskills, protecting the "nurse" of the Hudson.[1]

The preserve was created not only to safeguard the Hudson's watershed and manage the forest but also to guarantee a wilderness experience for wealthy New Yorkers. Two wings of the conservation movement clashed over these different goals—one side committed to planned long-term use of resources, the other committed to defending nature from development that threatened its pristine beauty.

The preserve was the result of a bold and precedent-setting state effort to protect nature. As confidence in the idea of limitless resources and the resiliency of nature faded, local, state, and national governments become agents of conservation, recognizing that they could no longer trust some invisible ecological hand to balance the demands of development and preservation. New York State would now be an active, if at times reluctant participant in the conservation

The impacts of quarrying on New Jersey's Palisades cliffs can be seen in this photo of the Carpenter Brothers' Quarry in Fort Lee, c. 1897. The Palisades Interstate Park Commission was formed in 1900 to preserve the striking scenery of this piece of Hudson River shoreline and transform it into a public playground.
(Palisades Interstate Park, New Jersey Section: Scanned Image Library.)

movement. Yet in spite of the state's role and that of groups like the Sierra Club, the movement continued to have an elitist underpinning. Public consciousness and participation in conservation remained low until the 1960s.

Dynamite, Dynamite, Dynamite

The most visible signs of destruction were to be found in the Palisades and Hook Mountain, just north of Nyack on the Hudson's western shore. Quarrying had intensified greatly in the 1870s and 1880s with the aid of dynamite and heavy-duty earth-moving equipment. A river traveler could not help but notice the scars and deep cuts in the Palisades, Hook Mountain, and Breakneck Ridge in the Highlands. Some of the Palisades' natural sculptures, including Washington Head and Indian Head, were destroyed.

Dynamiting, a daily reminder of the relentless destruction, galvanized residents of Palisades estates and the Women's Clubs of New Jersey on the western side and influential landowners from Riverdale on the east side into a pressure group determined to end the quarrying. In March 1890, state commissions from New York and New Jersey recommended the creation of a permanent interstate park to protect the Palisades from the blasters.

Preservation and Recreation

In 1900 the New York and New Jersey legislatures established the Palisades Interstate Park Commission (PIPC) to buy and administer land on the Palisades. The PIPC's jurisdiction extended from the top of the Palisades to the river's edge and by 1906 north to Hook Mountain in Rockland County. In addition to saving the Palisades

Especially during the Depression, the Palisades Interstate Park's beaches offered affordable recreation for hundreds of thousands, mostly New Yorkers who arrived by ferry. Use declined through the 1930s and the beaches closed as other recreational opportunities became available and the opening of the George Washington Bridge put an end to direct ferry service. This photo from July 2, 1939, shows the Alpine bathing area. It was the last beach closed (in 1944), and the only one closed due to pollution.
(Palisades Interstate Park, New Jersey Section: Scanned Image Library.)

and Hook Mountain from the quarrymen, the motive here was to encourage managed use and provide public recreation for Manhattanites in search of a respite from city life, eager to enjoy the Palisades and the Hudson River.

The recreational objectives, which included bathing, hiking, and camping, expanded and democratized use of the river while serving the interests of the elite conservationists who sought to preserve the landscape and connect new Americans with the morally uplifting experience of nature. It took the active leadership of well-connected citizens and the direct intervention of two state governments to produce this pioneering cooperative effort in conservation.

In 1909 the Palisades Interstate Park was formally dedicated as part of the Hudson-Fulton Celebration where parades, memorials, and speeches became civics lessons for old and new stock Americans, reminding them that the Hudson was America's river, whose majesty could instill pride in state and nation. At the same time that conservation efforts in the Adirondacks and on the Palisades attempted to protect the river's Romantic landscape, the Hudson-Fulton Celebration reinvigorated the historical associations which had taught so many Americans about our national history.

The Roads Roll On

The PIPC prepared surveys for new river roadways—the Henry Hudson Parkway in 1905 and the Palisades Parkway in 1909—to provide a motoring experience of the Hudson. The traveling public would come to know the river through automobile excursions that emphasized not engagement but rapid movement through the landscape.

The energy of the first wave of conservation extended into the 1920s. The PIPC expanded the park from its original 10,000 acres to 40,000, including Harriman and Bear Mountain Parks. Automobile access to these new parks was provided by construction of the Bear Mountain Bridge (1924)

New Deal public works projects transformed the American landscape. Bear Mountain caught the attention of WPA planners who sponsored the construction of Perkins Memorial Drive and the rustic Bear Mountain Inn in which they attempted to integrate design with the natural elements of the surrounding region. Most of the highway work was done by hand labor. *(Courtesy of the Palisades Interstate Park Commission.)*

an artist/vacation colony, into a bedroom community for New York City; the bridge quickly exceeded capacity.

While the forces of civilization dominated these decades with road and bridge building and ongoing quarrying at Little Stony Point and Mount Taurus in Cold Spring, the river defenders were not without voice. The Hudson River Conservation Society was founded in 1936 to challenge the quarrymen by appealing to the ideas of preservation and the Romantic sublime. In 1939 Carl Carmer published *The Hudson*, part of the "The Rivers of America" series. Carmer hoped that his work would reconstitute the Romantic and historical Hudson. Thirty years later this book became one of the cornerstones for the Hudson River's modern environmental movement.

The Hudson: "That River's Alive"

The environmentalists of the 1960s and 1970s would build on the tradition of the Romantic sublime, historical association, and the work of the first generation of conservationists. They also drew heavily on the relatively new science of ecology, with its concern for the balance of nature, and on public health issues first raised by Rachel Carson in her 1962 book *Silent Spring*. It is these kinds of health concerns that distinguish the environmental movement from the conservationism of the turn of the century. Over the next twenty years the history of the Hudson River would center on questions that engaged both the preservation of nature and the health of the environment.

Storm King

In 1962 Consolidated Edison (Con Ed), searching for new sources of power to satisfy New York City's enormous appetite

and the Storm King Highway (1919–1922), which runs two hundred feet above the Hudson and cuts across the face of Storm King Mountain. The highway network was extended west and north by construction of the George Washington Bridge (1931) and the New Deal's Storm King Highway (1940), which was built around the back of Storm King by the Civilian Conservation Corps. The pace of change was so rapid that two additional lanes had to be added to the George Washington Bridge in 1946 and a six-lane lower level in 1960. The completion of the Tappan Zee Bridge in 1955 turned Rockland County, formerly

This rendering of the proposed Storm King plant appeared in Con Ed's 1963 annual report. In *Power along the Hudson*, Allan Talbot claims that the unknown artist "did more than anyone else to create the beginnings of the opposition. His picture showed a portion of Storm King missing, like a slice removed from a tub of cheese. In its place was . . . a glistening, sharp-edged steel-and-concrete structure contrasted against what remained of the natural beauty of the mountain."
(Courtesy of Scenic Hudson.)

for electricity, proposed to build a pumped storage electricity generating plant at Storm King.[2] The proposal launched one of the major environmental battles of this century, one which contributed to a rebirth of interest in the Hudson.

In 1963 Carl Carmer and a group of preservationists organized the Scenic Hudson Preservation Conference, known today as Scenic Hudson, to oppose Con Ed's plans to build a pumping station and reservoir on Storm King Mountain. The opposition appealed to the aesthetic tradition established by the nineteenth-century Romantic painters and argued that Storm King should be held inviolate given its special place in the history and landscape of the river. For Carmer and friends, Con Ed's proposal was another example of desecrating the Hudson Valley to serve the needs of the city at the river's mouth.

At first the battle centered on the traditional conservation objective of preservation. But as concerns for the plant's impacts on fish life and the health of the river intensified, especially after revelations in 1963 of fish kills at the Indian Point nuclear power plant, scientific and technical questions became more prominent. Indian Point and other generating stations on the Hudson have "once-through" cooling systems that utilize cool water from the river and subsequently discharge it at higher temperatures.[3] The fish kills occurred at the intake stations, where river water was sucked in at a rate of thousands of gallons per second. The proposed Storm King plant would also draw in enormous volumes of water.

While Con Ed's power plant was scrapped and Storm King spared, the mountain was not inviolate. The Storm King Highway was opened in 1922 to provide access for motorists wishing to enjoy the scenic view. But in spite of this road cut, Storm King retains its majesty. *(Photo by Charles Porter.)*

Biologists and environmentalists feared that the Hudson's fish populations, particularly young fish for which the estuary serves as nursery, would be endangered by the Storm King plan.

Con Ed obtained a license to build the plant, only to be met with legal challenges contesting the licensing process. The challenges led to a precedent-setting ruling recognizing that aesthetic and environmental impacts had standing during the review process alongside issues of economics, property, and technology. In addition, government agencies charged with environmental protection became increasingly concerned about the fish kills and moved to require the utilities to build cooling towers at their nuclear and fossil-fueled plants.

These controversies dragged on for over a decade of frustrating hearings and lawsuits. Faced with the prospect of more of the same, the parties to the dispute reached a mediated out-of-court settlement in 1980. In the settlement's major tradeoff, the utilities abandoned the plans for Storm King and instituted measures to reduce fish kills at other power plants in return for a ten-year moratorium on a cooling towers requirement. The Storm King battle was not only a defeat for Consolidated Edison, it also energized a critical mass of conser-

vationists, environmentalists, and preservationists to organize and be ever ready to defend the Hudson against new assaults.[4]

Unnatural History

In 1969, amidst the power plant controversies, one of the most vocal environmentalists, Robert Boyle, published *The Hudson*

As the river is cleansed of sewage, warning signs like this one have mostly come down. *(Photo by Paul Cohen.)*

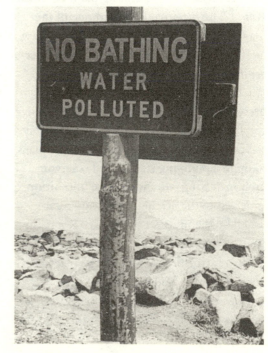

River: A Natural and Unnatural History. This book did for the Hudson's environmental movement what Rachel Carson's *Silent Spring* had done for the national movement in 1962. Boyle's work became the environmental handbook for the Hudson, documenting the long-term and systematic pollution which he effectively argued threatened the life of the river—what he called the "Unnatural Hudson." Boyle described in great detail the natural history of the river, and deepened people's understanding of its ecology and the public's responsibility for its health. This work shifted our focus from the aesthetic to the scientific and compelled us to recognize the Hudson as an ecosystem—one that was seriously endangered.

Public interest in and understanding of the Hudson was heightened by the battle over Storm King and Boyle's portrait of a polluted river. From its origins as a relatively small and elite group, the Hudson River environmental movement grew to encompass a wider segment of the region's populace. One of the signs of this renewed commitment was the growth of organizations such as Scenic Hudson, the Hudson River Fishermen's Association, and the Hudson River Sloop Clearwater.

Setting Sail to Restore the River

In the same year that *The Hudson: A Natural and Unnatural History* was published, the sloop *Clearwater* was launched to, in

Clearwater, launched in May 1969, is a reminder of the central role of the sloop in the rich maritime history of the Hudson, and also a symbol of contemporary efforts to restore the river to its past health. (Courtesy of Clearwater.)

Pete Seeger's words, "clean up this polluted stream" and make it "the way it was on the river a hundred years ago." The *Clearwater* combined the traditions of both classical conservation and the new environmentalism.

The sloop served as a Romantic reminder of a simpler preindustrial time when the Hudson was not yet transformed by modern technology. Thus the *Clearwater* connects us to the history of the river by re-creating the experience of sailing—reconnecting river travel with nature. But it also fights for a cleaner river by educating and informing the citizenry about key

environmental issues in an effort to broaden public consciousness and participation in decisions about the river's future. It seeks to make us all stewards of the river.

It is right indeed that this history of the Hudson should return to historical replicas, not only the sloop *Clearwater* but also the *Half Moon* and the *Clermont*. Both are soon to play a prominent role in the 2009 Hudson-Fulton-Champlain Quadricentennial, drawing us back to those seminal events in the history of the Hudson and reminding us all that we cannot experience the modern river or plan for its future without feeling the pull of its rich past.

Chapter 11

Resolving River Conflicts

The Chapter in Brief

In current environmental disputes, Romantic era arguments over whether nature and civilization can coexist are joined by debate over ecology, economics, property rights, and the quality of scientific data. Such disputes, originating in conflicting values systems, are resolved through the political process and within a framework of legislation interpreted and enforced by regulatory agencies and the courts. Federal and state laws require disclosure of possible environmental impacts before major projects get underway. Wetlands laws regulate activities potentially harmful to these habitats. Public trust doctrine establishes public ownership of and right of access to tidal wetlands. The Hudson is tapped as a municipal water supply. Coastal zone, estuarine management, and Greenway programs encourage input from many interested parties in formulating policies intended to guide development in a context of environmental protection.

A Question of Values

At the beginning of the twenty-first century, many contemporary Hudson River issues replay the conflict between civilization and nature which preoccupied the Romantic artists in the nineteenth century. However, nineteenth-century optimism that nature and civilization could exist in harmony has waned, allowing frictions at the root of this conflict to come to the fore. Will strict pollution controls cost jobs as industries move to regions with less stringent laws? Does owning marshland give one the right to fill it in, or can society prevent destruction of wetlands and the ecological values they provide? If river shallows are destroyed by landfilling, can scientists accurately predict whether fish there will perish or survive by moving elsewhere?

Typically a spectrum of opinion develops as decision makers weigh environmental values against other important concerns. At one end are those who desire an environment as unspoiled as possible. They believe that protecting ecosystems and organisms also protects the biological support systems necessary for human survival, or that these systems and species are as intrinsically valuable as humans and their civilization. To these individuals, the most admirable aspects of the quality of life in the Hudson Valley are symbolized by a healthy and attractive river. They feel that nature (as represented by the Hudson) has been severely stressed and needs stronger protection.

At the other extreme are those who believe that human endeavor should be minimally restrained by ecological concerns. They feel that negative ecological impacts are of minor importance relative to benefits accruing to society and to individual, institutional, and regional economic well-being. They have faith that the environment is resilient enough to adjust to alterations, or that in cases where ecological upset potentially has major repercussions for people, human ingenuity and technology can solve any problems.

But the majority of people and the greatest weight of opinion are balanced somewhere in the middle. Their shifts towards one end of the spectrum or the other, perhaps in response to arguments made by those at the extremes, will likely determine society's values on environmental matters.

Politics and Law

The first Earth Day in 1970 marked a major shift of society's values in favor of greater ecological protection. This shift translated into popular support for legislative action. In the late 1960s and early 1970s Congress enacted significant environmental laws including the National Environmental Policy Act, the Clean Water Act, and the Clean Air Act.

Existing executive branch agencies were reorganized and new ones created to administer these laws. The U.S. Environmental Protection Agency (EPA), New Jersey's Department of Environmental Protection (DEP), New York State's Department of Environmental Conservation (DEC), and county and municipal entities (health departments, planning boards, etc.) established standards, decision-making procedures, and enforcement measures to create a regulatory framework for resolving disputes.

However, conflicts over environmental values did not end. In the decades since, these conflicts have been politically expressed in attempts to tighten or loosen environmental restrictions. Public officials, environmental groups, business interests, and individual citizens continue to express their views and pressure legislators. The resulting laws reflect the political give and take necessary for enactment. They typically call not for absolute environmental protection but for protection that takes into account a variety of interests, a balance evident when the National Environmental Policy Act was written: "It is the continuing policy of the Federal government . . . to create and maintain conditions under which man and nature can exist in productive harmony, and fulfill the social, economic, and other requirements of present and future generations of Americans."

EPA	**PCB**	MGD	*EIS*
FHWA	*NYSDOH*	USFWS	USCG
LWRP	DEC	**DDT**	CZMA	FDA
NEPA	*HRFA*	**CPUE**	SEQRA
SPDES	**FWPCA**	PPM	NYSDOT
USGS	CERCLA	*NMFS*	DEPE

Debate about environmental controversies can present a confusing array of acronyms. Those used in this chapter and the next are defined where they first appear as well as in the glossary.
(Nora Porter Graphic.)

Such wording creates opportunities to influence environmental decision-making beyond the legislative realm. After enactment, even legislation clearly intended to protect the environment may give executive agencies room to balance competing interests in carrying out the law's aims, and often requires that agencies provide an opportunity for public comment as part of the regulatory process.

The need to balance conflicting public attitudes often requires judgment calls by agency managers. These decisions may additionally reflect the philosophies of elected officials who appoint key agency staff, particularly in high profile cases where major ecological or economic resources are at stake. While few in number compared to the day-to-day routine decisions, these cases can generate enormous pressures on agency decision makers, attract intense media attention, and greatly mold public opinion of how well government is managing environmental concerns.

When a party to a dispute feels that agencies have decided improperly or failed to enforce the law, they may take the matter to the third branch of government—the judiciary. The courts are the ultimate arbiters of whether a law's provisions have been properly interpreted and enforced.

In addition to political lobbying, regulatory process, law enforcement, and legal action, another avenue of conflict resolution is being explored as groups with divergent aims and roles sit down together to design management plans which will guide use of the Hudson's natural resources within a context of environmental protection. If accepted by the parties involved, such plans may in the future reduce the number of costly and time-consuming regulatory and legal wrangles.

Even within the bounds of the Hudson Valley, discussion of environmental law, values conflicts, and dispute resolution must cover a wide range of topics. For clarity's sake, this chapter covers issues of managing the river's natural resources and planning for development while protecting the environment. Chapter 12 covers pollution control.

Assessing Environmental Impacts: Storm King's Legacy

In the dispute over the proposed Storm King power plant (see chapter 10), a major achievement of conservationists worried about the plant's impacts on the mountain's scenery and the Hudson's striped bass was to earn a hearing for these concerns. They established that these environmental interests were valid and worthy of review alongside economic and engineering considerations as the proposal's fate was decided.

The National Environmental Policy Act

This achievement led to Congressional enactment of the National Environmental Policy Act (NEPA) in 1969. While the act does not require that projects with

the potential to harm the environment be stopped, it does mandate that the potential impacts be recognized and weighed in deciding whether or not to go ahead. The law mandates that a detailed environmental impact statement (EIS) be prepared regarding proposals for "major Federal actions significantly affecting the quality of the human environment." This public statement must cover the following:

(i) the environmental impact of the proposed action,
(ii) any adverse environmental impacts which cannot be avoided should the proposal be implemented,
(iii) alternatives to the proposed action,
(iv) the relationship between local short-term uses of man's environment and the maintenance and enhancement of long-term productivity, and
(v) any irreversible and irretrievable commitments of resources which would be involved in the proposed action should it be implemented.

NEPA's mandate is chiefly procedural: requiring full disclosure of potential impacts based on accurate investigation of the affected environment and its resources. Those who try to halt a project by claiming that NEPA has been violated must prove that the required EIS does not meet these standards—a situation illustrated in the fight over Westway.

A Case History: Westway— Right Way or Wrong Way?

In 1973, two vehicles traveling on Manhattan's elevated West Side Highway unexpectedly exited to the street below when a portion of the road collapsed beneath them. The collapse accelerated efforts to build a replacement roadway; the proposed design, dubbed Westway, called for a 4.2 mile-long

The Westway landfill would have extended from the current shoreline to the end of the West Side's piers for much of the proposed highway's 4-mile length. Proponents saw this area as a decaying waterfront in need of revitalization; opponents saw it as valuable habitat in need of protection.

expressway on two hundred acres of new landfill in the Hudson River. Creation of this new land, which would also support parks and residential, commercial, and industrial development, accounted for more than half of the project's cost, estimated at $2.3 billion in 1983.

The proposal quickly generated controversy. Opponents sought to protect air quality and the Hudson, and argued that such a huge sum was better spent on a less costly replacement highway built on shore, with the leftover money traded back to the federal government in return for mass transit funding. Supporters valued the economic benefits of development on the landfill and felt that Westway would result in a better highway and rehabilitation of a decaying waterfront.

Federal law required Westway's sponsors to obtain a landfill permit from the U.S. Army Corps of Engineers. The Corps' decision in this matter would be a "major Federal action" under NEPA, so an environmental impact statement was necessary.

The initial EIS dealt extensively with issues of air and noise pollution, traffic congestion, and mass transit alternatives. This multi-volume document also discussed—in just four paragraphs—the project's potential impacts on estuarine habitat, and concluded that they were not significant since the area to be filled was "biologically impoverished."

Westway Goes on Trial. To halt the project, Westway opponents sued, charging that the statement's analysis of these concerns was less than adequate. They claimed that meeting NEPA's procedural standards would require a new EIS based on more thorough and accurate research. The court dismissed most of these claims, finding that the highway agencies had satisfactorily assessed all potential impacts except those on estuarine habitat. Here the court agreed that the research supporting the conclusion that there would be little impact due to the area's biological impoverishment was inadequate, making its accuracy questionable.[1] Westway went on trial over this concern.

Further research established that this area was in fact home to a diverse and abundant array of creatures, notably winter flounder, white perch, and striped bass. But in spite of the new data, the highway agencies stood by their original conclusion that Westway's impacts on estuarine life were of little importance. Opponents believed that the new information required preparation of a supplemental EIS more fully assessing these impacts. After hearing the case the court agreed, finding that the highway agencies had presented data in a "misleading" manner, and had "acted in willful derogation of the requirements of [NEPA] in failing to issue a corrective supplemental environmental impact statement." The judge's 1982 decision directed them to complete such an EIS before Westway went forward.

After a third round of research and assessment, a draft supplemental EIS concluded that the landfill would indeed have "significant adverse impacts" on striped bass. The document underwent public review, and was then rewritten into final form. In the process, the conclusions about impacts were changed to "minor" without explanation or substantiation—a change examined closely when the new impact statement was brought before the court in 1985. Its authors argued that their basic conclusion had not changed: that the finding of minor impact was intended all along. Writing "the court finds this position incredible," the judge again halted the project. In his view, making such a change without substantiation constituted a failure to meet NEPA obligations for accurate assessment.

At this point, the highway agencies could have done more research, prepared yet another EIS, and tried again to satisfy the court. However, the deadline for applying to trade Westway funding for mass

transit money was now only weeks away. Another attempt to produce an acceptable EIS would have needed more time, with no guarantee of success; pursuing this course risked losing large sums of money. Not willing to gamble, New York opted for a less expensive roadway on shore and trade-in of leftover money for mass transit funds.

Policy and Politics. While the controversy was resolved largely through the courts, one should not exit Westway with the impression that the battle was a cut-and-dried legal matter. To its supporters the idea that concern for fish could stop a billion-dollar construction project was ridiculous. They tried end runs around the law: New York's governor persuaded like-minded members of Congress to introduce legislation exempting Westway from the environmental review required by NEPA. In response, the state's attorney general telegrammed New York's Congressional delegation to say, "Whatever your position on the merits of Westway, exempting any particular project

Westway's demise was followed by years of conflict over plans for a new waterfront park and what development should be allowed in the area west of the replacement highway. In 1998 the Hudson River Park Act designated the waters of the area as an estuarine sanctuary, established guidelines for use of the piers, and set up the Hudson River Park Trust to oversee development of a new park. The completed segments attract thousands of New Yorkers to the once decaying waterfront.

from the impartial application of environmental laws could do great and lasting harm to the national effort to clean our rivers and streams." Congress did not act on these bills.

Critics from environmental groups have observed that EIS documents often contain superficial or unsubstantiated findings, and seem to be written not with a true sense of NEPA's intent of complete and accurate disclosure but instead simply to meet the requirement for an assessment. The judge in the Westway case concluded that problems with the Corps of Engineers' assessments could "only be explained as resulting from an almost fixed predetermination to grant the Westway landfill permit." Challenging inadequate environmental assessments in court is often the only way to force full disclosure and review of impact statements.

Power Plant Review: Continued Controversy

In the wake of Storm King, the construction and operation of large power plants along the Hudson (there are seven north of New York City) remained a contentious matter. In 1992, fear of shortages led New York State to streamline permitting for new plants through enactment of Article X of the Public Service Law. Article X supplanted the state's Environmental Quality Review Act (SEQRA), modeled after NEPA, by setting up a Board on Electric Generation Siting and the Environment with representatives from the DEC, the Public Service Commission, the Department of State, the Empire State Development Corporation, and one member each from the judicial district and the county in which a facility would be located. The board had authority to grant or deny certificates of environmental compatibility and public need.

Only one new Hudson River power plant proposal went through Article X review.[2] In August, 1998, the Athens Generating Company applied to build a 1,080 megawatt gas-fired plant in Athens, located in Greene County. As with Storm King, the ensuing debate focused on potential fisheries and scenic impacts. The Hudson at Athens provides significant spawning habitat for American shad, and the site was in a region celebrated for its beauty, especially the vistas from Olana, the landmark estate of Hudson River School painter Frederic Church, the most famous American artist of the mid 1800s.

At this time, all of the estuary's power plants still used once-through cooling systems, sucking in enormous volumes of water—up to a peak of 2.5 billion gallons per day (mgd) at Indian Point—and in the process killing large numbers of fish, especially larvae and juveniles. These fish kills have been an ongoing source of friction between utilities and environmentalists since Storm King. As the Athens hearings progressed, negotiations focused on a hybrid wet/dry cooling system that would require about 4.8 million mgd of river water. However, when DEC finally issued a permit for the intake, it limited withdrawals to 0.18 mgd, a limit very protective of fish and one that mandated use of a dry cooling system with little need for river water.

The proposed plant would be visible in three designated Scenic Areas of Statewide Significance, the most important being the views from Olana. Studies conducted by the Athens Generating Company concluded that there would be minimal impacts on these vistas. Opponents challenged these conclusions, citing the height of the plant's smokestacks and the visual intrusion of towering plumes of water vapor from the cooling system originally proposed.

The impacts of the Athens Generating facility on vistas from Olana were a major point of contention in debate over the project. Shown here are the renowned view to the southwest and the view to the northwest, where the power plant is center right in the photo.

In reviewing these arguments, the Siting Board noted that the protections for scenic vistas were not absolute. The laws were "intended to harmonize preservation of natural and scenic resources with human population growth;" they "include siting guidelines which necessarily contemplate development with mitigation;" and they "emphasize that the character and public accessibility of views of the natural landscape must be evaluated in determining the extent of protection they are to be afforded." In balancing aesthetics and development, the board reached three main conclusions. First, the most famous views from Olana were to the southwest, looking out over the Hudson to the Catskills. The Athens plant would be located to the northwest, away from this main vista and in a less impressive landscape. Also, it would be visible only from hiking trails a fair distance from the mansion, or with tree-cutting to open up views in this direction. Finally, the requirement for dry cooling would eliminate the steam plumes.

In June, 2000, the Siting Board approved the plant. The assessment process had taken less than two years, a far cry from the lengthy Storm King review. Construction began in 2001, and the Athens facility went into service in 2004. Article X went out of service, however; with no new power plant proposals on the horizon, it was allowed to expire on January 1, 2003. Review of such projects is again governed by SEQRA.

Environmental Assessment: The Local Perspective

Westway and the Athens power plant were major projects with large-scale costs and impacts. Other environmental controversies involving development, different only in their smaller scale, simmer all along the Hudson, perhaps made fiercer since the parties involved are not just impersonal law firms, government agencies, or corporations but familiar faces—neighbors in a community. The debates have an immediacy which engages community residents in a personal way, and may come to dominate local politics. Typically, the officials making the decisions are more exposed to the wrath of dissatisfied constituents than are the administrators of major state and federal agencies. When the outcome of the required regulatory process leaves many citizens unhappy, the next election may offer the most immediate recourse.

Environmental assessments of local development projects may be mandated by state laws like New York's SEQRA, or—as in New Jersey—by similar requirements established under executive order. These reviews can be required by state agencies or by local governments—for example, as town planning boards consider approval of site plans for large subdivisions. Projects may also require variances under existing zoning laws, in which case zoning boards of appeal provide a forum for environmental review.

The local role in environmental review is important, since along the Hudson most planning and land use decisions are made by individual communities, following a strong tradition of home rule—local primacy in such decisions. The public hearings required during review often address community values beyond the ecological. The process provides a formal opportunity

Through economic upturns and downturns in recent decades, riverfront real estate projects like this one in Croton-on-Hudson have remained attractive to developers. In 2005, Scenic Hudson estimated that 15,000 units of housing were under review or in construction on the Hudson's shores. The largest, a 2,182 unit development planned for an abandoned cement-making site in Kingston, could increase the city's population by 25 percent if built as proposed.
(Photo by David Bernz.)

Historic attitudes about wetlands are illustrated by this sign, which suggests that filling in a tidal swamp to create a sanitary landfill—a dump—is a worthy use of such habitats.
(Courtesy of Clearwater. Photo by Steve Singer.)

Several Hudson River wetlands, including the North Bay marsh bordering the City of Hudson, have been impacted by such use.
(Photo by Charles Porter.)

for residents to comment on how a project might affect their deeply held sense of what the community should be—a quiet residential village or a bustling commercial center, for example. These local decisions have taken on increasing importance in recent years as the pace and reach of urbanization in the Hudson Valley has increased. While the impacts of any one housing subdivision or shopping center may be relatively small, the sum of development's impacts on water quality, habitat, biodiversity, and scenery in the region is substantial.

Like NEPA, state environmental review regulations are chiefly procedural. They mandate comprehensive and accurate disclosure of potential impacts, and may also require mitigation of potentially serious negative impacts. Other laws provide the regulatory framework for halting environmentally damaging projects. Of such statutes, those most important in protecting the Hudson have been state wetlands laws and the federal Clean Water Act.[3]

Protecting Wetland Habitats

Wetland habitats serve as feeding areas for waterfowl and other creatures, nurseries for young fish, and breeding sites for birds and mammals. They filter out sediment and pollution as they slow tidal currents. These habitats also offer economic benefits such as buffering damage from storms and floods and maintaining fish stocks that support valuable commercial fisheries. In addition, many wetlands possess great scenic beauty.

However, recognition of these values has been a long time coming. Wetlands were once seen as mosquito-infested wastelands, a view that countenanced destruction of over 50 percent of the coastal and estuarine wetlands acreage in the continental U.S. By the mid-twentieth century, urbanization had claimed most of the best building land along the northeast coast. Wetlands were among the last large open spaces available to absorb the building boom of the 1950s and 1960s; many were filled in then. In the Hudson Valley, it is estimated that 4,850 acres of such habitat have been filled in to create land for highways, railroads, industrial facilities, housing, and parks. Another 6,800 acres have been buried by sediment and dikes as a result of dredging operations. Wetlands have also suffered from activities on adjacent uplands that changed runoff or drainage patterns and increased pollution.

In response to growing awareness of their importance and the pressures on these habitats, governments have enacted regulations protecting wetlands. Such laws are lightning rods for disputes, perhaps because it is here that disparate underlying values are most clearly exposed. These battles come right down to belief that ecological health should be maintained versus belief that property interests should prevail.

Dredging and Filling

The major federal wetlands protection law is the Clean Water Act. As implied in the name, it is primarily an antipollution law. However, Section 404 of the act mandates that projects requiring landfilling or discharge of dredged material obtain a permit from the Army Corps of Engineers. In considering whether to grant the permit, the Corps must weigh costs and benefits, both ecological and economic, and the desirability and availability of alternatives. In addition, legal guidelines established under Section 404 state that "no discharge of dredged or fill material shall be permitted which will cause or contribute to significant degradation of the waters of the United States . . . [including] loss of fish and wildlife habitat."

Prior to passage of the Clean Water Act, the Corps of Engineers had issued dredge and fill permits based on its historic mission of keeping navigational channels open. To insure that these permit decisions also reflected an ecological perspective,

Congress directed the EPA to develop guidelines for issuing Section 404 permits and gave the agency the power to veto Corps permit decisions. By vesting power in two agencies with different missions, Congress tried to strike a balance which insured consideration of both the needs of commerce and the ecological values of wetlands.

This arrangement does not eliminate conflict, however, and disputes between the Corps and the EPA reflect their different perspectives. A case in point was dredging in Newark Bay, part of the port of New York and New Jersey. Without dredging, silt would accumulate at the bay's docks and prevent their use by large ships. Tests performed for a 1990 dredging permit application found dioxin in the silt. Concerned about this toxic chemical's effects in the ocean where the dredged silt would be dumped, the EPA withheld approval of the permits. The Corps felt that the risks posed by dioxin levels in the sediments did not justify the economic damage likely if the docks were closed. The ensuing discussions between the Corps, the EPA, and other agencies took years, during which time silt continued to accumulate, eventually requiring new rounds of testing and evaluation. The EPA finally allowed the project to go forward with the provision that the disposal site be covered with clean sand to prevent release of dioxin into the environment.

This episode was just one act in a longer-running drama. Dredged sediment had traditionally been discharged at the Mud Dump, a site five miles off the northern New Jersey shore. However, that practice became contentious with increasing awareness of contamination in the sediments and of negative ecological impacts on the ocean floor at the Mud Dump.

Spurred by this controversy, in 1996 the EPA, the Corps, and the U.S. Department of Transportation signed a letter ad-

New York Harbor's port facilities contribute about $20 billion annually to the region's economy. Smooth operation of this economic engine requires regular dredging to remove accumulating sediment. In addition, the harbor's shipping channels and berths are now being deepened to accommodate the larger ships coming into wide use.

dressing harbor dredging issues. The Mud Dump would be closed and covered with clean dredge spoil, and a harbor deepening project would proceed.[4] Progress on other initiatives outlined in the letter has included release—after input from many stakeholders—of a dredged materials management plan in 1999, startup of a watershed-wide contaminant trackdown and elimination program in 1997, and funding to demonstrate decontamination technologies and beneficial use of dredged materials.

State Wetlands Regulations

The states also play important roles in wetlands protection. Under Section 401 of the Clean Water Act, states must certify that fill, dredge spoils, and other discharges into waterways will not violate their water quality standards. In addition, New York and New Jersey have their own comprehensive wetlands laws, and these require permits for activities that may have impacts on these habitats.

Two New York State statutes apply to the Hudson: a freshwater wetlands law that covers the river south to the Tappan Zee Bridge, and a tidal wetlands law that applies below the bridge. Both use scientific parameters of flooding and vegetation types to define wetlands, and mandate preparation of inventories and maps of the state's wetlands. The laws allow DEC to develop land use rules for wetlands, and to regulate activities occurring on adjacent uplands.

These laws do not provide complete protection. In New York, for example, the freshwater wetlands statute requires that wetlands larger than 12.4 acres (one hectare in the metric system) must be mapped and protected, but some scientists consider current maps and inventories to be far from complete. Smaller wetlands of special significance can be included in the inventory, but are for the most part ignored. As a result, less than 50 percent of New York's freshwater wetlands are protected under this statute.[5]

To be successful, these regulations must be aggressively enforced. Be they saltwater or fresh, large or small, wetlands are frequently subject to piecemeal degradation that goes unnoticed or is low on the priority lists of enforcement agencies with limited staff and funds. Pressure from citizens is often key to enforcement of wetlands laws.

Protection by Purchase

One form of protection for wetlands and other coastal habitats is ownership or management by environmental agencies or conservation groups. Four of the river's largest wetlands—Piermont Marsh, Iona Island Marsh, Tivoli Bays, and Stockport Flats—are included in the Hudson River National Estuarine Research Reserve, managed by New York State's DEC in cooperation with other regional and federal agencies. The Scenic Hudson Land Trust, National Audubon Society, and Nature Conservancy are among the organizations which own or manage Hudson River wetlands and bordering uplands as preserves or sanctuaries.

Protecting habitat by purchase can be controversial. Here again, values come into conflict as people debate the wisdom of buying land to preserve it when land prices have soared, tax burdens seem high, budget shortfalls are a problem, and development might add to the tax base.

The Public Trust Doctrine

Even in the best of times only a limited amount of wetland habitat can be protected by purchase. However, under a long-standing principle of common law the public already owns lands subject to tidal influence (strictly, lands below average high tide). This public trust doctrine, by which

the state holds these underwater lands in trust for the public, guarantees access for swimming, boating, fishing, and other water-related pursuits, although the public cannot cross adjacent private land without the owner's permission.[6]

States can sell or rent public trust lands, a practice common in the seventeenth and eighteenth centuries when large parcels were sold to adjacent upland owners to promote commerce and economic growth. New York State's Office of General Services, which administers this property, estimates that 25 to 30 percent of tidal lands around Manhattan and along the Hudson have been conveyed into private hands.

Day-to-day management of public trust lands is difficult when agencies must rely on tenets of common law rather than specific statutes. In 1992 New York took a step towards codifying the public trust doctrine through enactment of an Underwater Lands Act. The law requires that anyone proposing to place a large structure or fill on these lands obtain a lease, easement, or other interest from the Office of General Services; it also provides for DEC review and regulation of such proposals to prevent harm to wetland habitats.

Putting the Hudson on Tap

The very substance of the Hudson—its water—is also held in trust for the public by the states. As is the case with wetlands, debates over use of this resource have generated much controversy.

In 1983, local residents alerted the Hudson River Fishermen's Association and their Riverkeeper to unusually frequent appearances of large tankers off Hyde Park and Port Ewen. Upon investigation, the Riverkeeper discovered that the tankers, owned by Exxon, were filling up with Hudson River water and carrying it to the Caribbean island of Aruba, which has limited fresh water supplies. There the firm used the water in refinery operations and offered it for sale, reportedly receiving $2 million that year. Exxon did not have the necessary state permit to transport and sell the water, but avoided a court trial over that issue by ending the practice and agreeing to pay settlements of $500,000 to the Fishermen's Association and $1.5 million to New York State.[7]

In breaking the story, the Riverkeeper characterized Exxon's operations as "a deliberate theft of water, a valuable commodity." Hudson River water *is* a valuable commodity, considered a viable drinking water supply (after treatment) over much of the freshwater river. For the water system serving Poughkeepsie's thirty thousand residents, the Hudson is the only source. Other communities use the river for backup or partial supply, and more may do so in the future. Over the years, the largest proposed withdrawals have been for New York City.

A Thirsty City

New York is a thirsty city: its water consumption reached a peak of 1.8 billion gallons daily in summer 1988. Ninety percent of this water comes from reservoirs in the Catskills, the rest mainly from the Croton Reservoir complex in Westchester County. However, the estimated safe yield of this system—the amount it could deliver each day during the worst drought on record—is only 1.3 billion gallons. New York's response to this gap was twofold: identifying new sources of supply, notably the Hudson River, and lowering consumption through conservation efforts.

The city has one tap on the Hudson, a pumping station in Chelsea, a hamlet just above the Beacon-Newburgh Bridge. One proposal for increasing New York's supply was to operate the Chelsea station continu-

ously and to construct additional pumping plants in Newburgh or Kingston, adding up to 300 million gallons daily (mgd) to the system. A more ambitious plan called for construction of an intake, pump station, filtration plant, and aqueducts in or near Hyde Park. This complex, estimated to cost $2.5 billion, might have taken in as much as one billion gallons daily during spring, when freshwater flow into the river usually peaks (an operation known as "high-flow skimming"). It would not have operated in late summer and early fall, when freshwater flow typically is minimal. Thus the project's annual yield would have averaged about 400 mgd.

Intake Impacts

The potential environmental impacts of these plans generated much controversy. As in the power plant debates, there were worries that the intake pipes would have sucked up fish, especially juveniles, larvae, and eggs. Given the river's role as a nursery for young fish, damage to fish populations could have been considerable.

Other potential impacts on estuarine organisms would have been more indirect. Detouring large quantities of water from

Riverkeeper

In Britain, riverkeepers have traditionally protected fish and habitat in trout and salmon streams. Inspired by this model, in 1973 four Hudson River environmental groups joined together to hire a Hudson Riverkeeper to protect the river in the public interest. This first venture ended after about two and a half years, but in 1983 the Hudson River Fishermen's Association hired a new Riverkeeper to patrol the Hudson. Subsequent successes in bringing pollution to light have inspired other such programs around the country and the world, and the Fishermen's Association has been absorbed into the Riverkeeper organization.
(Courtesy of Riverkeeper. Photo by Dan Shearer.)

Intended for emergency use during droughts, the pumps at New York City's Chelsea station can contribute 100 mgd of Hudson River water to the city's supply. By comparison, Poughkeepsie's plant, next largest on the Hudson, is permitted to pump 16 mgd.
(Photo by Cara Lee.)

Chelsea (or points further north) to faucets in New York could shift the salt front's position.[8] One might assume that plants and animals would simply move with the salt front. However, salinity is but one of many factors controlling their distribution, and staying in water of the proper salinity may put an organism in areas where other factors—substrate, current, or depth—are unsuitable.

The withdrawals proposed by New York City also caused concern among communities upriver. Poughkeepsie depends entirely on Hudson River water and cannot dilute salty water with fresh water from another source, as New York can by mixing river water with reservoir water. In

past droughts the salt front has reached Poughkeepsie's intakes; the city worried that increased pumping by New York might have made that a more regular occurrence. Other communities looking to the river as a potential supply worried that New York's demands would preempt theirs.

Increase the Supply or Lower the Demand?

Another approach to closing the 200 mgd gap between the reservoirs' safe yield and the city's demand was not to increase supply but to lower demand by conserving water and improving system management. By the city's own estimates, up to 240 mgd were being lost to leaks, water running in vacant buildings, open fire hydrants, and illegal connections—more than enough water to fill the gap.

Developing new supplies would also have been a costly proposition, and not simply for new intakes, pump stations, and aqueducts. Should the Hudson have become a permanent source of supply, the state Department of Health would have required the city to build expensive filtration plants. New supplies would have increased flow into New York City's sewage treatment plants and required expansion there. Six of these plants were already receiving greater flows than they were designed to handle.

Faced with such realities, New York increased emphasis on conservation efforts. In 1986 it began a leak detection survey in the supply pipes running under its streets, followed up by repairs to leaky pipes. In 1988 it began to install water meters to track how much water was being used, wasted, or lost due to leaks; metering also makes people pay for water according to how much they use, encouraging conservation to save money. The city also passed laws requiring installation of water-saving plumbing fixtures in new construction and in renovation of existing structures.

Through these measures, conservation education programs, and individual water-saving efforts, New York City's water consumption fell fairly steadily through the 1990s. As of 2003, consumption was roughly 1.1 billion gallons per day.

While the city has successfully lowered demand, it continues to investigate the feasibility of river withdrawals. In 2004, New York announced a plan to drill test wells into sand and gravel beds underlying the Hudson near Chelsea. The wells would draw river water through the sand and gravel, using them as a natural filtration system. This technique might mitigate impacts on fish, reduce the presence of microbes and suspended solids, and eliminate concerns about introducing zebra mussels into the water system. However, the practice would not allay worries about shifting the salt front.

As one means of addressing water supply issues, representatives of New York City, other local governments, state agencies, and environmental groups formed the Southeastern New York Intergovernmental Water Supply Advisory Council. This group attempted, with some success, to balance conflicting mandates, needs, and values through joint planning and priority setting as an alternative to more adversarial approaches.

Managing the Estuary

Applied to the Hudson River, such a process might head off at least some conflicts by establishing policies for protecting the ecosystem's vitality in ways that would allow sustainable development and use of its resources. The end products of the process would be management plans intended to guide decision making along the river. Optimism about this approach has led to

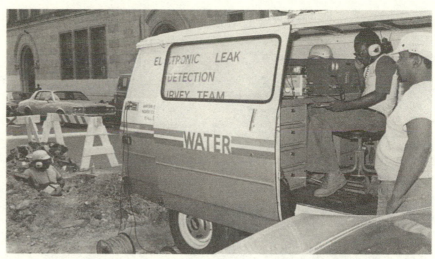

In 1986, New York's leak detection program surveyed 5.25 million feet of supply pipe, finding and repairing leaks losing over 24 mgd of water. By 1990, the length of piping surveyed yearly had doubled to 10 million feet, but the amount of leakage discovered had dropped by nearly half, to 12.6 mgd. The trend indicated the program's success in reducing overall leakage.
(Courtesy New York City Department of Environmental Protection/Carl Ambrose.)

the creation of coastal zone management programs, state and federal estuarine management programs, and the Hudson Valley Greenway.

Coastal Zone Management

Of all the resources the Hudson offers to those who live along its shores, perhaps the one in most limited supply is that very shoreline. With public recognition that the river is becoming cleaner, coupled to increased awareness of its beauty and recreational potential, riverfront property is now a valuable commodity. Jostling for space along the river are developers with proposals for housing, restaurants, and new marinas, industries which require waterfront locations, and groups seeking to increase public access and protect scenic values and habitats.

Conflicts over shorefront land use have been a concern not only here in the Hudson Valley but throughout the nation. In response, Congress passed the Federal Coastal Zone Management Act in 1972. This law provides financial assistance to the states to develop management programs that will preserve, restore, or enhance coastal resources. Participation is voluntary;

The Hudson and its shoreline offer an abundance of resources and support a great variety of human uses, among them:

environmental education programs like this one at the Tivoli North Bay Marsh;

shipping, which requires docking facilities for tugboats and other vessels;

swimming and picnicking at riverfront parks like this Kingston beach;

housing, here in a renovated industrial building at Yonkers;

boating, with services provided by marinas such as this one in Haverstraw;

and industry, represented by this cement plant and loading dock just south of Catskill.
(Photo by Charles Porter.)

incentives to get on board include the funding assistance and a provision that, once a state program receives federal approval, any federal actions affecting the state's coast must be consistent with that program. New Jersey and New York both have approved management programs. Since the Hudson is tidal, New York's extends up the river to the Troy Dam.

In parallel fashion, river communities in New York may prepare Local Waterfront Revitalization Plans (LWRPs) that spell out preferred uses of their riverfronts. Since most land use decisions occur at the local level, these plans can be helpful in dealing with intense development pressures along the Hudson, adding an additional layer of consideration to that required by the environmental review laws described earlier. Preparation of an LWRP allows a community to clarify its values and appropriately balance ecological protection, public access, and economic development in shaping the future of its riverfront. Community adoption of such a plan, once approved by the state, asserts a fair degree of local control since all state and federal agency actions within that community's coastal zone must then be consistent with the local plan.

The state provides technical assistance to communities trying to establish LWRPs. Such aid might include guidance in interpreting wetlands laws or in developing criteria for local ordinances to protect shoreline habitats. This aid is particularly helpful in small communities where planning boards and waterfront advisory boards are not usually trained specialists but rather citizens from many walks of life, elected or appointed on a volunteer basis.

In the two decades or so since New York State established its Coastal Management Program, half of the towns and cities lining the Hudson have participated in the program, and twenty-two communities had state approved LWRPs as of early 2005.

In New Jersey, coastal management is governed by the Coastal Area Facility Review Act, administered by the DEP. Projects with impacts on the coastal zone must receive permits from the agency, which evaluates proposals based on coastal resource and development policies promulgated under the Facilities Review Act. Unlike New York, New Jersey has no provision for delegating such review to communities through approval of local waterfront plans.

St. Lawrence Cement

New York's coastal management policies played a critical role in the fate of one of the largest industrial projects proposed for the Hudson in recent years. In 1998 the St. Lawrence Cement Company announced plans to manufacture two million metric tons of cement annually in Columbia County. The proposal called for an open mine on 1,222 acres in the town of Greenport, containing a cement plant and its 363-foot tall smokestack. A two-and-a-half-mile long conveyer for raw materials and powdered cement would link the plant to a 14-acre dock on the City of Hudson's riverfront.

Cement manufacturing has at least a hundred-year history in this part of the Hudson Valley. However, the proposal called for a massive plant producing three to four times as much cement as a now-closed facility in Greenport. Its potential impacts on air, water, and scenic quality were considerable; in addition, the project

New Jersey's Hudson River Waterfront Walkway: Preserving Access in the Face of Development

New Jersey's Hudson River shoreline offers spectacular views of the river, New York Harbor, and Manhattan's skyline. Recognizing its scenic and recreational value and foreseeing that residential and commercial development would replace declining port and industrial facilities, New Jersey's DEP moved to require that public access be provided in exchange for permits to develop on the waterfront. Its goal is establishment of a continuous waterfront walkway running 18 miles from the Bayonne Bridge to the George Washington Bridge. Since 1988 the project has been facilitated by the Hudson River Waterfront Conservancy, representing developers, property owners, nonprofit groups, state and local governments, and interested citizens. While progress has been fitful, coming primarily when proposals for private development are put on the table, over 11 miles of walkway are in place, along with an additional 5.5 miles along roadways of southern Jersey City and Bayonne.

The St. Lawrence Cement project would have replaced this closed plant in the Columbia County town of Greenport and expanded operations at an industrial dock next to a new City of Hudson park. New York's Department of State argued that the dock and the new, much larger plant would diminish the attractiveness of the area, with negative effects on sustainable long-term economic redevelopment.

fetched when the nearby Athens Generating Plant got a green light in 2000.

Columbia County's pastoral landscape and the scenic and historic sites around the City of Hudson started attracting second home buyers and tourists in the 1990s. In Hudson, this led to restoration projects and investment in new antique shops, galleries, restaurants, and home furnishings stores, sparking a revival in the community's economy. In its master plan, the city saw the waterfront as key to continued revival, and called for new parks, recreational docks, and mixed use development. Toward that end, Hudson had acquired a former oil storage site on the waterfront, cleaned up contamination there, and built a park. The city had also moved to obtain other waterfront parcels to realize its vision.

By one estimate, St. Lawrence Cement needed seventeen local, state, and federal permits and approvals. The DEC—the lead agency in the environmental review process—had responsibility for five of them. The public was eager to weigh in: a DEC public hearing in June, 2001, lasted nearly twelve hours, with over one thousand people in attendance. The agency then moved on to formal administrative law hearings that would consume several years.

To prepare its dock to receive raw materials from ships and load barges with powdered cement, St. Lawrence Cement was planning to dredge a portion of the river, reinforce the shoreline, and construct new docks. This required a permit from the Army Corps of Engineers, a federal action that, under the Coastal Zone Management Act, needed to be consistent with New York's coastal management policies. The Corps submitted a request for a consistency determination to New York's Department of State (DOS) in October, 2004.

came to be seen as a bellwether for the region's economic future. Most recent economic growth here had been based on tourism, recreation, retail establishments, and additional service industries. Critics argued that this new plant could be a wedge opening up re-industrialization of the Hudson Valley—a prospect that didn't seem far-

By this time, public debate was intense—DOS received over 13,000 comments from citizens, businesses, community groups, professionals, unions, and officials from New York and neighboring states. Of the issues raised, those relevant to the agency's deliberations had to do with the scale of St. Lawrence Cement's operation on the Hudson, its effects on the river's scenic resources, its impact on plans for waterfront revitalization, and how the facility would affect overall economic growth in the region.

In April 2005, the DOS issued its finding that the St. Lawrence Cement project was inconsistent with New York's coastal management policies. The project would turn a small harbor into a major industrial facility serving ships up to 750 feet long and as many as four large barges per week. Frequently in operation around the clock, it would dominate the riverfront, detracting from recreational and mixed small-scale residential and commercial use of the area as envisioned in Hudson's master plan. This could depress the city's recent economic growth, blunting the benefits of millions of dollars in public funds invested in waterfront revitalization.

The DOS decision effectively doomed the project by preventing issuance of the Army Corps permit. St. Lawrence Cement had the option of appealing the decision to the U.S. Secretary of Commerce, but later that spring announced that it would abandon the project.

Estuarine Management Plans

Given the importance of the Hudson, the need to maintain its ecological health while supporting sustainable human uses, and the history of controversy over such concerns, development of management plans for the estuary has received particular attention.

In progress are several efforts to identify estuarine resources and values in need of protection, determine what factors degrade those resources and values, and recommend possible solutions to problems.

In 1987 New York State established the Hudson River Estuary Management Program within the DEC to "protect, restore and enhance the productivity and diversity of natural resources of the Hudson River Estuarine District to sustain a wide array of present and future human benefits."[9] In 1996 Governor George E. Pataki released the Hudson River Estuary Action Plan listing twenty specific goals that addressed this mission, to be accomplished through partnerships linking the DEC's various divisions and other state and federal agencies, local governments, and private institutions and organizations.

Updated regularly, the Action Plan's goals are ecosystem based and watershed wide. They address three major areas: conserving natural resources and ecosystem health, cleaning up pollution and other impairments, and promoting public use and enjoyment of the river. Estuary projects have expanded understanding of key species like sturgeon and shad, delineated the boundaries and acreage of submerged aquatic vegetation beds, mapped the river bottom and tidal wetlands, inventoried biodiversity in adjacent uplands, upgraded boat launches, and preserved valuable open space on the shoreline. The most recent update, the Hudson River Estuary Action Agenda 2005–2009, expands the program's efforts to include conservation of pastoral landscapes and scenic vistas that help define the Hudson Valley's unique sense of place.

With similar goals in mind, the EPA designated both New York Harbor (including the Hudson south of the Piermont

Using side-scan sonar and other advanced technologies, the Hudson's bottom is being mapped to provide information essential to managing the estuary. This image includes Diamond Reef, a notorious hazard to shipping. Partnerships are essential to accomplish such major projects. This effort involved the Hudson River Estuary Program, the Hudson River National Estuarine Research Reserve, and a team of scientists from several institutions led by the Lamont-Doherty Earth Observatory of Columbia University.
(Image by Professor Roger Flood, State University of New York–Stony Brook.)

Marsh) and the Long Island Sound as estuaries of national significance. A five-year research and planning process led to creation of a management plan for both estuaries. The process involved a host of agencies, authorities, interstate commissions, and private groups.

These are ambitious undertakings given the scale and dynamics of these ecosystems, overlapping and often conflicting agency mandates, budget constraints, and underlying disagreements between the stakeholders involved. But the Hudson estuary is an entity greater than the sum of its many parts. Preserving its ecological health, a task now parceled out among many regulations and bureaucracies, may analogously require a system greater than the sum of these parts. Comprehensive management plans can establish the overarching goals and policies necessary to the task.

The Hudson Valley Greenway

The web of jurisdictions overseeing the Hudson River stems in part from the fact that ecological boundaries and regional identities often do not correspond to political boundaries. The Hudson Valley is recognized as a distinct region from historical, cultural, commercial, and ecological perspectives. Yet from the Mohawk River's mouth to the Battery, some eighty-two political jurisdictions (villages, towns, boroughs, and cities) govern the Hudson's shorelines—not counting counties or New Jersey jurisdictions. In this context, local decisions made without reference to a regional identity could, in piecemeal fashion, erode the assets that make the region as a whole so attractive and distinctive.

Recognizing this problem, the New York State legislature established the Hudson River Valley Greenway program in 1991. While intended to preserve open space in and around densely inhabited regions, greenways are more than a patchwork of open lands. Greenways try to link these lands both physically, via creation of trails and preservation of small parcels linking larger open areas, and perceptually, fostering the sense that all these parcels are valuable parts of a larger entity defined by its natural heritage.

Responsibility for designing and implementing a regional planning strategy rests with the Greenway Community Council. Past efforts to regionalize Hudson Valley planning and land-use decisions have been stymied by firm belief in home rule and distrust of bureaucratic control by outsiders. Aware of this history, the Council began at the local level, encouraging (with financial incentives) communities to develop their own plans addressing Greenway objectives. These plans guide preparation of subregional plans and ultimately a planning document for the entire region. This regional plan then goes back to the localities for review. Those that elect to be guided by the plan's provisions will be entitled to special funding consideration for projects which advance Greenway goals.[10]

The Greenway also manages the Hudson River Valley National Heritage Area, a federal effort to recognize, preserve, and promote the region's nationally significant historic, cultural, and natural resources. This initiative has focused on creating a regional sense of identity based on the valley's rich history, and, in turn, tourism centered on this heritage. More federal recognition of the Hudson came when it was named an American Heritage River in 1998. This designation is intended to facilitate better access to existing federal services for the valley's communities.

In a 1991 Greenway report to New York State's governor and legislature, one hears echoes of Romantic era belief in an equilibrium between preservation and development:

> The Valley is a place where the future must be built in harmony with region's

natural and historic heritage. We are convinced that economic development will not occur in areas that tolerate a deteriorated environment.

We emphasize that there must be places for the residents of the Valley to live and to work just as there must be places for them to have access to the Hudson River and the Valley's beauty and history.

But any such equilibrium will be a dynamic one. The struggle between development and preservation has characterized the Hudson's history for the past 150 years. It will no doubt continue to challenge both the activists at opposite poles and the many conscientious citizens in the middle as they make democratic choices to shape a Hudson River environment in keeping with their values.

Chapter 12

Is the Hudson Getting Cleaner?

The Chapter in Brief

The Hudson, once an "open sewer," is cleaner now. The Clean Water Act deserves much of the credit, requiring sewage treatment and funding treatment plant construction. Overflows from combined sanitary and storm sewers remain a problem. The act also established the National Pollution Discharge Elimination System to control point sources of pollution. As these have been regulated, nonpoint pollution has become a major source of water quality problems. Oil pollution, a major concern given the volume of oil transported on the Hudson and New York Harbor, is also covered by the Clean Water Act. Superfund, intended to clean up hazardous waste left by past disposal practices, is being applied to PCB contamination in the upper Hudson. Preventing discharges rather than just regulating them is seen as the best solution to pollution problems, especially those involving toxic chemicals.

An Open Sewer

"Life Abandoning Polluted Hudson" ran a 1966 headline in the *New York Times*. Government reports of that time referred to the river as an "open sewer." Old-time river rats pull the legs of newcomers by telling how, before going for a swim back then, one tossed in a few boulders to clear holes in the scum.

Much of this ill repute came from the enormous volume of untreated human sewage discharged into the Hudson. Sewage may carry pathogens that make swimming in or eating shellfish from polluted waters dangerous to human health. It also contains nitrates, phosphates, and other nutrients that may cause unpleasant blooms of algae (see chapter 2). Additionally, sewage becomes food for microorganisms in the river, and more sewage means more microbes. As their numbers increase, they use up more and more of the dissolved oxygen in the water.[1] Ultimately, oxygen levels can be reduced nearly to zero, killing off most higher forms of life in the affected area.

Sewage pollution, aggravated by other untreated organic wastes from pulp mills and tanneries, once made the Albany Pool (stretching roughly from Cohoes southward past Albany) infamous as the most severely polluted section of the Hudson. In *The Hudson River: A Natural and Unnatural History*, Robert Boyle quotes from a press report which described a hearing about the pool's problems: men "grit their teeth and women left the room."

The Albany Pool mess was but one of the Hudson's horror stories. The river's sewage problems along Manhattan were as bad as those in Albany; off Tarrytown the water would be colored with whatever paint the General Motors plant there happened to be using on its cars that day; grease and oil poured into the Hudson from railroad repair facilities in Croton. But the rising tide of environmental concern in recent decades has produced a flood of anti-pollution laws. Today, when those who teach about the Hudson are asked "Is the river getting cleaner?" the answer is "yes," though there is still plenty of room for improvement.

At plants such as New York City's North River facility, here shown under construction, incoming sewage first undergoes primary treatment, entering tanks where some solids settle to the bottom. Water and suspended solids go on to secondary treatment, in which microbes digest organic material. This may occur in a trickling filter — a bed of rocks coated with a slime of micro-organisms — or in an activated sludge tank, where a suspension of solids is aerated to promote the desired microbial action. After another round of settling, clarified water is chlorinated to kill bacteria and then discharged to the river. The solids left behind become sewage sludge.
(Photo by S. Stanne. Diagram courtesy of Clearwater.)

The Clean Water Act

Much of the credit for improvements over the past two decades should go to the Clean Water Act (formally the Federal Water Pollution Control Act) enacted in 1972 to "restore and maintain the chemical, physical, and biological integrity of the Nation's waters." The act aims to directly curb pollution by improving municipal sewage treatment, regulating *point discharges* of pollutants (from a specific pipe, discharge canal, or similar facility), managing *nonpoint source pollution* (polluted runoff from streets, parking lots, farm fields, lawns, and the like), and preventing oil pollution.

Municipal Sewage Treatment

The Clean Water Act requires that municipalities provide secondary treatment for their sewage, a process that can remove 85 percent of its organic materials. Originally, the act also committed federal funds toward the great expense of building sewage treatment plants.[2] Most river communities quickly moved to construct such plants, the notable laggard being New York City owing to the scale of its discharges and a fiscal crisis. Some 150 million gallons of sewage per day flowed untreated from Manhattan's West Side until 1986, when the North River plant, located on the Hudson in Harlem, began operation.[3] Completion of this plant and Brooklyn's Red Hook facility, finished in 1987, rounded out the city's planned set of fourteen treatment plants.

Certain measures of water quality have improved greatly as a result of sewage treatment. Dissolved oxygen levels have increased in the Albany Pool and New York Harbor. Fecal coliform bacteria counts are lower. These nonpathogenic bacteria live in the human digestive tract; when numerous in water samples they usually indicate the presence of sewage and, potentially, of more dangerous microbes that sewage might contain. As numbers of coliforms go up or down, there is a correspondingly greater or lower probability of pathogens being present.[4] Off Manhattan, startup of the North River plant resulted in a 78 percent decrease in fecal coliform counts between 1985 and 1986.

Dealing with Sewage Sludge. Left behind after these plants have discharged treated water is sewage sludge, now given the classier name biosolids. This semisolid substance is rich in organic matter and nutrients. For decades, New York City and parts of Long Island, Westchester County, and New Jersey shipped their sludge to dumpsites in the Atlantic Ocean, but Congress banned the practice and the last sludge barge sailed from New York in summer 1992. Of the 1,200 tons of biosolids produced daily by the city, 43 percent is heated and dried to form fertilizer pellets, used in plantings along city streets and in Florida citrus groves, among other sites. An additional 37 percent is spread on land to enrich nutrient-depleted soil—on Texas rangeland, for example. The remainder is composted to form mulch, or combined with highly

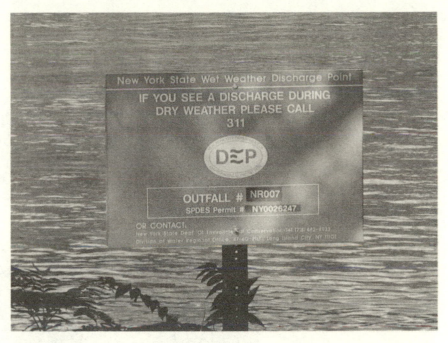

Outfalls where combined sewer overflows enter the river must have permits and be marked with signs.

alkaline material for use as an agricultural liming agent.

In New Jersey, about 77 percent of the biosolids produced in Bergen and Hudson Counties is shipped to other states where it is used in ways similar to those described above. The remainder is incinerated. Many upriver communities in New York dispose of their sludge in landfills.

Sludge sometimes contains heavy metals and other hazardous substances that the sewage treatment process cannot break down or neutralize. These pollutants limit its use in agriculture and pose problems even when sludge is disposed of as solid waste. They may leach out of poorly designed or operated landfills or spread widely through the air if incompletely incinerated. Sources of such pollutants include water and sewer pipes (copper and lead leach from these) and industries which discharge wastes into sewer systems.

Industrial discharges to sewage systems can cause other problems. Treatment plants are mainly designed to remove biological

Effective sewage treatment, including curtailing combined sewer overflows, is necessary to maintain and increase safe use of Hudson River swimming areas like this Kingston beach.

wastes. Industrial chemicals may pass through unaffected to pollute the river, or they may disrupt the treatment process and even pose explosion or fire hazards. By law, industries discharging into municipal sewage systems must establish effective pretreatment programs to clean their wastewater before it empties into the sewers. These programs are administered by local governments on the basis of federal and state standards.

Combined Sewer Overflows. Continued progress in sewage cleanup will require solving the problems posed by combined sewer overflows (CSOs) in New York City and other older urban areas. After storms, runoff from storm drains enters the sanitary sewers and can increase total flow beyond the capacity of the sewage plant at the receiving end. When this happens, the treatment process may not work thoroughly; it may even be bypassed, sending this combined sewer overflow, waste and all, into the river. According to the environmental group Riverkeeper, a steady rain of at least one quarter inch per hour can lead to the discharge of 520 million gallons of untreated combined sewer overflows. Scientists estimate that 90 percent of the coliform bacteria found in New York Harbor at present come from CSOs. Solving this problem will require separating stormwater pipes from sanitary sewers, or building storage tanks which collect overflows for later treatment in drier weather. The cost of such tanks is reckoned in billions of dollars.

Much of the litter floating on the Hudson and New York Harbor also comes from storm sewers. In New York City, catch basin hoods are used to limit the amount of trash entering the sewers, and at a few dozen sites booms and nets are placed to collect trash where the sewer pipes enter waterways.

Treatment plant capacity is also exceeded as more residences are built and hooked into sewage systems, more water is used in new commercial and industrial facilities, and people form habits that consume more water. All of this water ultimately flows to sewage plants. Expanding capacity through new plant construction is very expensive. In addition, many of the plants built in the years immediately after passage of the Clean Water Act now need repair and upgrading. Finding the money to maintain this infrastructure and the health of the Hudson will be a major concern in coming years.

Ready for a Swim? On hot summer afternoons at Kingston's bathing beach on the Hudson, lifeguards keep watch over hundreds of people crowding the sand and water, trying to ensure their safety. Also vital to their safety is regular water testing by the county health department, making sure that this swimming spot is free of contamination by sewage. Such contamination, which may carry harmful bacteria and other pathogens, is a major factor limiting swimming in the Hudson. Other concerns include the poor visual clarity of the water and strong tidal currents.

Nonetheless, New York State classifies the length of the river from Castleton to the New Jersey line as swimmable, though a check with the county health department about conditions at one's favorite beach is advisable. A study released in 2005 by the DEC's Hudson River Estuary Program found three actively used official swimming beaches and thirteen other sites that could be developed as public swimming beaches.

Controlling Discharges under the Clean Water Act

While sewage pollution is of major concern to swimmers, it is only one of many waste discharges—hazardous chemicals, heavy metals, and heated wastewater, for example—that have degraded the Hudson. The Clean Water Act requires regulatory agencies to address such problems by establishing water quality standards that designate the uses of a waterbody, set criteria to protect those uses, and establish control measures to insure that the criteria are met.

The process has three parts. Part one is a classification scheme intended to designate the best use of every waterway. These use classifications are:

A. Suitable for drinking, cooking, or food processing;
B. Suitable for primary contact recreation (swimming);
C. Suitable for fishing and fish propagation; and
D. Suitable for secondary contact recreation (i.e., boating) and fish survival.

Citizen Action for Cleaner Water

After the Clean Water Act became law, some polluters ignored it or were slow to comply. Clearwater initiated a People's Pipewatch Program in which volunteers searched out noxious discharges, identified their sources, and investigated whether or not the dischargers had the required permits. Their detective work led to prosecutions and fines against polluters. Clearwater and Riverkeeper have also used the Clean Water Act's citizen suit provision to force an end to serious discharges. The Act allows citizens to sue for enforcement of the law should responsible agencies fail to uphold its provisions, and to recover legal costs from polluters if a suit is successful.
(Photo by Karin Limburg.)

Classifications reflect the current best use of the waterway; much of the mid-Hudson, which supplies drinking water to Pough-keepsie and other communities, is classified A. They are also intended to be goals for the eventual quality of a particular stretch of water. A waterbody in which people regularly swim may not always be safe for swimming, but if that use merits a classification of B, then pollution must be controlled to attain the necessary water quality. Classifications are made with input from the public, and reviewed every three years.

The next step in the process is setting water quality criteria: numerical limits for the concentrations of pollutants found in the Hudson or other water bodies. These criteria may vary according to use classification.

With classifications established and criteria in place, environmental agencies carry out part three of the program: issuing permits to control the quantities of wastes going into a waterway. Point discharges are regulated by the National Pollution Discharge Elimination System (or State Pollution Discharge Elimination System—SPDES—when administered by states, as it is in New York and New Jersey). Every pipe through which any facility discharges wastes into the river must have a SPDES permit specifying what pollutants can be discharged, the limits for each pollutant, and the frequency and type of testing that must be performed to monitor the discharge. Violations can result in fines and prison terms. Permits must be renewed every five years, at which time discharge limits can be made more stringent. By this means the SPDES "E"—for elimination—could be realized, as was intended in the Clean Water Act's national goal that "discharge of pollutants into the navigable waters be eliminated by 1985."

Has SPDES worked? The year 1985 has come and gone; discharges into the Hudson River continue. Whether a glass of river water remains half filled or half emptied of pollution depends on one's point of view.

New York's water quality assessments once focused on impaired water bodies, reported in the Priority Water Problems List. The DEC still prepares that report—now called the Priority Waterbodies List—biennially, but starting in 1996 it modified its assessment process with the aim of covering all waters, among them 52,000 miles of rivers and streams and over 1,530 square miles of estuaries.

According to the 2004 list, 35 percent of New York's streams met their water quality standards, 7 percent were impaired or threatened, and 9 percent could not be assessed due to insufficient data; 49 percent remained to be covered. Point discharges accounted for less than 3 percent of these impairments. Nonpoint sources—primarily agricultural and streambank erosion—were the main culprits.

Estuaries had more problems: by area, about 41 percent were impaired. Urban runoff, CSOs, and toxic chemicals and heavy metals in sediments caused the lion's share of the problems. The presence of toxics has led to widespread issuance of health advisories intended to limit consumption of contaminated fish. Point sources caused 11 percent of the impairments; these were mostly municipal sewage discharges, which limit swimming and shellfishing.

The fact that point sources cause a relatively small number of impairments can be viewed as evidence that the SPDES system has been successful. But some worry that this could change. Responsibility for testing and reporting on compliance rests with the polluter, a situation akin to the fox guarding the henhouse. Environmentalists acknowledge that this arrangement can work, but only if regulatory agencies have the will and resources to examine polluters' reports thoroughly and back up this review with on-site inspections, random sampling of discharges, and firm action when violations are found.

Monitoring SPDES. In 1990, DEC data showed that 83 percent of significant dischargers sampled statewide were in compliance with their permits, apparently a fairly good record. However, the data covered only 37 percent of major dischargers. In addition, the DEC was falling far behind in renewing SPDES permits on schedule; during the 1980s and 1990s, the agency told holders of 6,000 permits deemed to be of low risk to the environment that their renewals would not be processed but that they could operate under expired permits indefinitely. In the mid 1990s, a time of budget austerity, the DEC instituted a policy intended to focus increasingly scarce staff and funds on renewal of high risk permits (about 1,800 statewide as of 2005). The agency has claimed a better than 90 percent renewal rate. However, most of these are administrative renewals—simply checking an application form for accuracy and completeness, with no technical review or inspection of a permitted facility.

In 2003, New York State's Comptroller released an audit of this process, based on SPDES permit renewals in the first half of 2002. The audit concluded that even major permits were inadequately monitored, and—given the lack of timely technical review—there was a good chance that the renewals did not reflect new assessments of discharge impacts or improvements in pollution control technology. The report noted that eight years after the DEC initiated its policy of focusing on high-risk permits it could not produce documentation that any five-year technical permit reviews had been completed.

Environmentalists have expressed concern over the lack of opportunity for citizen participation in the process, and about the DEC's tendency—even in technical reviews—to ignore substantive documentation of problematic discharges by the public. They also point out that overall enforcement actions by DEC in recent years have been fewer than in the early 1990s.

In a 2005 report, the organization Environmental Advocates of New York blamed such problems on political failure to provide funding and staff. "The DEC remains an endangered agency. The hard-working professionals at the DEC are regularly called upon to do more work with fewer people while the administration continues to reject any suggestion that the DEC's drastically reduced workforce is having a negative impact on the environment and human health." The group estimated that there were approximately 870 fewer employees compared to 1994 staff levels—far too few for the agency to fulfill its mandate. Early in 2006, then Governor George Pataki did propose an increase in DEC staffing, emphasizing water pollution control positions.

Controlling Nonpoint Source Pollution

Nonpoint source pollution can be seen on a rainy day in the parking lot of any Hudson Valley shopping mall. Rather than simply dodging puddles in a rush to get out of the rain, take a look at what they often contain: oil, antifreeze, and other fluids leaked from cars, as well as plastic wrappers, cigarette butts, and other solid waste, all bound for the nearest storm drain and ultimately the Hudson. Now multiply that scene by the

Nonpoint sources of pollution include:

sediment eroding off construction sites and into streams;

motor oil, antifreeze, and other liquids leaking from automobiles;

and fertilizers and pesticides washed off lawns and agricultural lands.

valley's many square miles of parking lots and highways to begin to understand the problem's magnitude.

Other major components of the problem are fertilizers and pesticides applied to farm fields and lawns, animal wastes (especially where many animals are kept together in a small area, the case in cattle feedlots), and soil washed off land left bare by farming or construction activities. These pollutants typically are not discharged through a specific pipe; instead, they are carried by runoff as it drains downhill and enters waterways at many scattered locations. These many small contributions add up; nonpoint source pollution is now the major factor impairing water quality across New York.

While state and federal agencies encourage local governments to prevent nonpoint pollution through land use controls, the Clean Water Act does not require specific remedies. Appropriate solutions will vary greatly depending on the degree of urbanization in a region and its particular land uses. The act directs the states to inventory waters affected by such discharges and to prepare plans for dealing with the problems. Once plans are approved by the EPA, they can receive funding grants from the federal government.

The DEC's Nonpoint Source Management Program, approved by the EPA in 1990 and most recently updated in 2000, identifies New York waters adversely impacted by nonpoint pollution, sets goals for reducing its impacts, maintains working relationships with other agencies to correct problems on a watershed basis, and provides guidance, incentives, and funding for control efforts. For the most part, the program relies on funding incentives rather than regulation to achieve its aims.[5] New Jersey has a similar program.

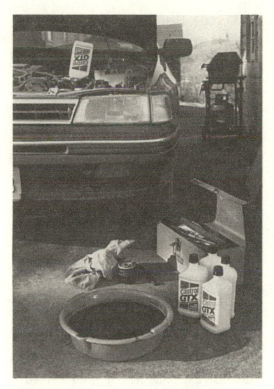

Taking Individual Action against NonPoint Pollution

Basements and garages may contain potential pollutants: paints, paint thinners, motor oil, antifreeze, and
lawn and garden pesticides, to name a few. All too
often these find their way into storm drains (or down
the sink where they may contaminate sludge or septic
systems). Such substances should be used only in pre-
scribed amounts. Leftover chemicals can be turned in at
household hazardous waste pickup days sponsored by
county environmental councils or other local agencies;
used motor oil should be returned to auto repair shops
for recycling.

Stormwater Runoff

In undisturbed watersheds, soil absorbs
rainfall and stores it as groundwater, releasing it slowly and steadily to streams. As watersheds become urbanized, construction of
homes, roads, malls, parking lots, and other
structures covers the land with impervious
surfaces that prevent water from soaking
into the ground. Instead, rain is channeled
through gutters, downspouts, and catch
basins into nearby streams as stormwater
runoff.

Besides transporting trash, oil, and
other nonpoint pollution, stormwater runoff is itself a problem. Its sheer volume
can damage streams, eroding banks and
carving out channels like a router cutting
across wood. Stream creatures, especially
invertebrates at the base of food webs, are
swept away or smothered as mud eroded
from the banks blankets gravel bottoms.
Aquatic life is further stressed as flows alternate between flood and trickle; when
rain runs off swiftly without recharging
groundwater, flow to streams in dry weather
is reduced. Such impacts appear when impervious surfaces cover about 15 percent of
a watershed.

Regulatory agencies are now trying
to control stormwater runoff through a
permit system. Industrial sites and construction sites larger than one acre are
required to have a permit for stormwater
discharges, specifying how runoff will be
controlled. Municipalities are also required
to develop plans for stemming stormwater
runoff.

Adding It All Up: TMDLs

One might wonder if consideration is
given to the totality of impacts to the
Hudson from all these pollution sources.
An answer is found in one of the more
recent acronyms to appear in the vocabulary of river cleanup: TMDL—total maximum daily load—the maximum amount
of a pollutant that a waterway can receive
and still meet water quality standards.
When a waterbody does not support its
designated uses, the Clean Water Act requires states to consider setting TMDLs
for pollutants that are impairing water
quality.

A TMDL is calculated using mathematical models that factor in the following components:

1. A *load allocation* including natural background levels of a pollutant, along with any contributions from atmospheric deposition or nonpoint sources;
2. A *waste load allocation* including permitted sources such as industrial point discharges, sewage plants, and combined sewer overflows;
3. A *margin of safety* that provides headroom in the case of errors in the calculated allocations and allows for additional sources of the pollutant in the future.

The process of setting TMDLs can be complex. Pollutants of concern and their sources must be identified. The allowable concentration of each pollutant must be established using scientific data about its effects on humans, fish and wildlife, and other resources. In most cases, this concentration will be equivalent to a water quality standard. Scientists must calculate how pollutant loadings translate to concentrations in the water. Finally, decisions must be made about how loadings will be allocated among the sources, and how regulatory agencies will implement any necessary reductions. Strategies might include stricter discharge limits in SPDES permits, more controls on air pollution from stacks in other states, or targeted programs to reduce certain types of nonpoint pollution.

The public can participate in the process of setting TMDLs. This can be contentious, as dischargers anticipate how waste load allocations might require more extensive—and perhaps expensive—control measures. And before a TMDL becomes effective, the EPA must review and approve it.

In 2004, New York released a list of impaired waters requiring development of TMDLs. The Hudson and lakes and streams in its watershed are prominent on the list. Many lakes and reservoirs that drain into the Hudson are impacted by atmospheric deposition—acid rain in the Adirondacks, and mercury in the Catskills. Fish consumption advisories due to PCB contamination prevent the main stem from fully supporting its designated use for fishing. Developing TMDLs and addressing these impairments will take considerable resources, and, in the case of atmospheric deposition, require solutions that are national in scope.

Preventing Oil Pollution

The Port of New York handles more petroleum than any other harbor in the United States, so it is no surprise that oil spills are a problem here. In two months early in 1990, spills of 565,000, 25,000, and 120,000 gallons blackened the Arthur Kill between Staten Island and New Jersey. While only the largest spills gain public attention, this type of pollution occurs virtually every day in the harbor.

Only a small portion of the oil entering New York Harbor goes up the Hudson, but by volume and value, petroleum products are the most important cargo shipped on the river. In 2003, about eight million barrels worth some $465 million went to upriver destinations. The Hudson has not been spared from spills, including 28,000 gallons from a barge that hit Diamond Reef in 2005, 102,000 gallons from a grounding on the same reef in 1987, and an infamous encounter between a barge and a reef in the Highlands in 1977 that released 480,000 gallons.

Oil's impacts go beyond the oil-soaked birds and beaches shown during nightly newcasts. During the Arthur Kill spills, the herons that nest there avoided oiling; they were wintering in warmer climes. But food webs on which the birds depend were damaged: large swaths of *Spartina* grasses in the area's marshes were killed; populations of killifish, on which some heron species depend, were decimated, as were fiddler crabs and some types of clams. In the two years following the spills, nesting success of snowy egrets suffered: more than 80 percent of chicks died, and some scientists speculate that the young egrets died of starvation associated with the destruction of food supplies. The slicks are gone now, and killifish numbers are rebounding, yet oil remains in the marsh sediments and will probably contaminate this habitat for years, affecting benthic creatures and the animals that feed upon them.

Clean Water Act regulations prohibit the discharge of oil into navigable waterways, require inspections of vessels and waterfront oil terminals, and provide for fines when violations occur. The law mandates preparation of contingency plans to deal with spills, including the creation of cleanup "strike forces" and prompt notification of authorities when accidents occur. The act also authorizes government takeover of cleanup efforts when responsible parties' efforts are inadequate, with later recovery of cleanup costs from those parties.

While a number of federal and state agencies have authority over oil production, transportation, refining, and storage, the U.S. Coast Guard has the most prominent role in dealing with oil pollution in these waterways.[6]

An Ounce of Prevention is Worth a Pound of Cure

Given human imperfection, a few spills are inevitable. Yet noting the regularity of such

On February 4, 1977, the Hess Oil barge *Ethel H.* grounded on Con Hook Rock just north of the Bear Mountain Bridge. Before the barge was freed and towed away four days later, 480,000 gallons of heavy fuel oil had spilled, forming a slick that covered some 30 miles of the Hudson.
(Photo by Charles Porter.)

accidents and the sorry record of cleanup efforts (only 10 to 15 percent of spilled oil is usually recovered), it is worth recalling the adage that an ounce of prevention is worth a pound of cure. Environmentalists advocate adoption of more preventive measures to reduce the number of spills, their scale, and the severity of their impacts.

More rigorous inspections of vessels and facilities handling oil are one such measure. The largest of 1990's Arthur Kill spills poured from a ruptured Exxon pipeline that was not inspected due to gaps in agencies' statutory responsibilities, and in which a faulty leak detection system went uncorrected for more than twelve years. Improvements in navigational aids would also reduce the chance of collision or grounding. The potential for human error could be reduced through better training and tighter licensing requirements for mariners, along

Reporting Pollution

In response to a call from a concerned citizen, DEC staff direct a cleanup of home heating oil leaking into a marsh along a tributary of the Hudson.

Oil spills and other environmentally damaging incidents should be reported to appropriate authorities, though it can be difficult to determine which one has responsibility. For example, sewage discharges from pipes could be the concern of a municipal agency, or of the state if violation of a SPDES permit is involved, while such discharges from boats on the Hudson are regulated by the Coast Guard. One can also report incidents to environmental watchdogs. Below are some useful phone numbers.

New York State Department of Environmental Conservation:
to report polluters, 1-800-847-7332; to report spills, 1-800-457-7362.

New York State Attorney General:
environmental crimes hotline to report intentional or reckless release of hazardous substances that endanger people or the environment, 1-800-771-7755.

New Jersey Department of Environmental Protection:
24-hour hotline, 1-877-927-6337.

The National Response Center hotline:
to report oil spills, chemical spills, or illegal ocean dumping to the federal government, 1-800-424-8802.

Riverkeeper:
1-800-217-4837 ext 242.

New York/New Jersey Harbor Baykeeper:
1-732-888-9870.

with increased use of pilots skilled in the intricacies of navigating the harbor and the Hudson.

For decades, environmentalists called for tankers and tanker barges to be constructed with double hulls and bottoms, which offer a second layer of protection against tank rupture due to collision or grounding. The Coast Guard estimated that the infamous *Exxon Valdez* spill in Alaska, the largest in U.S. history, would have been reduced by 25 to 60 percent had the ship been constructed with a double bottom. In response to this spill, Congress passed the Oil Pollution Act of 1990, requiring that all new tankers delivered after 1994 for operation on U.S. waters be constructed with

double hulls. It also set new requirements for contingency planning by government and industry.

Implementation of contingency plans in real-life situations can be problematic, as was evident with the Exxon pipeline break. Since the leak alarm system was known to be faulty, its warnings were ignored and the pipeline was not shut off for six hours. When the spill was discovered, estimates of its size were far too low, resulting in delayed and inadequate deployment of containment booms. As the oil spread, Exxon and the Coast Guard discovered that the containment and cleanup equipment on hand in the harbor—on paper enough to handle the spill—was in actuality not sufficient or available; additional equipment had to be flown in from as far away as Alabama. Wetland areas identified as sensitive habitats in an existing Coast Guard contingency plan were not boomed off promptly, and were soaked with oil.

While improvements in technology and regulation have been put in place, the human element remains. Even on tankers of the latest design, human error and cutting corners to save time or money can have potentially disastrous results. Having extra equipment standing by or conducting more frequent training and rigorous inspections adds expense. The basic debate over preventing oil spills boils down to how great a margin of safety is desired, and at what cost.

Through regulation of oil pollution, point and nonpoint discharges, and sewage treatment, the Clean Water Act is intended to control ongoing pollution. But what about the legacy of years of toxic discharges into the Hudson?

A Superfund for Super Messes

To remedy problems caused by abandoned or uncontrolled hazardous waste sites, Congress passed the Comprehensive Environmental Response, Compensation, and Liability Act—more popularly known as Superfund—in 1980. Money for Superfund originally came from a tax on the chemical and petroleum industries. Since 2003, funding has come solely from general tax revenues, as the tax on industry was allowed to lapse. When those responsible for the waste can be identified, the EPA may seek reimbursement from the polluters for cleanup costs. New York has enacted a fairly similar state Superfund law.

Mention of Superfund brings to mind industrial wastelands piled with rusty bar-

rels leaking their noxious contents onto the ground, perhaps with workers in spacesuit-like protective garb examining the mess. Along the Hudson, the dangers posed by toxic chemicals have been masked by the river's beauty.

One site, Foundry Cove, is in Cold Spring, surrounded by the spectacular scenery of the Hudson Highlands. Before cleanup, the cove had the dubious honor of containing the world's highest known levels of environmental contamination by cadmium. The second site encompasses 200 miles of the Hudson from the Battery in Manhattan to Hudson Falls. Its epicenter runs from the Troy Dam north to Hudson Falls, where the river's surface reflects the lovely pastoral landscapes of Saratoga and Washington Counties. In the bottom here are "hotspots," areas of sediment with especially high concentrations of toxic PCBs.

Correcting hazardous waste problems through Superfund is a complicated process replete with jargon. Simply, once a site is placed on Superfund's National Priorities List, the EPA conducts a two part study: part 1 a remedial investigation into the nature and extent of the problem, part 2 a feasibility study examining cleanup options.[7] After completing these assessments and seeking public comment, the EPA issues a record of decision, identifying actions to be taken. At this point, the EPA may enter into consent decrees with polluters who caused the contamination; such decrees detail financial and other responsibilities for the cleanup. Lastly, a remedial design study details the engineering and implementation of the chosen solutions. The entire process can take many years, as is evident in the history of cleaning up cadmium and PCBs in the Hudson.

Cadmium Cleanup in Cold Spring: A Case Study of Superfund Success

Cadmium is a heavy metal known to cause kidney damage and suspected of causing cancer. The contamination in Foundry Cove came from a battery factory operated in Cold Spring between 1953 and 1979. After being placed on the National Priorities List in 1981, the initial remedial investigation (1985) found that "high levels of cadmium, nickel, and cobalt existing in the site sediments pose a health hazard from direct contact, inhalation of heavy metal contaminated dust from the sediment, and bioaccumulation in the biota with subsequent ingestion of contaminated crabs and other biota." In one 50-by-100 foot section, the cove's sediments contained up to 17,000 ppm of cadmium.

After several feasibility studies examined cleanup alternatives, the EPA issued three records of decision. The first called for highly contaminated sediments to be dredged out, chemically fixed, and deposited in a landfill outside the Hudson Valley. The second specified limited dredging in other, less heavily contaminated portions of river bottom and marsh, where removal might have caused more ecological harm than the cadmium present there. This portion of the project also included restoration of marsh habitats affected by dredging. The third required decontamination of the factory, its contents, and grounds, plus excavation of nearby residential yards, where there were high levels of heavy metals in the soil.

In 1991, a consent decree between the EPA, the Marathon Battery Company, and the U.S. Army (which built and initially operated the plant) provided nearly $11 million for cleanup of the factory and its grounds—about 70 percent of the costs of this part of the remediation. Federal and state Superfunds covered the remainder. Remedial designs for dredging and other cleanup and restoration efforts at the site were completed in 1992. In 1993 the EPA announced a $109 million settlement with the Army, Marathon, and Gould Inc. (another firm that once operated the factory) in a consent order covering this work. Cleanup was completed in 1995.

This former battery factory in Cold Spring discharged cadmium into Foundry Cove and adjacent portions of the Hudson. Decontamination of the plant's interior and nearby residential yards was completed in 1992. Cleanup of the plant grounds and dredging to remove cadmium-laden sediments from the cove—here shown staked out to guide the process—finished in 1995.

PCBs: A Case Study in Ongoing Struggle

The story of attempts to cleanse the Hudson of PCBs is more complex and far from over. Cleanup proposals have been put forward, shot down, and reincarnated in a manner recalling popular horror movies with their endless sequels.

PCBs are suspected of causing liver damage and cancer and have been shown to have serious negative effects on brain chemistry, reproduction, and infant development. Human exposure to the Hudson's PCBs comes mostly via consumption of fish and other river life—hence the issuance of health advisories.

According to the EPA, from 1946 to 1977 as many as 1.3 million pounds of PCBs were discharged from two General Electric Company (GE) plants in Hudson Falls and Fort Edward. Washed downriver, the chemicals entered food chains through-

out the Hudson. Levels of PCBs in fish began to worry environmentalists, anglers, and researchers in the early 1970s. Their concerns captured public attention in 1975 with a *New York Times* front-page story headlined "State Says Some Striped Bass and Salmon Pose a Toxic Peril." The article described a DEC alert advising the public not to eat Hudson River stripers. In 1976 the agency prohibited commercial fishing for all Hudson species other than American shad and adult Atlantic sturgeon.[8]

General Electric had a SPDES permit from the DEC to discharge PCBs. However, increasing evidence that PCBs damaged fisheries prompted the DEC to conclude that the discharges violated state environmental laws, and the agency took legal action against GE. The ensuing hearings concluded that the contamination resulted from corporate abuse *and* regulatory failure. In a 1976 settlement, GE agreed to

Highly Chlorinated

Lightly Chlorinated

Polychlorinated biphenyl molecules consist of two linked phenyl groups—rings of six carbon atoms (C) and some hydrogen atoms (not shown)—with chlorine atoms (Cl) attached in various numbers and positions. Over 200 varieties can be formed. Those with many chlorine atoms are implicated in causing cancer; less-chlorinated varieties alter levels of chemicals vital for proper brain functioning and negatively impact reproduction and infant development.

The bulk of the river's PCBs came from this General Electric factory in Hudson Falls and another one in neighboring Fort Edward. These plants manufactured heavy-duty capacitors, in which PCBs were used as an insulating fluid.

A citizen advisory committee, appointed to provide input to research and cleanup efforts funded by the 1976 settlement between the DEC and GE, views Site 10, once a potential location for a landfill to hold PCB-laden sediments from the river.

end its PCB discharges and put up $4 million for monitoring and investigation of the problem and possible remedies. The settlement also required the DEC to contribute $3 million to the research effort.

A PCB Cleanup Proposal. It was soon clear that cleanup costs would far exceed $7 million. Forty million dollars was the 1978 estimate for the DEC's proposal to dredge the hotspots and place the contaminated sediments in a landfill in Fort Edward. Though uneasy about the landfill, most Hudson River environmental groups supported the plan. They felt that, uncontrolled, the hotspots would continue to feed PCBs into the estuary, and that a major flood might scour out PCB-laden sediments and send a heavy slug of contamination downriver. Thus timely removal of PCBs, even if to a landfill, was vital. In 1980, Congress authorized $20 million for the project via an amendment to the Clean Water Act. The amendment specified that this money was not to be released if other funds were available from a hazardous substance cleanup fund.

Many Fort Edward residents opposed siting a hazardous waste landfill in their community. The location chosen—labeled Site 10—was an abandoned farm in a thinly settled part of town. However, opponents felt that the landfill would lower property values and threaten working farms nearby, and they were able to block use of Site 10. This initiated a new review and site selection process, adding another layer of scientific study and administrative procedures to those ongoing in preparation of a cleanup plan.

The DEC was required to prepare an environmental impact statement and submit it to the EPA for approval before the project could proceed. The EIS, completed in October 1982, recommended dredging the worst of the hotspots. In December, the EPA denied approval of the EIS and barred release of funds authorized by the Clean Water Act amendment on the basis that cleanup money was available under Superfund. Environmentalists cried foul: at the time, the contaminated sites were not on the National Priorities List, nor was there any guarantee that the project would qualify for Superfund status or funding. Claiming that the decision was a political shell game aimed at killing the project, Clearwater, Scenic Hudson, the Hudson River Fishermen's Association, and others sued the EPA for release of the cleanup money, and were joined in that suit by the DEC.

Superfund Enters the Fray. In 1983, the EPA did assess the problem under Superfund, and placed the Hudson River PCBs Site on the National Priorities List. Following the requisite studies, the agency's 1984 record of decision identified GE as the responsible polluter. However, the EPA found that the proposed remedies were not cost-effective given lack of a defined threat to public health, and at that time chose to take no action on a Superfund cleanup of the river bottom.[9]

Shortly afterwards, the lawsuit over the Clean Water Act funds was settled, allowing release of the money once the DEC resurveyed the hotspots and secured a landfill site. The agency proceeded to seek approvals for dredging and a landfill at a new location; hearings began in 1987. In fall, 1988, the hearing judge recommended issuing the required permits. His recommendations went to New York State's Hazardous Waste Facilities Siting Board for a final decision. Here progress was halted again, as the board agreed that the project was necessary but found the new landfill site unacceptable.

Meanwhile, the EPA was mulling over a DEC petition to review the 1984 Superfund no-action decision. In December 1989, the two agencies jointly announced that the EPA would reconsider a Superfund cleanup of the PCBs.[10]

Throughout this period, the politics of the PCB controversy involved every level of government from local town halls to Congress and the White House. GE, individual citizens, and organized activist groups on both sides tried to speed or stall the proposed cleanup by pressuring elected officials and agency administrators. Decisions about hazardous waste cleanup are usually thought to be above politics, since toxins affect people regardless of their political affiliation. However, evidence gathered for the lawsuit over the EPA's 1982 impoundment of the Clean Water Act funds showed that it was based on political pressure to stop the project rather than scientific or resource management concerns.[11]

Reassessing the PCB problem. The new remedial investigation and feasibility studies required for the reassessment were originally expected to take eighteen months. Given the history of the issue, it was no surprise that the process consumed more than a decade.

Phase 1 of the reassessment, primarily a review of existing data, was completed in August 1991. Phase 2, begun in December 1991, included the collection and analysis of new data on the location of PCB hotspots, the availability of the chemical to the ecosystem, and the risks it posed to humans and ecological communities. The later stages of these studies overlapped with Phase 3, preparation of the feasibility study evaluating cleanup alternatives.

Sources and Availability of PCBs. The Phase 2 studies revisited issues that had long been contentious, among them whether the hotspots were contributing to contamination in the river downstream. While discharges (halted in 1977) from GE's Hudson Falls and Fort Edward plants were clearly the sources of the hotspot PCBs, the company argued that Mother Nature was solving the problem by covering older, contaminated sediments with newer, clean material. It also pointed to reports estimating that there were significant contributions of PCBs to the estuary from tributaries and sources downriver.

The reassessment concluded that the primary source of PCBs to the lower Hudson was the portion of the Superfund site above the Thompson Island Dam, located just below Fort Edward. This area included the Hudson Falls and Fort Edward facilities and the sediments of the Thompson Island Pool formed by the dam. PCBs from the pool—identifiable by their unique chemical signature—were dominant among PCBs measured in water samples south to Kingston for most of the year. Furthermore, PCBs from the upper Hudson accounted for about half of the total PCB loading to New York Harbor.

The EPA found little evidence for widespread burial of PCB-contaminated sediment by clean material in the Thompson

Just below Fort Edward is a pool formed by the Thompson Island Dam, one of a series of dams and locks in the Hudson River portion of the Champlain Canal. The slow currents in the Thompson Island Pool make it the first settling basin below GE's plants in Fort Edward and Hudson Falls; the river's beauty here hides numerous hotspots of PCB contamination.

Island Pool. Comparing new data to earlier measurements, it documented significant losses from the PCB inventory in the hotspots and transport of the lost PCBs into the lower Hudson. Given the available inventory, significant PCB releases from sediment to water would continue for decades.

Earlier in the debate, GE scientists had demonstrated that microbes will degrade PCBs under controlled laboratory conditions. The company suggested that this process would remediate the Hudson's hotspots, but later experiments in the river cast doubt on whether biodegradation would take place in situ. In its Phase 2 reports, the EPA concluded: "Sediment inventories will not be naturally "remediated" via dechlorination. The extent of dechlorination is limited, resulting in probably less than a 10 percent mass loss from the original concentrations."

Human Health. Phase 2's Human Health Risk Assessment confirmed that eating fish is the primary pathway of exposure to the river's

PCBs. Using a realistic scenario of upper Hudson fish consumption, the risk to human health was calculated to be one more case of cancer than might otherwise be expected among every one thousand people exposed—a risk level one thousand times higher than the EPA felt was protective and ten times higher than the highest risk level allowed under Superfund law. Regarding non-cancer health effects, eating fish from the upper Hudson resulted in PCB exposures more than one hundred times higher than the standard for minimizing hazard.

A similar study examined the health risks of consuming fish from the estuary in the Mid-Hudson Valley. The calculated cancer risk was still more than one hundred times higher than the EPA's goal for protection; for non-cancer health effects, exposure levels were thirty times higher than desired. For both regions, the health risks of eating river fish were expected to exceed generally acceptable levels until 2039.

Impacts on Fish and Wildlife. Opponents of removing the PCBs pointed out that levels

From the Troy Dam to Hudson Falls, signs remind Hudson River anglers that the fish they catch are contaminated by PCBs and must be released. Below Troy, anglers are allowed to keep their catch but health advisories recommend limiting consumption of those fish.

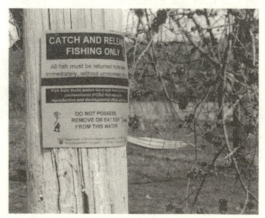

of contamination in striped bass and other river creatures have gone down, implying that effects on fish and wildlife have lessened. However, most of the decline occurred over the late 1970s and 1980s, following cessation of PCB discharges. Except for a spike in the early 1990s (see sidebar), levels have remained fairly constant since then, with considerable yearly fluctuation thought to be due to river flow conditions.

The EPA's ecological risk assessments for the upper Hudson concluded that current PCB levels in sediments, water, and food pose risks to a broad range of fish and wildlife. PCBs may negatively affect fish survival, growth, and reproduction, especially for species higher in food chains that eat other fish. As might be expected, fish-eating birds and mammals like the bald eagle, belted kingfisher, great blue heron, mink, and river otter are similarly at risk; so are those that feed on insects with an aquatic life stage spent in the river—the tree swallow and little brown bat, for example. Fragile populations of threatened and endangered species like the bald eagle and shortnose sturgeon are particularly susceptible to adverse effects from PCB exposure.

While the potential impacts to fish and wildlife are greatest in the upper river—especially in the Thompson Island Pool—and fall off as PCB concentrations decrease downriver, the EPA determined that even in the mid-Hudson region, most of the creatures mentioned above are at risk. The agency expected this to be the case through 2018 if no cleanup was undertaken.

The Feasibility Study. Phase 3 of the reassessment, the feasibility study, began in September 1998 and concluded with the release in December 2000 of the Proposed Plan for the Hudson River PCBs site.

In the feasibility study, the EPA listed five remedial action objectives:

1. Reduce the cancer risks and non-cancer health hazards for people eating fish from the river by reducing the concentration of PCBs in fish.
2. Reduce risks to fish and wildlife by reducing the concentration of PCBs in fish.
3. Reduce concentrations of PCBs in river water that are above existing state and federal standards.
4. Reduce the inventory of PCBs in sediment that are or may be bioavailable.
5. Minimize the long-term downstream transport of PCBs in the river.

The study identified the following possible remedies for the problem: taking no action; monitored natural attenuation (tracking the progress of natural processes in fixing the problem); containment by placing an engineered cap on the riverbed over targeted hotspots; and complete or partial removal of PCB-contaminated

Additional Contamination from Hudson Falls

In 1992, routine tests found unexpectedly high PCB levels in the water of the upper Hudson. When concentrations in fish also jumped that year, a search began for a "new" source of PCBs other than the identified hotspots. The hunt led back to GE's Hudson Falls plant. The collapse of an old wooden gate in the adjacent abandoned Allen Mill had released accumulated PCBs seeping from the plant's grounds and drains. In 1994, when water flowing over the falls next to the plant was diverted for work on a dam, nearly pure PCBs were found oozing from the exposed bedrock. The DEC has required GE to undertake a succession of remedial actions to address these sources of PCBs.

sediments. Except for the no action alternative, all options included control of ongoing PCB seepage from bedrock at GE's Hudson Falls plant site and continued fish consumption advisories and fishing restrictions. The study screened scenarios for implementing these potential courses of action, evaluating how well each would achieve the remedial action objectives. Based on this analysis, the EPA announced its Proposed Plan for the PCBs Superfund Site.

The proposed remedy consisted of targeted dredging of 2.65 million cubic yards of sediment containing over 100,000 pounds of PCBs using environmental dredging techniques that minimize adverse environmental impacts such as resuspension of sediments. It called for monitoring the natural attenuation of residual contamination in both dredged and unremediated areas until PCB concentrations in fish reach an acceptable level. Some of the dredged areas would be backfilled with clean material to isolate residual PCBs and to replace habitat. Dredged sediments would be dewatered and stabilized at treatment/transfer facilities and then transported to approved toxic chemical disposal facilities outside of the Hudson River Valley. No new landfill would be sited here, skirting the major obstacle to past cleanup proposals.

The Public Debate. Release of the proposed plan began the run-up to a record of decision, and ushered in one of the most intense and visible public debates over an environmental issue that the Hudson Valley has seen in its long history of such controversies.

According to a 2005 GE Web site posting, the company spent nearly $32 million on public relations addressing the Hudson River PCB issue from 1990 to 2005, much of it between release of the preferred plan and the record of decision. Their television campaign suggested that the cleanup cure

would be worse than the disease of PCB contamination. Ads showing a clamshell dredge dripping muddy water implied that that dredging would just stir up the PCBs. GE also emphasized the scale of the project, claiming that the volume of material to be dredged would fill Yankee Stadium, and that the equipment and facilities necessary would be a blight on the upper Hudson riverscape.

Lacking GE's financial resources, environmental groups supporting the project took to the grassroots. They mobilized letter-writing campaigns to EPA officials, staged candlelight vigils along the length of the Hudson, distributed fact sheets, and spearheaded demonstrations at public relations sessions organized by GE. By the conclusion of the EPA's public comment period in April 2001, nearly 73,000 individuals and groups had submitted comments, the great majority favoring the proposed plan.

The Record of Decision. The EPA's record of decision, released in February 2002, hewed closely to the proposed plan. It called for dredging the upper Hudson to remove contaminated sediments estimated to contain approximately 65 percent of the total PCB mass present there. This remedy assumed that the DEC would negotiate and oversee a separate action to control the PCBs leaking from GE's Hudson Falls plant site.

The EPA entered into consent orders with GE to design and implement the project, starting with detailed mapping and a new round of samples from the area to be dredged, and proceeding to design of specific approaches to removing sediment, transporting and disposing of the material, and replacing disturbed habitat. According to the 2003 consent order covering design work, this part of the project would be funded by GE and was expected to take three years. In 2006, the EPA announced that dredging would be delayed to 2008, but it finalized a consent decree for the first phase of that undertaking.

The issue continues to earn front page coverage over performance standards for the project and what environmentalists see as flaws in GE's intermediate design plans. After decades of argument, the PCB story may seem like stale news to the larger public. It shouldn't be. The chemicals continue to flow over the Troy Dam and into the lower Hudson. Thirty years after PCBs became headline news, they remain the most serious toxic hazard in the river.

Pollution Prevention vs. Pollution Control

The history of the Hudson's PCB problem makes clear the difficulties in trying to clean up *after* a pollutant has been released. As a result, environmentalists and regulatory agencies now look beyond controlling ongoing discharges of hazardous pollutants and focus on preventing their release.

In his 1990 book *Making Peace with the Planet*, well-known environmental scientist Barry Commoner evaluated the success of the Clean Water Act, Clean Air Act, and other similar laws. Choosing common pollutants known to be dangerous to human and ecological health, he reviewed studies which allowed comparisons of their levels in the environment before and about a decade after passage of these laws. While some specific waterways had shown improvement, the picture nationwide was disappointing. In the few cases where levels of a pollutant had substantially declined, he attributed the decrease to elimination of the pollutant in production processes. Lead levels, for example, dropped dramatically due to elimination of leaded gasoline. Commoner summed up by making the case for pollution prevention rather than pollution control: "When a pollutant is attacked

In the months leading up to the EPA's release of its record of decision, environmental groups organized numerous demonstrations and vigils calling for cleanup of the Hudson's PCBs.
(Photo by Chris Bowser.)

at the point of origin—in the production process that generates it—the pollutant can be eliminated; once it is produced, it is too late. This is the simple but powerful lesson of the two decades of intense but largely futile effort to improve the quality of the environment."

New Jersey enacted a Pollution Prevention Act in 1991. The law requires certain industries to reduce the generation of pollution at the source by 50 percent over five years, and provides incentives for developing new industrial processes which reduce use and discharges of harmful pollutants. New York passed a Hazardous Waste Reduction law in 1989, establishing reduction and elimination as the most preferred methods of hazardous waste management. In both states, industries must develop and implement hazardous waste reduction plans that are subject to scrutiny and approval by environmental agencies.

Reducing pollution at the source can be accomplished by using different raw materials, changing manufacturing processes, redesigning products, and improving

(Photo by Charles Porter.)

maintenance and housekeeping at factories. If production of wastes cannot be avoided, its management may be improved through reuse and recycling. Such changes often result in savings for manufacturing firms through more efficient use of raw materials and lower waste disposal costs, making environmental protection good for business as well as for the Hudson.

In cases where reduction or reuse of wastes is not possible, they must by treated and disposed of in an environmentally sound manner. Here pretreatment, SPDES permits, and other Clean Water Act programs discussed above come into play. To avoid the possibility that these controls may encourage industries to discharge their wastes elsewhere—in the ground or up a smokestack instead of into the river—New York's DEC coordinates its regulatory divisions and programs in a Multi-Media Pollution Prevention effort. This allows comprehensive review and regulation of a polluter's impacts on air, water, and land.

Adoption of these pollution prevention measures, complementing the pollution control programs of the Clean Water Act and removal of the river's PCBs under Superfund, promises a real reduction in toxic contamination. The more insidious, death-by-a-thousand-cuts threat to water quality posed by watershed urbanization is being addressed through nonpoint pollution cleanup plans and stormwater regulations. With progress on these fronts, those who ask "Is the Hudson cleaner?" in the future will be answered with a more resounding "yes!"

Afterword

When a large quantity of information is packed between the covers of a book like this one, readers may view it as a final authority on the topic covered. While we hope and trust that *The Hudson* will be an invaluable reference, it is not intended to and cannot possibly be the last word.

One obvious reason is length: a work of this magnitude lacks comprehensive detail. But in addition, and contrary to what one might expect, the experience of researching and writing this book did not make the authors feel more expert and comfortable in their increasing knowledge of the Hudson. Rather, it made clear the degree to which many specific statements of fact must be qualified because important questions about the ecology and history of the river are at present unanswered.

Thus the book should serve as a basic skeleton of information, suggesting the direction of deeper investigation and supporting fuller understanding of fields in which the reader has a personal interest. At the same time, it points out the connections to be made between relevant yet diverse fields of knowledge.

We encourage readers to undertake such investigation, leavening the academic research with trips to the river, letting it spark curiosity and inspiration. In earlier times, this happened as a matter of course, since much of everyday life centered on the Hudson. The river is not so "in the face" of valley residents today, yet it still defines this region and remains at the mercy of natural and social forces that have determined its past and present condition. Through fuller understanding of these forces, we hope our readers will be better able to insure that the Hudson River continues to inspire in the future.

Sources and Notes

Materials used in preparing this book are described below, accompanied by notes. For each chapter, the first paragraph lists the most important and readily available works, using an abbreviated citation. See Suggested Readings for complete, annotated citations of these sources. The second paragraph lists materials that provided more limited amounts of information, or that may be more difficult to obtain. Complete citations are provided for those readers who wish to find these items.

1. A Physical Overview of the Hudson

The first chapter of Karin Limburg et al., *The Hudson River Ecosystem*, provided information on length, width, depth, flow, and salinity. In Levinton and Waldman's *The Hudson River Estuary*, the chapter on the Hudson Valley's geological history by Les Sirkin and Henry Bokuniewicz and another on the physical oceanography of the estuary by W. Rockwell Geyer and Robert Chant were invaluable sources. The New York State Geological Survey's *Geology of New York: A Simplified Account*, Y.W. Isachsen et al., describes the impacts of ice age glaciers on southeastern New York and the Hudson Valley. Tide data came from the National Ocean Survey's online tide tables.

More specifics concerning the geological history of the Hudson came from scientific papers, most notably "Late Quaternary Geology of the Hudson River Estuary: A Preliminary Report" by W. S. Newman, D. H. Thurber, H. S. Zeiss, A. Rokach, and L. Musich in *Transactions of the N.Y. Academy of Sciences*, series 2, vol.31 (1969), and "Oceanographic and Geologic Framework of the Hudson System"

by Nicholas K. Coch and Henry J. Bokuniewicz in *Northeastern Geology*, vol.8, no. 3 (1986). Added detail came from John H. Johnsen's *The Hudson River Guide*, a 1987 edition of a field book for geological trips on the Hudson. Discussion of the salt front and flushing rate depended on the report *Salt Front Movement in the Hudson River Estuary*, New York by M. Peter de Vries and Lawrence A. Weiss (Troy, N.Y.: U.S. Geological Survey, 2001).

1. All depths given in this book are referenced to average low tide level, usually called mean low water.

2. Glacial Lake Hudson became Glacial Lake Albany as it expanded northward through the Highlands. The lake is thought to have extended nearly 200 miles from Glens Falls to New York City.

3. Other deltas formed in Glacial Lake Albany near the present-day sites of Newburgh, Kingston, Red Hook, Hudson, Kinderhook, Albany, and Schenectady.

4. Because the moon is in motion, revolving around the earth, a complete tidal cycle actually takes twenty-four hours and fifty minutes. Imagine yourself on the spinning earth's surface, checking your watch as you pass directly under the moon. As you wait for the earth to whirl you around full circle, the moon is not standing still. It is moving ahead, towards the east as you view things, so that you will need more than twenty-four hours and 360 degrees to catch up. You must wait an additional fifty minutes for the spinning earth to put you directly under the moon again. For this reason, the timing of a given tidal event will fall back by fifty minutes each day, on average. For example, if low tide on Monday morning is at 9:00, low tide Tuesday morning would be at 9:50.

5. The flood tidal current should not be confused with flooding due to heavy rains. Destructive floods of the latter sort do occur in the Hudson above the Troy dam; their effects are dampened by tidal action further to the south. Except in the highest floods, river levels south of Catskill fall within ranges determined by ocean tides.

6. Parts per million are units commonly used to describe a chemical's concentration in a given substance such as water. Imagine one part per million as one letter of a million printed in a book. There are about 500,000 printed in this book; thus the letter "v" in volume would be one per million in a book twice the length of this one. Concentrations are also commonly expressed as milligrams per liter (mg/1); with very dilute solutions, the units are practically equivalent.

7. As of 2005, Port Ewen, Rhinebeck, Hyde Park, Highland, and Poughkeepsie depend on the estuary for all or part of their water supply. New York City has a pump station at Chelsea, just above the Beacon-Newburgh Bridge, to draw water from the river during drought emergencies.

2. Energy Flows and Nutrient Cycles in the Hudson

In this revised edition, recent data on food webs, productivity, and inputs of organic carbon, nitrogen, and phosphorous to the estuary came from Levinton and Waldman's *The Hudson River Estuary*, in particular a chapter on bacterial abundance, growth, and metabolism by Stuart E. G. Findlay, a second on primary production in the freshwater tidal Hudson by Jonathan J. Cole and Nina M. Caraco, and a third on influences on primary productivity in the lower Hudson estuary by Robert W. Howarth, Roxanne Marino, Dennis P. Swaney, and Elizabeth W. Boyer. The more general descriptions of food webs, energy flow, and nutrient cycling depended on standard ecology texts, notably Eugene P. Odum's *Fundamentals of Ecology*.

While their content is included in the Levinton and Waldman chapters listed above, two papers referenced in the first edition of this book remain important sources. Limiting factors controlling algal growth were covered by Jonathan J. Cole, Nina M. Caraco, and B. Peierls in "Can Phytoplankton Maintain a Positive Carbon Balance in a Turbid, Freshwater, Tidal Estuary?" *Limnology & Oceanography*, vol.37, no. 8 (1992). The importance of detritus and associated bacterial production was addressed by Stuart E. G. Findlay et al. in "Weak Coupling of Bacterial and Algal Production in a Heterotrophic System: the Hudson River Estuary," *Limnology & Oceanography*, vol.36, no. 2 (1991). Data on production in the freshwater estuary came from Robert W. Howarth, R. Schneider, and D. Swaney in "Metabolism and Organic Carbon Fluxes in the Tidal Freshwater Hudson River," *Estuaries*, vol.19, no. 4 (1996).

1. The amphipod example also points out a major difference between taxonomic classification, by which organisms are given a scientific name, and categorization based on ecological considerations. In taxonomy, organisms are grouped based on anatomy, physiology, and evolutionary development; ecological categorizations depend on roles and placement within ecosystems and can group taxonomically unlike organisms together. Amphipods and bald eagles are far apart taxonomically but could be grouped together ecologically as scavengers; both will eat dead fish.

2. Heat energy is expressed in random motion and vibration of molecules. This is transferred to other nearby molecules and results ultimately in the dispersion, not the destruction, of energy.

3. Energy loss along the food chain has practical effects on the numbers and size of consumers. For instance, the Hudson River can support many more Canada geese than great blue herons. Though similar in size, geese eat plants; their position lower in the food chain means that there is more energy available for them than for herons.

4. These estimates, stated in U.S. tons, come from a synthesis of data collected and calculations made in different years and places. There are gaps; for example, the figures for watershed and marsh contributions do not include data from points south of Newburgh, and inputs of sewage and phytoplankton from New York Harbor south of the Battery, which are very difficult to measure, are left out. The estimated total is probably on the low side.

5. Nitrogen is an important component of many compounds vital to the functioning of living organisms, among them amino acids (the building blocks of protein), and nucleic acids (constituents of genetic material). Phosphorus is found in phospholipids (part of cell membranes) and vertebrate bone, and is important in energy transformations within cells.

6. This description is very simplistic. The nitrogen cycle can be traced through many steps involving bacteria and fungi which alter the form of the fixed nitrogen before it is reused by green plants.

3. The Hudson's Habitats and Plant Communities

A wide-ranging source of information for this chapter was *Hudson River Significant Tidal Habitats: A Guide to the Functions, Values, and Protection of the River's Natural Resources*, produced jointly by the Division of Coastal Resources and Waterfront Revitalization, New York Department of State, and the Nature Conservancy. Also useful was *The Ecology of Tidal Freshwater Marshes of the United States East*

Coast: A Community Profile by W. E. Odum et al. In Levinton and Waldman's *The Hudson River Estuary*, chapters on phytoplankton production by Jonathan J. Cole and Nina F. Caraco; submerged vegetation by Stuart E. G. Findlay, Cathleen Wigand, and W. Charles Nieder; tidal wetlands by Erik Kiviat, Findlay, and Nieder; and alien species by David L. Strayer were very helpful. Information in the species descriptions came primarily from the *Atlas of the Biological Resources of the Hudson Estuary* (Yonkers, N.Y.: Boyce Thompson Institute for Plant Research, 1977; out of print) and *A Field Guide to Coastal Wetland Plants of the Northeastern United State*s by Ralph W. Tiner, Jr.

Valuable for its descriptions of wetland habitats and species was Erik Kiviat's *Hudson River East Bank Natural Areas, Clermont to Norrie* (Arlington, Va.: The Nature Conservancy, 1978). Robert E. Schmidt and Erik Kiviat's 1988 report to the Hudson River Foundation, "Communities of Larval and Juvenile Fish Associated with Water-Chestnut, Water-Milfoil, and Water-Celery in the Tivoli Bays of the Hudson River," offered specific information on those plants and communities associated with them.

1. Technically, the euphotic zone extends to the point where light available to plants allows photosynthesis to produce just enough energy to meet their respiratory needs. This is roughly the point at which 1 percent of surface light remains.

2. While these are generally used, terms may vary from reference to reference (the intertidal zone may be called the littoral zone, for instance) and some authors include more divisions.

3. Also encountered in discussions of this community are the terms *periphyton* and *aufwuchs*, referring to plants and animals living underwater attached to surfaces, including plant leaves and stems, that project above the bottom. Epiphytes would be included in the category defined by these two terms.

4. This quote is from George E. Davenport, writing in the *Bulletin of the Torrey Botanical Club*, vol.6 (Boston, 1879). Water chestnut came to the Hudson via the Mohawk drainage, where it was reportedly introduced to Collins Pond in Scotia in 1884.

5. Low and high marsh are the most basic divisions of the marsh community. Scientists who study these communities have subdivided further, using a number of classification systems.

6. Extensive single-species stands of marsh plants—stands which appear to be many individual plants packed closely together—may actually be one plant with above-ground stems and leaves growing from an underground network of rhizomes.

7. Notable examples of tidal swamp communities are found at Tivoli Bays near Red Hook, and at Rogers Island and Ramshorn Creek near Catskill.

4. The Hudson's Invertebrate Animals

Ralph Buchsbaum's *Animals without Backbones* provided background information about invertebrates as a group. In Levinton and Waldman's *The Hudson River Estuary*, Michael L. Pace and Darcy J. Lonsdale's chapter on the Hudson's zooplankton and David L. Strayer's on benthic animal communities were important sources. Material about specific invertebrate species came from Robert Pennak's *Fresh-water Invertebrates of the United States*, Kenneth Gosner's *A Field Guide to the Atlantic Seashore*, and Leland Pollock's *A Practical Guide to Marine Animals of Northeastern North America*. John Waldman's *Heartbeats in the Muck* provided background on oysters in New York Harbor.

Some details on specific organisms or groups of organisms came from a variety of scientific papers, fact sheets, and articles. Particularly useful was David Strayer's "Ecology and Zoogeography of the Freshwater Mollusks of the Hudson River Basin," a report prepared for the Hudson River Foundation in 1986, and "Oysters in the Hudson" by Chuck Keene in the winter 1993 member bulletin of the Museum of the Hudson Highlands, Cornwall on Hudson, New York. *An Atlas of the Biological Resources of the Hudson Estuary* (see chapter 3 notes above) also provided facts about individual species.

1. For these reasons and more, even we will not cover the protozoans. However, they play a key role in food chains and other aspects of Hudson River ecology, and readers interested in them should check the references above.

2. *Polychaete* and *oligochaete* are imposing words, but easy to interpret once one knows that *chaeta* means "bristle" to a zoologist, while the prefix *poly* means "many," the suffix *oligo* "few." The bristles of polychaete worms grow in a bundle from a sac in the skin; only a few bristles grow from each sac in the skin of oligochaetes.

3. The moon snail drills into the shells of bivalves with its radula; the whelk hammers at bivalve shells, chipping a hole into its prey.

4. Compound eyes are made up of many individual lenses and provide the crab with sight. The simple eyes respond to the absence or presence of visible light and to ultraviolet light.

5. The New York State Department of Health recommends limiting consumption of Hudson estuary crabs to

six per week and advises against eating the soft green substance—commonly called tomalley or mustard—found in the body. It contains high levels of chemical contaminants, including PCBs and heavy metals.

5. The Hudson's Fishes

General information about fish came from the text *Ichthyology* by Karl F. Lagler et al. In Levinton and Waldman's *The Hudson River Estuary*, Waldman's chapter on migratory fishes was a valuable reference, as was the chapter on the river's fisheries by Karin E. Limburg, Kathryn A. Hattala, Andrew W. Kahnle, and Waldman. Bigelow and Schroeder's *Fishes of the Gulf of Maine*, and C. Lavett Smith's *The Inland Fishes of New York State* provided details on individual species.

A list of fish species recorded from the Hudson (north of the Battery) and its tributaries can be found in C. Lavett Smith and Thomas R. Lake's paper, "Documentation of the Hudson River Fish Fauna," *American Museum Novitates*, no. 2981, from the American Museum of Natural History in New York City. This list is maintained and updated regularly by Lake. It does not include species recorded only from New York Harbor. Discussion of the critical zone was drawn from testimony titled "Analysis of Fisheries Sampling Programs Conducted in the Hudson River with an Overview of the Biological Productivity of That System," prepared for the EPA by William Dovel. Information about consumption of Hudson River fish came from the New York State Department of Health's *2005–2006 Health Advisories: Chemicals in Sportfish and Game*.

1. Though significant from an evolutionary point of view, lampreys are of minor importance in the Hudson. The anadromous sea lamprey (*Petromyzon marinus*) can be seen spawning in tributaries. At sea, this lamprey is parasitic, fastening on to host fish with a round mouth filled with rows of rasplike teeth and feeding on blood and tissue. It does not feed when spawning, but uses its mouth to pile rocks into a nest for its eggs.

2. Sharks and their kin take water in through the mouth and pass it out through five to seven pairs of gills, each in its own pouch. Muscle contractions pump water over the gills, but this pumping ability is limited in many sharks. They are only able to take in sufficient water for respiration while in motion, and suffocate easily when immobilized. Sharks, rare in the Hudson above the Battery, are occasionally caught in New York Harbor.

3. Fish breathe molecular oxygen (O_2) dissolved in water, not the oxygen atom of the water molecule (H_2O).

4. Assuming that growth rings are close together only in winter is not always correct. A more accurate method of assessing age in fish is by examining growth rings on otoliths, calcareous structures that are part of the organs for hearing and balance.

5. In many species the young must at first fill their swim bladder with air taken in at the surface. They can then maintain inflation with blood gases.

6. A parent stream is the stream or area within the stream where an individual fish was born. Many anadromous fishes return to their parent stream to spawn. If the stream is altered in any way, it may be unrecognizable to the returning adults, the result being reproductive failure.

7. The jelly-covered hairs may be exposed on the surface of a fish's body, embedded in sheltering pits, or enclosed in canals running under the skin.

8. To obtain details or the latest updates on these advisories, visit the New York State Department of Health Web site at www.health.state.ny.us.

6. The Hudson's Birds and Beasts

Most information in this chapter came from scientific reports rather than books intended for the general public, though the *The Audubon Encyclopedia of North American Birds* by John K. Terres (New York: Alfred A. Knopf, 1980; out of print), and Roger Tory Peterson's *Field Guide to the Birds* provided data on individual species. Through the DEC's Web site, New York State's Breeding Bird Atlas provided information on nesting status; its field work, conducted from 1980–1984 and again from 2000–2005, documents changes in breeding bird populations over the last two decades.

Discussion of the Hudson's amphibians, reptiles, and mammals depended largely on the work of Erik Kiviat, including *Hudson River East Bank Natural Areas, Clermont to Norrie*, published by the Nature Conservancy in 1978, and "Where Are the Reptiles and Amphibians of the Hudson River?" in two parts from *News from Hudsonia*, vol.12, nos. 2–3 (1997) and vol.13, no. 3 (1998). The section on birds owes much to checklists produced by bird clubs and nature centers. "Birds of the Hudson River National Estuarine Research Reserve" is especially useful, and available free from the Reserve (c/o Bard College Field Station, Annandale, NY 12504). Reports by Bryan L. Swift of the New York State Department of Environmental Conservation, "Avian Breeding Habitats in Hudson River Tidal Marshes" (1989), and Charles Keene of the Museum of the Hudson Highlands, "1984–1985 Survey of Bald Eagles, Peregrine Falcons, and Osprey along the Hudson River," both prepared for the Hudson River Foundation, were important references. Swift's study was repeated by Alan Wells of Lawler, Matusky, & Skelly Engineers in "Marsh Breeding Bird Survey in the

Hudson River Estuary, 2005," final report to the New England Interstate Water Pollution Control Commission, 2005. Data on the New York Harbor heron rookeries came from "Harbor Herons Project: 2004 Nesting Survey," a report prepared for the New York City Audubon Society by Dr. Paul Kerlinger. Updated bald eagle and peregrine falcon information came from 2004 status reports available on the DEC's Web site.

1. Some aquatic turtles "breathe" through the lining of the pharynx in the throat and also through the lining of the cloaca, an internal cavity into which the genital and excretory systems discharge.

2. The poisonous copperhead (*Agkistrodon contortrix*) is found locally in rocky areas bordering the Hudson, but is a mild mannered, retiring snake. The chances of being bitten are minimal unless one inadvisably tries to handle the snake. The timber rattlesnake (*Crotalus horridus*) occurs away from the river in a few upland locations in the Hudson Valley.

3. The diving ducks need a running start because they have smaller wings for their size than surface-feeding ducks.

4. Another warning involving toxic chemicals and birds comes from the New York State Health Department, which advises hunters not to eat mergansers. These ducks feed chiefly on fish, and tend to concentrate the PCBs found in the Hudson's fish.

5. Report beached seals or other marine mammals or sea turtles, ill or healthy, to the Riverhead Foundation for Marine Research and Preservation, the only organization in New York State authorized to rescue stranded sea animals. Its 24-hour hotline number is 631-369-9829.

7. *Exploration, Colonization, and Revolution*

The historical framework and factual details for a description of the colonial period were drawn from Carl Carmer's *The Hudson* and Russell Shorto's *The Island at the Center of the World*. Discussions of Native Americans depended on Herbert C. Kraft's *The Lenape: Archaeology, History and Ethnography*, and Julian Harris Salomon's *Indians of the Lower Hudson River: The Munsee*. Descriptions of land use and settlement patterns in the 1600s and 1700s relied on Raymond O'Brien's *The American Sublime: Landscape and Scenery of the Lower Hudson Valley*, and D. W. Meinig's innovative geography of early American history, *The Shaping of America: A Geographical Perspective on 500 Years of History: Atlantic America, 1492–1800*, vol. 1.

Other sources included John Seelye's *Prophetic Waters: The River in Early American Life And Literature* (New York: Oxford University Press, 1977), which influenced the chapter's emphasis on the centrality of the Hudson in colonial and revolutionary New York, and Paul Wilstach's *Hudson River Landings* (Indianapolis: The Bobbs-Merrill Co., 1933), which provided a clear overview of the revolutionary battles.

1. Muhheakantuck is spelled in various ways including Muhheakunnuk, Mahicannittuck and Mahicantuck.

2. A lively addition to the literature of local native history is a five-part series of articles by Robert S. Grumet in the magazine *Hudson Valley* (January–May, 1991). Grumet is an archaeologist who draws on the findings of this discipline to create a political and cultural history of the valley's natives.

3. Even after Columbus's discovery Europeans continued to hope for a natural passageway through the barrier of the American continent to the South Sea. An alternative Northeast Passage, sailing to the north of Europe and Asia, was not as popular as the northwest route.

4. The Dutch applied the term Walloons to Huguenot refugees from the southern Netherlands. The Huguenots were French Protestants persecuted by Catholic monarchs.

5. The Hudson's reaches included (from south to north) the Great Chip Rock, the Tappan Reach, the Haverstroo, Seylmakers, Crescent, Hoges, Vorsen, Fishers, Claverack, Backerack, Playsier, Vaste, and Hunters.

6. The term North River distinguished the Hudson from the Delaware, which was the South River and the southern boundary of Dutch holdings in seventeenth-century America. It may also have been a term used by traders to distinguish the Delaware from the Hudson. Even today, the term North River is used to refer to a portion of the Hudson along Manhattan; the term is reflected in the naming of the North River Sewage Treatment Plant at West 135th Street.

7. Rooted in medieval practices, the manorial system was based on the grant of land and feudal rights to a lord by royal charter. The land in turn was rented or leased by the lord of the manor to tenants or peasants for a fixed dues or service.

8. The first federal census found seven free, non-white households in Albany in 1790. Legislation abolished slavery there in 1799, and the 1810 census counted more than three hundred free residents of African ancestry. This information comes from the Colonial Albany History Project, which has been studying the ethnic makeup and daily lives of Albany's minorities prior to 1800. Using innovative research methods, the project has offered insights into the lives of slaves and free people of color, whose history had long been neglected.

9. This quote is from Meinig's *The Shaping of America*.

8. The Romantic River

Discussion of the sublime and basic analysis of the work of the Hudson's painters comes from Barbara Novak's *Nature and Culture: American Landscape and Painting 1825–1875.* Raymond O'Brien provides a definition of the sublime more directly tied to its use in the Hudson Valley in his *American Sublime: Landscape and Scenery of the Lower Hudson Valley.* The section on literature relied on Arthur Adams's *The Hudson River in Literature,* and treatment of estate architecture on John Zukowsky and Robbie Pierce Stimson's *Hudson River Villas.*

Additionally, Leo Marx's *The Machine in the Garden* (New York: Oxford University Press, 1967) shaped discussion of the struggle between nature and civilization.

1. Luminism, sometimes referred to as "air painting," flourished in the middle decades of the century. It concentrated on capturing weather, light, and air effects. The leading painters in the movement included Sanford Robinson Gifford, John Frederick Kensett, Fitz Hugh Lane, and Martin Johnson Heade.

2. Alexander Jackson Davis (1803–1892) was a most prolific New York architect, notably successful in his Greek Revival style and in his anticipation of the use of cast iron. He designed many river estates, the best examples of which include Locust Grove in Poughkeepsie and the neo-Gothic Lyndhurst in Tarrytown. Andrew Jackson Downing (1815–1852) was the nation's most popular theorist of architecture and landscape gardening. He also urged the development of public open spaces. His magazine, *Horticulturist,* and his many publications on rural residences and landscape gardening exercised enormous influence over the Romantic Movement and nineteenth-century estate building in the valley. Downing and Davis were close friends and collaborators. *Charmed Places: Hudson River Artists and Their Houses, Studios, and Vistas,* edited by Sandra Phillips and Linda Weintraub, discusses their influence on river estates (see Suggested Readings.)

9. Industrialization and the Transformation of the Landscape

Information about development of cities, towns, and villages as well as industrial growth in the nineteenth century was found in D. W. Meinig's *The Shaping of America: A Geographical Perspective on 500 Years of History: Atlantic America, 1492–1800,* vol. 1, and Carl Carmer's *The Hudson.* Discussion of the railroad's impact on the valley landscape was based on John Stilgoe's *Metropolitan Corridor: Railroads and the American Scene.*

Additional sources included F. Daniel Larkin's *John B. Jervis: An American Engineering Pioneer* (Ames: Iowa State University Press, 1990), offering background on Jervis' work; John Seelye's *Beautiful Machines: River and the Republican Plan 1755–1825* (New York: Oxford University Press, 1991), which examines the cultural and political significance of rivers, canals, and steamboats in the early republic; and Paul Wilstach's *Hudson River Landings* (Indianapolis: The Bobbs-Merrill Co., 1933), covering the development of communities and industrial growth along the river.

1. Brickmaking in the valley began to decline in the 1920s with the importation of European bricks and innovations in use of building materials including glass, aluminum, and poured concrete. The Depression also hit the industry hard; production in Haverstraw had just about ended in the 1940s. By the early twenty-first century there were no operating brickyards left on the Hudson.

2. Some economic historians describe three stages of economic development: a primary, or agricultural, stage; a secondary, or industrial, stage; and finally a tertiary, or service, stage. Thus we tend to refer to the present as a postindustrial, or tertiary, stage.

3. Fulton and Livingston's monopoly rights had passed to Aaron Ogden, who sued Thomas Gibbons to restrain him from engaging in steam navigation between New York and New Jersey. In *Gibbons v. Ogden* the court invalidated the New York monopoly and curbed state authority to restrict interstate transportation. This ruling contributed to the expansion of steam navigation on eastern rivers, harbors, and bays.

4. Overemphasis on the Erie Canal may lead one to not only ignore other canals but miss the sense of canal fever which gripped the region at this time. Another example was the Delaware and Hudson Canal, completed in 1828 to transport anthracite coal from Pennsylvania coal fields to tidewater at Rondout for transshipment to New York City.

5. The technological sublime celebrated the machine as a mark of progress and American creativity. This definition countered the generally held view that the sublime could be found only in nature.

6. Faced with dual competition from railroads and steamboats, the sloops were relegated to freight service, and by century's end were largely gone. Steamboats were to meet the same fate as automobiles and trucks joined the railroads in providing a greater share of transportation services. The steam engine itself was replaced by the more cost-efficient diesel engine. The last Hudson River passenger steamboat, the *Alexander Hamilton,* ended service in 1971. In 1989 its successor, the diesel-powered excursion vessel *Dayliner,* ceased regular passage on the river. Commercial traffic is now dominated by diesel tugs with their barges.

7. John B. Jervis, the chief engineer of the Hudson Line, saw no tension here. In fact, he argued that the railroad would enhance the experience and beauty of the shoreline and river.

8. The most prominent of the remaining industrial facilities along the Hudson are power plants which use the river as a source of cooling water (see chapter 10). Oil tank farms are also common; the river is still an important shipping route for petroleum products—bulk cargoes most cheaply shipped by tanker barges.

10. Conservation and Environmentalism

The historical background for themes of conservation and environmentalism was drawn from Roderick Nash's *Wilderness and the American Mind*. Raymond O'Brien's *American Sublime: Landscape and Scenery of the Lower Hudson Valley* helped connect these two national movements to the Hudson. Sections on the Storm King controversy and pollution of the Hudson relied on Robert Boyle's *The Hudson: A Natural And Unnatural History*, and Allan Talbot's *Power Along The Hudson*. More recent treatment of environmental issues in the Highlands can be found in Frances Dunwell's *The Hudson River Highlands*.

Discussion of the history of the conservation and preservation movements also drew from Hans Huth's *Nature and the American: Three Centuries of Changing Attitudes* (Berkeley: University of California Press, 1957), and Kate H. Winter's pioneering discussion of women and the wilderness experience, *The Women in the Mountain: Reconstruction of Self and Land By Adirondack Writers* (Albany: State University of New York Press, 1989). The July 1998 issue of *cliff*notes*, the visitor's newsletter for the New Jersey section of the Palisades Interstate Park, provided information on the history of the park's bathing beaches.

1. The Forest Preserve consisted of 681,374 acres that were designated "forever wild"—never to be leased to any person or corporation—by constitutional amendment in 1894. In 1892, New York created the Adirondack State Park, 2.8 million acres which included the Forest Preserve and other lands held by private individuals. The state did not treat public and private lands within the park in the same fashion, allowing development to continue on the privately owned sections.

2. The proposal involved pumping river water up to a storage reservoir to be located behind Storm King Mountain. This would occur during times of low electrical demand (late at night, for example). During times of peak demand, water released from the reservoir would drive turbines to produce electricity. The turbine house was to have been carved out of Storm King's northeast flank, which looks out over Cornwall and Newburgh Bays.

3. In power plants using fossil or nuclear fuels, the heat produced boils water to create steam which drives turbines to generate electricity. The steam, and the water used to make it, run through a closed system of pipes which includes a condenser. Here the steam condenses to liquid water by losing its heat to cooler water flowing through the condenser in a separate set of pipes.

4. The settlement also required the utilities to contribute $12 million to endow an independent research foundation (the Hudson River Foundation), spend $2 million per year on biological monitoring, and to fund the establishment of a hatchery (now closed) to stock the river with 600,000 young stripers annually.

11. Resolving River Conflicts

Much of the information in the Westway case study came from *The Hudson River Ecosystem* by Karin Limburg et al. Descriptions of wetland values, coastal management, and responsibilities of agencies overseeing Hudson River environmental quality can be found in the New York Department of State's *Hudson River Significant Tidal Habitats: A Guide to the Functions, Values, and Protection of the River's Natural Resources*. Robert Boyle's *The Hudson River: A Natural and Unnatural History* includes some information on landfill controversies.

Since many of the disputes described in this chapter are ongoing, books about them can quickly become dated. Thus periodicals, regulatory agency documents, environmental impact statements, and studies by environmental groups were most useful in writing this chapter. Much of the information on the Athens Generating facility came from the Siting Board's *Opinion and Order Granting Certificate of Environmental Compatibility and Public Need*, available from the New York State Public Service Commission. The EPA and Army Corps of Engineers Web sites provided details on New York Harbor dredging issues. *Wetlands of the United States: Current Status and Recent Trends* by Ralph W. Tiner, Jr. (Washington, D.C.: U.S. Fish and Wildlife Service, 1984) provided historical data on loss of wetlands. Data on lost wetland acreage along the Hudson is from Jennifer Anne Young's M.A. thesis, "Human Manipulation of the Historical Hudson Shoreline" (University of Connecticut, 1990). Discussion of water supply issues depended on bulletins produced by Scenic Hudson (14 Civic Center Plaza, Poughkeepsie, NY 12601), and online reports from the New York City Department of Environmental Protection. Information on coastal zone management came from "Coastal Resources and Development Policies," published by New Jersey DEP's Division of Coastal Resources (Trenton, NJ 08625) and documents from the Division of Coastal Resources of New York's Department of State. Details on the St. Lawrence Cement case came from the Department of State's consistency determination of April 19, 2005, DEC administrative law rulings, and documents produced by the advocacy group Friends of the Hudson. Discussion of estuary management programs drew information from the "Hudson River Estuary Action Agenda 2005–2009," from the Hudson River Estuary Program at the DEC (21 South Putt Corners Road, New Paltz, NY 12561), and *The Tidal Exchange* newsletters of the New York/New Jersey Harbor Estuary Program (290 Broadway, 24th Floor, New York, NY 10007). Finally, Hudson River Greenway information came from documents put out by the Greenway Council (Capitol Building, Capitol Station, Room 254, Albany, NY 12224).

1. Study had been limited to two summer months when low oxygen conditions made the area inhospitable to fish and other aquatic life. Also, researchers had used only a limited array of equipment for collecting estuarine creatures.

2. Article X was also used in reviewing proposals for significant additions and modifications to existing Hudson River power plants, notably the Bethlehem Energy Center (formerly the Albany Steam Generating Plant) and the Bowline power plant in Haverstraw.

3. The Endangered Species Act and similar state regulations have had a small role in controversies on the Hudson itself. However, in land use issues in the watershed, threats to rare and endangered species have often been at the center of controversy.

4. In the letter, the EPA agreed to standardize toxicity testing of dredge spoils. Clean sediments are those that pass such testing. Much of the material to be removed for the harbor deepening project is clean as it consists of rock or sediments deposited before the industrial age.

5. This law also allows localities to take over regulation of wetlands within their boundaries. While this has rarely been done, conservationists feel that towns might not strongly enforce wetlands regulations.

6. Adjacent property owners also have the right to wharf out to navigable waters, and may apply to lease or purchase underwater lands for private use.

7. The $1.5 million eventually endowed the Hudson River Improvement Fund, administered by the Hudson River Foundation. The fund supports projects that will enhance public use and enjoyment of the natural, scenic, and cultural resources of the river.

8. One engineering study suggested that pumping 300 mgd from the river at Chelsea would shift the salt front two

miles north, though New York City acknowledged a great deal of uncertainty in this estimate. The effects of the larger withdrawals envisioned by the high-flow skimming plan are not known.

9. The Estuarine District stretches from the Troy Dam to the Narrows, including adjacent tidal wetlands, tidal portions of tributaries, and associated shorelands.

10. The greenway legislation also established a Greenway Heritage Conservancy to provide financial and technical assistance for projects—land acquisition or environmental studies, for example—that would further Greenway goals.

12. Is the Hudson Getting Cleaner?

Robert Boyle's *The Hudson River: A Natural and Unnatural History* provided historical information on pollution of the Hudson. *The Hudson River Ecosystem* by Karin Limburg et al. offered a well-researched case history of the PCB issue through 1984. Barry Commoner's *Making Peace with the Planet* was helpful in developing the section on pollution prevention.

Given the contemporary nature of such issues, full-length book treatments can become outdated quickly. Up-to-date information is scattered through a wealth of reports, impact statements, periodicals, and agency bulletins, many now available on the World Wide Web. Data on New York State water quality and resource management programs and issues came from DEC's report *New York State Water Quality Section 305b Report* (2004). A description of New York's nonpoint source pollution control efforts can be found in DEC's *Nonpoint Source Management Program 2000*. Analysis of the SPDES program depended on the October 2005 report "Endangered Agency II: Are Staff Cuts at the DEC Threatening Your Safety?" by Environmental Advocates of New York, and Karl S. Coplan's article "Of Zombie Permits and Greenwash Renewal Strategies: Ten Years of New York's So-Called 'Environmental Benefit Permitting Strategy,'" *Pace University Law Review* (Spring 2005). Discussion of oil pollution prevention depended on the study "No Safe Harbor: Tanker Safety in America's Ports" (Natural Resources Defense Council, New York, 1990), and information on the EPA's Web site. The EPA's Region 2 office in New York City published fact sheets about cadmium cleanup in Cold Spring; its Hudson River PCBs Superfund Web site provided access to many relevant reports and documents. Also useful in preparing the discussion of PCBs were John E. Sanders' paper "PCB-Pollution Problem in the Upper Hudson River: From Environmental Disaster to Environmental Gridlock," *Northeastern Environmental Science*, vol. 8, no. 1 (1989), and "PCBs in the Upper Hudson River: The Science Behind the Dredging Controversy," a white paper prepared for the Hudson River Foundation by Joel E. Baker et al and released in October 2001.

1. The dissolved oxygen used by aquatic microorganisms feeding on sewage and other organic matter is measured as biological oxygen demand (BOD). High BOD indicates the presence of large amounts of organic matter in the water.

2. Until 1984, federal grants covered 75 percent of construction costs, states typically another 15 percent. Localities covered the remaining 10 percent. New York State voters should be credited for earlier attention to sewage cleanup; a spate of treatment plant construction began soon after they passed a billion dollar bond act for the purpose in 1965. Currently, the federal government allots construction money to the states on a loan basis; New York funds construction and upgrades with a combination of loans and grants.

3. The plant was originally to be constructed further south on the West Side. Moving it to Harlem, some observers claim, reflects a tendency to inequitably site sewage plants, hazardous waste treatment sites, incinerators, and similar facilities in low-income neighborhoods, often with high minority populations, where opposition will likely be less organized, vocal, and powerful.

4. Health agencies do not routinely count the numbers of pathogens; it is a demanding and expensive task given their variety and relative scarcity. In 2004, federal beach water quality standards required that *Enterococcus* be used as the primary pathogenic indicator for beach safety. *Enterococcus* has a higher correlation with presence of human pathogens than fecal coliform.

5. The federal government requires that goals for managing nonpoint pollution to coastal waters like the Hudson be enforceable, relying on regulatory rather than voluntary management measures. However, recognizing the need to maintain flexibility, agencies allow a wide range of specific practices to be used in meeting the management goals.

6. New York's DEC has three spill response teams for different sections of the Hudson and New York Harbor; New Jersey also has such teams on the harbor. While the Coast Guard has lead responsibility, cleanups are coordinated efforts including the Coast Guard, state response teams, and industries involved in oil transport and storage. State agencies identify sensitive habitats which need prompt protection during spills and inspect oil storage facilities.

7. The EPA must also consider taking no action, an option perhaps appropriate if, for example, the environment or public health risks posed by cleanup outweigh those associated with the contamination.

8. Commercial fishing for blueback herring, alewife, Atlantic tomcod, and blue crab reopened in 1978.

9. Based on concerns over exposure to contaminated dust, the EPA did call for capping deposits of PCB-laden sediments left high and dry after destruction of a dam in Fort Edward, and in a 1990 consent decree directed GE to pay $10 million for the task.

10. The reasons for revaluating the 1984 decision included new advances in treating PCB-contaminated sediments, a policy of reviewing Superfund records of decision every five years, and a preference—established when the law was reauthorized in 1986—for remedies which permanently and significantly reduce the volume, toxicity, and mobility of hazardous substances.

11. It was during this period of the Reagan Administration that the EPA official in charge of hazardous waste cleanup, Rita Lavalle, was found guilty of improperly linking cleanup funding decisions to political considerations. Anne Gorsuch Burford, the EPA Administrator responsible for impounding the PCB cleanup funds, was forced to resign due to similar allegations.

Glossary

adipose fin: a fleshy fin lacking rays; found behind the dorsal fin on some fishes.

aesthetic: a sense or taste for the beautiful; a love of beauty.

amphipod: a small, vaguely shrimplike crustacean, usually flattened from side to side with thorax in segments instead of a single piece; also called scud or sideswimmer (order Amphipoda).

anadromous: describes fishes which live in the sea (or large lakes) as adults but move into freshwater streams to spawn.

anal fin: an unpaired fin located on the underside and towards the tail of many fish.

arachnid: an arthropod which typically has eight legs and two body sections, one combining the head and thorax, the other an abdomen; spiders and water mites are examples (class Arachnida).

arthropod: an animal characterized by paired, jointed legs and an exoskeleton made of chitin; crustaceans, insects, and horseshoe crabs are examples (phylum Arthropoda).

barbel: a fleshy sensory appendage of some fishes, catfish "whiskers" for example.

benthos (adj. **benthic**): organisms living underwater on or in the bottom.

bioaccumulate: to build up quantities of a contaminant in the body of an individual organism.

biological concentration: process by which contaminant levels increase in the organisms along a food chain, reaching highest concentrations in top predators.

bivalve: a mollusk with two shells (valves) joined at a hinge; clams are examples (class Bivalvia).

bloom: a rapid and sizable increase in a population of microscopic aquatic plants.

bouweries: farms or plantations owned by early Dutch settlers.

calcareous: containing calcium carbonate.

carnivore: an organism that eats animals.

cartography: the science of mapping.

catadromous: describes fishes which live in fresh water as adults but move into salt water to spawn.

caudal fin: tail fin.

chevaux-de-frise: obstacles of wood, wire, or spikes placed in a pathway or waterway to prevent an enemy's advance.

chitin: a horny, flexible substance that is the major component of arthropod exoskeletons; in crabs and other crustaceans chitin is hardened by deposits of calcium carbonate.

chlorophyll: found in green plants, this chemical gives such plants their color and captures light energy for conversion into chemical energy.

chloroplast: a structure, found in many plant cells, in which chlorophyll is concentrated and which provides energy necessary to the workings of the cell.

chromatophore: one of the specialized cells in a fish's skin which contain pigment and cause color changes.

cilia: tiny hairlike structures which, arranged in groups and beating rhythmically, provide locomotion and other functions for living things.

cladoceran: one of a group of tiny crustaceans characterized by a nonsegmented body, a pair of large antenna used for locomotion, and, in most, a bivalvelike shell covering the abdomen and thorax; also called water fleas (order Cladocera).

cold-blooded: describes animals that do not maintain a set internal body temperature.

comb jelly: see ctenophore.

community: in ecology, an assemblage of organisms living and interacting in a given habitat.

compound eye: an eye composed of many separate units, each with its own lens and light-sensitive cells.

consumer: in ecology, an organism that obtains energy by eating other organisms; primary consumers eat plants, secondary consumers eat the plant-eaters, tertiary consumers eat secondary consumers, etc.

copepod: one of a group of tiny crustaceans that most commonly have elongated, segmented bodies, a pair of prominent antennae, swimming legs on their undersides, and a pair (or two sets) of taillike spines (subclass Copepoda).

critical zone: in estuaries, a highly productive, low salinity region important as a nursery for larval and juvenile fishes.

crustacean: one of a group of arthropods that are primarily aquatic and very diverse in form; typically the body has three sections (head, thorax, and abdomen) and a calcified chitinous exoskeleton; crabs and water fleas are examples (class Crustacea).

ctenophore: one of a group of small jellyfish-like creatures that lack stinging cells and have eight rows of cilia used in locomotion; comb jellies (phylum Ctenophora).

cyanobacteria: photosynthetic single-celled organisms; also called blue-green algae, but their simple cell structure is more like that of bacteria than that of algae (division Cyanophyta).

DEC: New York State Department of Environmental Conservation.

decomposer: an organism that obtains energy by breaking dead organic matter down into simpler components; usually refers to bacteria and fungi.

delta: a deposit of sediment, often triangular in shape, laid down where stream currents enter and slow down in relatively still water.

DEP: New Jersey Department of Environmental Protection.

dermis: in fish, the underlying fibrous layer of skin.

detritivore: an organism that feeds on dead organic matter; usually refers to organisms other than bacteria and fungi.

detritus: cast off or dead and decaying plant and animal matter.

diatom: one of a group of algae with a cell wall made largely of silica; they are often yellow in color (division Bacillariophyta).

dinoflagellate: one of a group of microorganisms that usually possess both chlorophyll and hairlike flagella for locomotion (division Pyrrophyta).

dorsal fin: unpaired fin(s) with rays; found on the backs of most fish.

DOS: New York Department of State

dredging: digging up sediments from the bottom of a water body.

ebb current: a tidal current moving towards the ocean.

echinoderm: one of a group of marine animals which possess tube feet connected to a system of vessels carrying water through the body; sea stars and sea urchins are examples (phylum Echinodermata).

ecology: the study of relationships between living organisms and their environments.

ecosystem: a functional unit of ecology, encompassing interacting living organisms and the physical environment which they inhabit.

EIS: environmental impact statement.

emergent: describes aquatic plants that have erect stems, leaves, or other parts that project above the water.

energy: the ability to do work, to power activity; takes several forms: light energy in solar radiation, chemical energy in food, for example.

EPA: U.S. Environmental Protection Agency.

epibenthic: living underwater on the substrate's surface.

epidermis: the outer layer of skin on fish.

epiphytic: living attached to submerged plants, but not deriving any nutrition from them.

estuary: a body of water freely connected to the sea and partially surrounded by land, in which salt water is diluted by fresh water running off the land.

ethnocentric: believing in the superiority of one's own group.

euphotic zone: in water bodies, the area near the surface in which there is enough sunlight for plants to grow.

eutrophication: the process in which a body of water is enriched with nutrients, encouraging plant growth; when caused by pollution, called cultural eutrophication.

exoskeleton: an external framework which contains and supports the tissues of many invertebrate animals.

fecal coliform: bacteria found in the digestive tracts of warm-blooded animals; elevated levels of these bacteria in water often indicate pollution by sewage.

filamentous: a habit of growth in which cells are arranged in a line; often describes algae.

fission: a process by which one cell divides into two.

fix: in ecology, to capture energy or nutrients and convert them into forms usable by plants and the animals which depend on plants.

fjord: a valley eroded below sea level by glaciers and later submerged by rising seas.

flat: a level area of sediment in subtidal shallows or in the intertidal zone.

flood current: a tidal current moving in from the open ocean.

flushing rate: the time necessary for water to move from the upstream end of an estuary to its mouth.

fly boat: a fast sailing vessel used chiefly in the sixteenth and seventeenth centuries for the rapid transportation of goods in coastal trade; usually a Dutch flat-bottomed boat.

food chain: a linear pathway by which food energy moves from plants to plant-eating animals to predators; in grazing food chains, animals feed directly on green plants; in detritus food chains, dead organic material from plants and other organisms nourishes decomposers and detritivores eaten by other animals.

food web: interconnected food chains in which each organism has several sources of food and, except for top predators, is in turn eaten by a variety of other organisms.

gastropod: a mollusk distinguished by a well-developed head, a broad, muscular foot, and a radula; snails and slugs are examples (class Gastropoda).

green algae: microscopic, single-celled plants with nuclei and chlorophyll concentrated in chloroplasts (division Chlorophyta).

habitat: the place or setting in which an organism lives.

herbaceous: nonwoody.

herbivore: an organism that eats plants.

historical association: enhancement and celebration of a landscape's identification with local, regional, or national history.

home rule: a legal doctrine giving local governments responsibility for land use decisions within their communities.

hydroid: the attached, polyp form of a hydrozoan.

hydromedusa: the planktonic, jellyfish-like form of a hydrozoan.

hydrozoan: one of a group of small jellyfish and sea anemone–like animals (class Hydrozoa).

intertidal: within the zone between average low and average high tide level.

Knickerbocker: a descendant of the Dutch settlers of New York.

larva (plural *larvae,* adj. *larval*): an early life stage or immature form of an animal.

lateral line: a sensory system, attuned to vibration, appearing as a series of pores or canals arranged in a line along the side of many fish.

limiting factor: of factors necessary for an organism to survive and grow, the one in lowest supply relative to need.

luminism: a style of painting which emphasizes the transcendent quality of pure and constant light.

LWRP: local waterfront revitalization plan.

mantle: in mollusks, a fold in the body wall that secretes the calcareous shell.

marsh: a wetland dominated by emergent herbaceous plants; in tidal areas, low marsh is found below the mean tide level, high marsh above.

mean tide level: the water level determined by averaging high and low tide.

medusa: free-floating form of a jellyfish or related organism; resembles an open umbrella with tentacles hanging below.

metamorphose: in biological development, to change profoundly in form when moving from one life stage to the next—caterpillar to butterfly, for example.

mgd: million gallons daily.

midden: a refuse heap, often one left by early inhabitants of an area.

mollusk: one of a group of animals characterized by having a mantle and a muscular foot; clams and snails are examples (phylum Mollusca).

molt: to shed a body's outer covering and replace it with a fresh one, as a bird replaces feathers or a crab its shell.

nares: nostrils.

nationalize: the act of identifying an object, event, or place with a country's history and identity.

neap tide: a less extreme tide—a lower high tide or a higher low—occurring when the moon is in its first or last quarter.

nektonic: capable of swimming strongly enough to move against the current.

nematocyst: one of specialized cells used by jellyfish and their relatives to sting or ensnare prey.

NEPA: National Environmental Policy Act.

nonpoint source pollution: pollution carried in runoff from an area of land rather than being released through a pipe from a factory, sewage plant, or similar facility.

nuclei (singular *nucleus*): in cells, specialized bodies that contain genetic material and direct cell growth and metabolism.

nutrient: an element—nitrogen, or phosphorous, for example—required for an organism's growth and development.

nutrient trap: a phenomenon in which large amounts of nutrients are retained in an estuary by salt water pushing into the system.

nymph: an immature insect, similar in form to the adult, that attains adulthood by molting rather than by metamorphosis.

oligochaete: a segmented worm characterized by bristles that grow singly from a sac in the skin; the earthworm is an example (class Oligochaeta).

omnivore: an organism that eats both plants and animals.

operculum: in fish, the gill cover; in snails, a flap that is attached to the foot and seals the shell opening.

ostracod: one of group of tiny crustaceans with body parts enclosed in a bivalve shell (subclass Ostracoda).

pathogens (adj. *pathogenic*): organisms, such as certain bacteria and viruses, which cause disease.

patron: a member of the West India Company who was given manorial rights to lands in exchange for planting a colony of fifty settlers.

PCBs: polychlorinated biphenyls, a class of chemical compounds in which chlorine atoms are attached to two connected phenyl rings.

pectoral fins: in fish, the paired fins closest to the head or highest on the body.

pelvic fins: in fish, the paired fins located on the underside either below or behind the pectoral fins; also called ventral fins.

picturesque: interesting in an unusual way; irregular.

photosynthesis: the process, energized by sunlight and aided by chlorophyll, in which green plants convert carbon dioxide and water into sugar and oxygen.

phytoplankton: microscopic plants that live drifting in the water.

PIPC: Palisades Interstate Park Commission.

plankton: aquatic organisms which, unable to swim strongly, drift at the mercy of currents.

point discharge: pollution released via a pipe from a specific factory, treatment plant, or similar facility.

polychaete: a segmented worm with bristles that grow in a bundle from a sac in the skin; the clam worm is an example (class Polychaeta).

polyp: the attached form of a jellyfish or its kin; hydroids and sea anemones are examples.

ppm: parts per million.

ppt: parts per thousand.

pretreatment: in pollution control, treatment of industrial wastes prior to their release into a sewage system.

primary producer: an organism capable of converting light energy into chemical energy that can serve as food for other organisms; green plants.

primary production: the rate at which energy is accumulated through photosynthetic activity by plants.

projectile points: commonly called arrowheads, but more often spearpoints and knives; important archaeological indicators of time and culture.

protoplasm: the semisolid and liquid component of a cell.

public trust doctrine: in common law, ownership of certain waters and lands by the state in trust for its citizens.

pupa (plural *pupae*): a resting, usually immobile stage or form occurring during some insects' transformation from larva to adult.

radula: in mollusks other than bivalves, a toothed tongue or ribbonlike organ used for feeding.

rays: thin, bony structures that support the fins of fish.

reach: the stretch of water visible between bends in a river channel.

reef: in the Hudson, a partially or fully submerged ridge of rocky substrate.

respiration: uptake of oxygen in organisms, a process which breaks down organic molecules, produces carbon dioxide and water, and makes energy available to the organism.

rhizome: the underground portion of a plant's stem; it usually grows horizontally, and from it spring erect stems and true roots.

Romantic: the primacy of thoughts and feelings of the imagination; the subjective experience.

sachem: a chief of a tribe or confederation of Native Americans.

salt front: in estuaries, the leading edge of dilute saline water moving landward from the sea.

SEQRA: New York state's Environmental Quality Review Act.

sessile: living attached to the substrate.

shaman: a priest or medicine man among certain North American tribes.

simple eye: in arthropods, a primitive eye in which a single lens refracts light for sensory cells in the retina.

SPDES: State Pollution Discharge Elimination System, a pollution control program established by the Clean Water Act.

spring tide: an extreme tide (higher high or lower low) occurring when the moon is in its full or new phase.

sublime: grand, majestic, noble, and awe-inspiring.

substrate: an underlying layer of material; the mud or sand on a river bottom, for example.

subtidal: pertaining to portions of tidal waters below low tide level and thus always submerged.

succession: replacement of one ecological community by another over time.

swamp: a wetland dominated by woody plants.

swim bladder: (also air or gas bladder) a gas-filled sac located in the body cavity of many fish; provides buoyancy and in some species serves as a sound producing or sensing organ, or as a primitive lung.

technicological sublime: the beauty and majesty in machinery and mechanical progress.

terminal moraine: a deposit of glacially eroded soil and rock marking the limit of a glacier's advance.

thermodynamics: the study of energy flow and transformation in mechanical and chemical systems.

TMDL: total maximum daily load of pollution allowed within water quality standards for a waterbody.

topography: the physical features of an area's landscape.

transpiration: loss of water vapor by land plants.

tributary: a stream that flows into another stream or body of water.

tunicate: a primitive chordate: (backboned animal), usually sessile and possessing a tough, translucent outer layer of body wall—a tunic; sea squirts are examples (subphylum Urochordata).

turbid: clouded with sediment.

water column: the portion of a water body between the surface and the bottom.

water flea: *see* cladoceran.

watershed: the area of land from which water runs off into a given body of water.

wetland: land and submerged land supporting aquatic or semiaquatic plants.

zooplankton: animals, mostly tiny, which are unable to swim strongly and thus drift in the water column.

Suggested Readings

A thorough study of the Hudson River should encompass history, literature, art, architecture, political science, biology, chemistry, geology, and many other fields of knowledge. This brief reading list can include only a fraction of the valuable reference books in river-related disciplines; it does cite those most useful in preparing this book. In the years since the first edition appeared, the World Wide Web has become an essential source of information; a few of the many relevant Web sites are cited with titles that will allow search engines to readily find them.

General overviews of the Hudson ecosystem and its inhabitants can be found in Robert H. Boyle's *The Hudson River: A Natural and Unnatural History* (New York: W. W. Norton & Company, 1979), *The Hudson River Ecosystem* by Karin Limburg, Mary Ann Moran, and William H. McDowell (New York: Springer-Verlag, 1986), and *The Hudson River Estuary,* edited by Jeffrey S. Levinton and John R. Waldman (New York: Cambridge University Press, 2006). Boyle's book—once the bible for the river's environmental movement—is out of print but well worth a search. *The Hudson River Ecosystem* and *The Hudson River Estuary* are intended for an audience comfortable with formal science writing. The former is now dated, but its case histories of Westway, PCB, and power plant issues provide valuable analysis of the role of science in the decision-making process. Levinton and Waldman offer a comprehensive and up-to-date set of papers covering the physical and biological workings of the estuary; their volume is essential for serious scientific study of the Hudson.

John Waldman's *Heartbeats in the Muck: A Dramatic Look at the History, Sea Life, and Environment of New York Harbor* (New York: The Lyons Press, 1999) lives up to its subtitle. It is a colorful, accessible, and wide-ranging description of the southern end of the Hudson estuary.

For readers who want their science embedded in lyric prose, or language arts teachers involved in curriculum focused on the estuary, Rachel Carson's classic *Under the Sea Wind,* first published in 1941, is still an excellent choice (New York: Penguin, 1996). While not specifically about the Hudson, this book describes the lives of creatures common here in very literate style.

General histories of the Hudson tend to quickly wander from the river into the wider setting of the valley's communities. We still do not have a history of the river per se but rather histories of the river valley. A good recent synthesis of the history is *The Hudson* by Tom Lewis (New Haven: Yale University Press, 2005). Out of print but well-focused and filled with ideas is Raymond O'Brien's *The American Sublime: Landscape and Scenery of the Lower Hudson Valley* (New York: Columbia University Press, 1981). But the touchstone for histories of the river is Carl Carmer's *The Hudson* (New York: Fordham University Press, 1992). This work, originally published in 1939, has a timeless quality which still provides inspiration for river lovers. A more journalistic account is Allan Keller's *Life along the Hudson* (New York: Fordham University Press, 1997). Finally, D. W. Meinig's innovative geography of early American history, *The Shaping of America: A Geographical Perspective on 500 Years of History: Atlantic America, 1492-1800,* vol. 1 (New Haven: Yale University Press, 1986) describes patterns of settlement that are clearly observed in Hudson Valley history.

One can supplement these traditional histories with firsthand accounts from Roland Van Zandt's *Chronicles of the Hudson: Three Centuries of Travel and Adventure* (Hensonville, N.Y.: Black Dome Press, ,1992), images from Jeffrey Simpson's *The Hudson River 1850-1918: A Photographic Portrait* (Tarrytown, N.Y.: Sleepy Hollow Press, 1987; out of print), and river guidebooks including Arthur Adams' *The Hudson River Guidebook* (New York: Fordham University Press, 1996) and Wallace Bruce's *The Hudson By Daylight* (New York: Walking News, 1982), a reprint of the 1907 edition. Finally, Clearwater's *Panorama of the Hudson River from New York to Albany* (Poughkeepsie, N.Y.: Clearwater, 1979; out of print but available in some libraries) reprints William Wade's 1845 series of maplike drawings depicting the river's shores, accompanying them with old prints, current photographs, and commentary. An essential source for the study of the river with maps, guidebooks, drawings, and travelers' accounts is the "Hudson River Portfolio" Web site of the New York Public Library.

Chapter 1. Those interested in Hudson Valley geology will find *Geology of New York: A Simplified Account*, Y. W. Isachsen, E. Landing, J. M. Lauber, L. V. Rickard, and W. B. Rogers, eds. (Albany: New York State Geological Survey, State Education Department, 2000), a valuable reference. The forces which cause tides are described in many books on oceanography; *An Introduction to the World's Oceans* by Keith Sverdrup, Allison B. and Alyn C. Duxbury (Columbus, Ohio: McGraw-Hill, 2005) has particularly clear diagrams of these phenomena. Tidal information, invaluable to anyone planning trips on or along the Hudson, can be found on the National Ocean Service Web site. Also handy is *Hudson River Tide and Current Data, 1 April-30 November*, distributed annually by Sea Explorer Ship 168 (contact Jack Feldborg, 63 South Gate Drive, Poughkeepsie, NY 12601, or Clearwater). The U.S. Geological Survey maintains a "Hudson River Salt Front" Web site with real-time data on movements of the front, and the Stevens Institute of Technology distributes real-time data on tides, weather, salinity and other parameters in New York Harbor through its "Urban Ocean Observatory" Web site.

Chapter 2. Energy flow, food webs, and nutrient cycles are covered in ecology texts such as Eugene P. Odum and Gary W. Barrett's *Fundamentals of Ecology* (Stamford, Conn.: Thomson/Brooks Cole, 2005). Levinton and Waldman's *The Hudson River Estuary* (cited above) provides detailed discussions of these topics more specific to the Hudson. Aldo Leopold's description of nutrient cycling in the essay "Odyssey" from his classic *A Sand County Almanac* (New York: Oxford University Press, 1989) merits the attention of those teaching both science and literature.

Chapter 3. River habitats and plant communities are well-described in *Hudson River Significant Tidal Habitats: A Guide to the Functions, Values, and Protection of the River's Natural Resources* (Albany: New York Department of State/Division of Coastal Resources and Waterfont Revitalization and the Nature Conservancy, 1990). More generalized treatment of these habitats is available in *The Ecology of Tidal Freshwater Marshes of the United States East Coast: A Community Profile* by W. E. Odum, T. J. Smith III, J. K. Hoover, and C. C. McIvor (Washington, D.C.: U. S. Fish and Wildlife Service, 1984). Helpful in identifying wetland plants along the Hudson is *A Field Guide to Coastal Wetland Plants of the Northeastern United States* by Ralph W. Tiner, Jr. (Amherst: University of Massachusetts Press, 1987).

Chapter 4. A fine general introduction to the invertebrates is Ralph Buchsbaum's *Animals Without Backbones* (Chicago: University of Chicago Press, 1987). Kenneth L. Gosner's *A Field Guide to the Atlantic Seashore* (Boston: Houghton Mifflin Company, 1999), with the beautiful illustrations typical of the Peterson Field Guide series, is useful to laypeople interested in invertebrates of the Hudson's saltier regions. Leland Pollock's *A Practical Guide to Marine Animals of Northeastern North America* (New Brunswick, N.J.: Rutgers University Press, 1998), more specific to this geographical area, has abundant black and white illustrations and useful keys. While its focus is not the Hudson, William W. Warner's *Beautiful Swimmers: Watermen, Crabs, and the Chesapeake Bay* (Boston: Back Bay Books reprint edition, 1994) blends the natural history of the blue crab and the human interests of those who catch them in an evocative manner.

Chapter 5. C. Lavett Smith's *The Inland Fishes of New York State* (Albany: New York State Department of Environmental Conservation, 1985) is out of print but remains an excellent reference, with a section devoted to the Hudson estuary's fishes—hence the adjective "inland" rather than "freshwater" in the title. *Bigelow and Schroeder's Fishes of the Gulf of Maine*, edited by Bruce B. Collette and Grace Klein-MacPhee (Washington, D.C.: Smithsonian Institution Press, 2002), remains an outstanding reference on marine and estuarine fishes ranging into the Hudson and nearby waters. Robert G. Werner's *Freshwater Fishes of the Northeastern United States: A Field Guide* (Syracuse, N.Y.: Syracuse University Press, 2004) is a fine field guide with an identification key. Peter Moyer's *Fish: An Enthusiast's Guide* (Berkeley: University of California Press, 1993) is a good choice for the layperson interested in general fish biology; more detail is provided in texts such as Moyer's *Fishes: An Introduction to Ichthyology* (Upper Saddle River, N.J.: Prentice Hall, 2003). Finally, a number of books about fish and fishing enter the realm of literature; John McPhee's *The Founding Fish* (New

York: Farrar, Straus and Giroux, 2002) is a worthy choice, examining the natural history of the American shad and its interaction with humans, though it does not have much to say about the Hudson's population. The "Freshwater Fishes of New York" Web page on the New York State DEC's Web site has lots of information and lovely images of many species common in the Hudson.

Chapter 6. There is a wealth of general reference works dealing with amphibians, reptiles, mammals, and birds. But for recent information specific to the Hudson one needs to dig into scientific literature, the newsletters and species lists of local organizations interested in these creatures, and regional periodicals that deal with natural history topics. For field identification, the Peterson Field Guides are good choices, starting with series originator Roger Tory Peterson's *A Field Guide to the Birds of Eastern and Central North America,* (Boston: Houghton Mifflin, 2002) and including *A Field Guide to the Mammals,* by William H. Burt and Richard P. Grossenheider (Boston: Houghton Mifflin, 1998) and *A Field Guide to Reptiles and Amphibians of Eastern and Central North America* by Roger Conant and Joseph Collins (Boston: Houghton Mifflin, 1998). The "New York State Breeding Bird Atlas" pages on the DEC's Web site offer species distribution maps that allow comparison of a species' occurrence in 1980-1985 versus 2000-2004.

Chapter 7. Two of the best histories of the native peoples of the valley, Herbert Kraft's thorough *The Lenape: Archaeology, History and Ethnography* (Newark: New Jersey Historical Society, 1987) and Julian Harris Salomon's more specialized *Indians of the Lower Hudson River: The Munsee* (New City, N.Y.: Rockland County Historical Society, 1983) are out of print. Henry Hudson has been the subject of many biographies but *Juet's Journal: The Voyage of the Half Moon from 4 April to 7 November 1609* (search for Juet's Journal online to find the text at Newsday's Long Island History Web site) and Donald S. Johnson's *Charting the Sea of Darkness: The Four Voyages of Henry Hudson* (New York: Kodansha International, 1993) are the best accounts of his exploration of the river. All studies of the colonial Dutch in New York will have to start with Russell Shorto's *Island at the Center of the World: The Epic Story of Dutch Manhattan and the Forgotten Colony That Shaped America* (New York: Doubleday, 2004), which most effectively builds on the remarkable research efforts of the New Netherland Project in Albany. A good, detailed study of early Dutch settlers is Charlotte Wilcoxen's *Seventeenth Century Albany: A Dutch Profile* (Albany: Albany Institute of History and Art, 1984). The Bicentennial failed to produce a definitive regional history of the Revolution. Lincoln Diamant's *Chaining the Hudson: The Fight for the River in the American Revolution* (New York: Fordham Uni-

versity Press, 2004) is as close as we come to an account of the Hudson's role in the Revolution.

Chapter 8. The glorious age of the romantic Hudson is best approached through the work of the painters and writers. John K. Howat's *The Hudson River and Its Painters* (New York: Viking Press, 1972; out of print) gives a good basic overview while Barbara Novak provides a framework for interpreting the paintings of the Hudson River School in *Nature And Culture: American Landscape and Painting 1825-1875* (New York: Oxford University Press, 1980; out of print). These two works should be supplemented with Angela L. Miller's The Empire of the Eye: Landscape Representation and American Cultural Politics, 1825-1875 (Ithaca, N.Y.: Cornell University Press, 1993). The more personal relationship between artist and river valley is examined in *Charmed Places: Hudson River Artists and Their Houses, Studios, and Vistas* (New York: Harry Abrams Inc., 1988; out of print) edited by Sandra S. Phillips and Linda Weintraub. A selection of the pertinent literature is available in Arthur G. Adam's *The Hudson River In Literature: An Anthology* (New York: Fordham University Press, 1988). The remarkable legacy of the nineteenth century's frenzied estate building is lavishly presented in John Zukowsky and Robbie Pierce Stimson's *Hudson River Villas* (New York: Rizzoli, 1985; out of print).

Chapter 9. Hudson Valley agriculture has received fresh attention from Thomas Wermuth in *Rip Van Winkle's Neighbors* (Albany: State University of New York Press, 2001) and Martin Bruegel's *Farm, Shop, Landing: The Rise of a Market Society in the Hudson Valley, 1780-1860* (Durham, N.C.: Duke University Press, 2002). Nineteenth-century industrialization of the river valley has not yet been treated fully in a single detailed work. The catalog of a Bard College exhibit, *Industrial Transformations: Nineteenth-Century Business and Industry in the Mid-Hudson Valley* is helpful. Regional industrialization is best studied through histories of individual business activities such as brickmaking, ice harvesting, lumbering, and shipyards. The Romantic impulse was not limited to the arts but extended to technology as well. Images of technical progress are examined in Kenneth W. Maddox's *In Search of the Picturesque: Nineteenth-Century Images of Industry along the Hudson River Valley,* another Bard College exhibit catalog (Red Hook, N.Y.: 1983). Anthony J. Peluso's *Bard Brothers: Painting America Under Steam and Sail* (New York: Harry N. Abrams Inc., 1997; out of print) examines the way river steamboats were among the most celebrated objects of romantic technology. Donald C. Ringwald's *The Mary Powell* (Burbank, Ca.: Howell-Norton1972; out of print) is a study of the queen of river steamers. The impact of the railroad on river travel and the valley landscape is one of the main themes in John Stilgoe's *Metropolitan Corridor: Railroads and the American Scene* (New Haven: Yale University Press, 1983).

Chapter 10. The Hudson's twentieth-century history has seen an increased emphasis on conservation and preservation. To study these forces one should begin with Boyle's *The Hudson: A Natural and Unnatural History* (cited above), a work that changed the way we looked at the river. Allan R. Talbot's *Power along the Hudson: The Storm King Case and the Birth of Environmentalism* (New York: Dutton, 1972; out of print) offers analysis of this important case. The first chapter of his *Settling Things: Six Case Studies in Environmental Mediation* (New York: Ford Foundation, 1983; out of print) reviews the resolution of the issue. Frances F. Dunwell's *The Hudson River Highlands* (New York: Columbia University Press, 1991) provides a good introduction to environmental issues in the Hudson Highlands, along with much information on the natural and human history of the river. Roderick Nash's *Wilderness and the American Mind* (New Haven: Yale University Press, 2001) places the modern environmental history of the river in the context of its historical background. Thomas Berry's *The Dream of the Earth* (San Francisco: Sierra Club, 1990), discusses the eco-theology movement and contains several chapters that focus on the Hudson. Berry sees the valley as a bio-region, a natural community in which we are functioning members.

Chapters 11 and 12. With ongoing disputes over Hudson River environmental concerns, the most timely information about them comes from Web sites, newspaper reports, articles in periodicals, reports from agencies and organizations involved in the disputes, and scientific literature. Given the degree of research and the logistics involved in producing books about these battles, such longer works tend to reflect the history and basic science involved rather than the most up-to-date information on progress towards resolution. However, three books cited above should be mentioned again. Boyle's *The Hudson River: A Natural and Unnatural History* offers vivid descriptions of historic political and legal clashes along the river and a compelling statement of values held by one of the river's most outspoken environmental advocates. Limburg et al., *The Hudson River Ecosystem* presents more objective, detailed reviews (through 1985) of three major controversies—Westway, PCBs, and power plant operations—and the roles played by scientific research in attempts to resolve these disputes. Levinton and Waldman's *The Hudson River Estuary* provides updates on PCBs, fisheries management, and other relevant topics. The New York Department of State publication *Hudson River Significant Tidal Habitats* (cited above-chapter 2) provides a broad overview of human impacts on the river and of the roles of specific agencies in resolving issues raised by these impacts. While its perspective is national and global rather than regional, Barry Commoner's *Making Peace with the Planet* (New York: New Press, 1992) offers a well-documented and provocative critique of environmental improvements—or lack thereof—under the Clean Water Act and other relevant laws.

Web sites are of particular value here. For descriptions of environmental laws, government programs, and texts of major decisions, visit the following agency's sites: the U.S. Environmental Protection Agency Region 2, the New York State Department of State Division of Coastal Resources, the New York State Department of Environmental Conservation, the New Jersey Department of Environmental Protection, and the New York City Department of Environmental Protection. For the perspectives of environmental advocates, visit the Web sites of Hudson River Sloop Clearwater, Scenic Hudson, Riverkeeper, and the New York/New Jersey Baykeeper. Also useful is the Hudson River Foundation's Web site.

Index

Page numbers in italics refer to illustrations.

Acartia tonsa, 46

Adirondacks, 1, 131, 170, 191n1

African Americans, 101, 104, 108; constructing West Shore Railroad, *129*

agriculture, 117; Dutch, 100; Dutch farm, *99*; and Erie Canal, 122; and pollution, 168

Albany, 3, 122; Pool, 161

alder, smooth, *40*

alewife, 41, *70*

algae, 12, 13, 29–31; blooms, 24–25, 30–31, 161; blue-green, 22, 29, 30, 34; epibenthic, 31, 34; epiphytic, 34; in food web, *15*; green, 29, 30. *See also* cyanobacteria; diatoms; phytoplankton

ammonia, 22

amphibians, 77–79

amphipod, 13, 16, 17, 44, 53; in food web, *15*

Anabaena, 30

Anacystis, 30

anchovy, bay, 45, *73*

Andre, John, 107

anemones, 49; white, *49*

Ankistrodesmus, 30

Anodonta implicata, 51

arachnid, 52

archaeology, 93

architecture, 114; bracketed cottage model, *114*

Army, U.S., 174; Corps of Engineers, 142, 144, 148, 156

Arnold, Benedict, 107

arrow-arum, *37*

arthropod, 46–48, 52–55

Arthur Kill: heron colonies, 84; oil spills, 170–171

ash: black, *40*; red, *40*

Asterionella, 29

Athens Generating Company, 144–145, *145*, 156

Atlantic Ocean, 3, 4, 23, 24

automobile, 129, 133; pollution from, *168*. *See also* roads

bacteria: coliform, 163, 164; decomposers, 21; *Enterococcus*, 193n4; in food web, *15*; in nitrogen cycle, 22; production by, 18–19; and sewage, 25, 162

Bard, James and John, 124, *126*

barnacle, 19, *53*, 53–54; larval, 44, *47*

bass, largemouth, 41, 65, 72; and polychlorinated biphenyls, 75

bass, smallmouth, 41, 72

bass, striped, 46, *59*, *60*, *71*, 75; and polychlorinated biphenyls, 75–76, 175, 179; and Westway, 143

bass: in food web, *15*; temperate, 70, *71*

Battery, 2, 7, 8, 107

Bear Mountain Bridge, 129, *130*, 133

beaver, 90, 96, 99

benthos, 28, 43, 48–57

bioaccumulation, 75, 76

biological concentration, 75, 76

biosolids, 163

birds, 80–89; nesting colonies, 84–85, 87; perching, 85–86; population declines, 87, 88–89; raptors, 87–88; swimming, 80–83; wading, 83–85

Bithnyia tentaculata, 51

bittern, least, *84*

bivalve, 50–51, 57–58

blackbird, red-winged, *85*

bluefish, 70–71, *71,* 75

bluegill, 14, 17, 72

borers, marine, 48

Bosmina longirostris, 47

Bougainvillia, 45

bouweries, 100

Boyle, Robert, 136–137, 161

brant, *81*

brickmaking, 5, 118, *118,* 190n1 (chapter 9)

bridges, 129–130. *See also* Bear Mountain Bridge; George Washington Bridge; Poughkeepsie Railroad Bridge; Rip Van Winkle Bridge; Tappan Zee Bridge

Brooklyn, 5, 105

Bryant, William Cullen, 111, 112

bufflehead, *82*

bullfrog, *78*

bullhead, brown, 65, 66, 67–68, *68*

bunker. *See* menhaden

Burgoyne, John, 104, 106

butterfish, 45

caddis fly, *56*

cadmium, 171, 174

canals, 3, 121–122; Champlain, 178; Delaware & Hudson, 190n4; Erie, 121–122, *122;* map of, *121*

canoe, dugout, 94, *95*

canvasback, *82*

carbon, 17; sources, 19–20; *20, 24;* cycle, 20–21

Carmer, Carl, 134, 135

carnivore, 14

carp, common, 36, *63,* 72

Carson, Rachel, 134, 137

castles, 115

catfish, 64, 66, 67–68; white, 65, *68*

Catskill, 9, *127;* chart of river at, *28*

Catskills, 109, *110,* 131, 145, 151, 170. *See also* Hudson River School; landscape; mountain house; wilderness

cattail, narrow-leaved, *38*

cement manufacture, 118–119, *154, 156. See also* St. Lawrence Cement

Ceratium, 30

channel, 3, 27–28

Chaoborus, 47

Chelsea, 151; pump station, 151, *152*

chlorophyll, 21

Church, Frederic, 111, 144. *See also* Olana

cladoceran, 46–47, 53. *See also* water flea

clam, 16, 50; fingernail, 50; hard, 51, 57; harvest, 57; soft-shelled, *51,* 57

Clean Water Act: citizen suits, 165; and nonpoint pollution discharges, 165–169; and oil pollution, 171; and polychlorinated biphenyls, 176–177; and point discharges, 165–167; Section 401 water quality certification, 149; Section 404 landfill permits, 148–149; and sewage treatment, 162; success of, 181; total maximum daily load, 169–170; water classifications, 165–166

Clearwater, 101, 137, 137–138; People's Pipewatch, *165. See also* sloops

Clermont, 120, 121, 138. *See also North River*

Clinton, DeWitt, 6, 72

coastal zone management, 153–157

Coast Guard, U.S., 171, 172–173

Cold Spring, 174

Cole, Thomas, 109–111, 113, 128; Cedar Grove, 114; *The Clove, Catskills, 110;* in *Kindred Spirits, 111*

Colvin, Verplanck, 1, 131

comb jellies, 45; Beroe's, *44;* Leidy's, *44*

Commoner, Barry, 181

community (ecological), 27. *See also* algae: epibenthic; benthos; marsh; phytoplankton; submerged aquatic vegetation; swamp; wetlands; zooplankton

Con Ed. *See* Consolidated Edison

Congress, U.S., 140, 143, 173, 176

conservation, 131–138; water, 152–153. *See also* Carmer, Carl; environmentalism; preservation

Consolidated Edison, 134–136

consumer (ecological), 14

Cooper, James Fenimore, 113–114

coot, American, 82–83, *83*

copepods, 15, 44, 45, *46*

copperhead, 189n2(chapter 6)

cordgrass: saltmeadow, *38;* saltwater, *38. See also Spartina* cormorant, double-crested, 80, *82*

Cornwall-on-Hudson, *120*

courts, 140–141; in Storm King case, 136; in Westway case, 142–143

crab: blue, *55;* consumption advisory, 187n5 (chapter 4); fishery, 58; hermit, *55;* horseshoe, *52,* 52–53, 58; larvae, *47;* redjointed fiddler, *55;* rock, *55;* soft-shelled, 54, 58; spider, *55*

crappie, black, 72

crayfish, *54*

Cropsey, Jasper, 111; Ever Rest, 114

Croton Point, 5; chart of river at, *32*

Croton River, 5

crustacean, 46–47; larval forms, 47; abundance in Hudson, 46, 52; as food, 58

ctenophore, 45

cyanobacteria, 22, 29, 30. *See also* algae: blue-green

Cyathura polita, 53

cycles: carbon, 20–21; nitrogen, 21–23; oxygen, 21; phosphorus, 23–24

Cyclops, 46

Cyclotella, 29

damselfly, *56*

Daphnia, 47

darter, tesselated, *69*

Davis, Alexander Jackson, 114, 190n2 (chapter 8)

DDT, 87, 88

decomposers, 16, 18, 23

deer, white-tailed, 15, 89

Delaware River, 5, 100, 189n6

delta, 5, 185n3

detritivores, 16, 18, 21, 23, 28, 48

detritus, *16,* 16–20, 23, 33; in food web, *15*

development, *146,* 153, 155, 159, 169; as source of conflict, 146–147; in wetlands, 147–148

Diamond Reef, 31, *158,* 170

Diaphanosoma, 47

diatoms, 29–30; in food web, *15*

dinoflagellates, 30–31

dioxin, 148

dogwood, silky, *40*

dolphin, common, 90

Downing, Andrew Jackson, 114–115, 123, 190n2(chapter 8)

dragonfly, *56;* and polychlorinated biphenyls, *75*

dredging, 3, 148–149, *149;* in pollution cleanup, 174, 176–181. *See also* Army, U.S.: Corps of Engineers

Drew, 124, 125

ducks, 81–82; black, *81;* hunting, 80–81; wood, *81*

Durand, Asher, 111, 112; *Arrival of Henry Hudson, September, 4, 1609, 97; Kindred Spirits, 111*

Dutch, 98, 99–101; place names, 102

eagle, bald, *87;* effects of pesticides on, 87; restoration, 88

Earth Day, 140

echinoderms, 56

ecology: definition, 13; use in conservation movement, 137

ecosystem, 13, 16, 137

Edotea triloba, 53

eel, American, 63, 65, *69,* 75

egrets, 84–85; great, *84;* snowy, *84,* 171

energy, 14–16; flow and loss, 17–20; pyramid of, *18*

enforcement (of environmental law), 140–141; by citizen suits, 165; of discharge permits, 167; local role, 146–147, 154–155; of wetland laws, 150

English settlement, 101–104. *See also* Revolutionary War

Environmental Advocates of New York State, 167

environmental impact statement (EIS), 140–141; for polychlorinated biphenyl cleanup, 176; for Westway, 142–144

Environmental Protection Agency, U.S. (EPA), 140; and cadmium cleanup, 174; and landfill permitting, 148; and polychlorinated biphenyl cleanup, 176–181; regulatory review, 168, 170; Superfund, 173

environmentalism: and preservation, 134–138; and values conflicts, 139–140, 148, 150

Esopus Island, chart of river at, *81*

Esopus Meadows, 7, 31, *32*

estates, 114–115

estuary, 9–11; productivity in, 11–12; and fish, 60–61

estuary management plans, 141, 157–158

euphotic zone, 28, 187n1(chapter 3)

Eurytemora affinis, 46

eutrophication, 24

exotic species. *See* introduced species
exploration, 96–99
Exxon: oil spills, 171, 172; water withdraw-
    als, 150–151
Exxon Valdez, 172

falcon, peregrine, 88
Feldspar Brook, 1
ferries, 129–130, 133
fish: anadromous, 60; barbels, *65,* 67; ben-
    thic, 67–69; catadromous, 69; chromato-
    phores, 62–63; classification, 61; color-
    ation, 62–63; countershading, *63;* critical
    zone for, *60,* 60–61; in diet, 94, *95;* esti-
    mating age, 63, 188n4; fins, 66; gills, *61,*
    61–62, *62;* health advisory, 76, 170, 175,
    178; nektonic, 67, 69–73; numbers in
    Hudson, 59–60; scales, *63,* 63–64; senses,
    64–66; skin, 62; sounds, 64; swim bladder,
    64, 66, 70, 188n5; and water withdrawals,
    135–136, 144, 151
fisheries, 70, 73–76, 94
flat (tidal), 31, *32*
flatfishes, 68–69
flooding, 32–33, 186n5 (chapter 1)
flounder, 62–63; chromatophores of, *63;*
    summer, *68;* winter, *68*
fluke. *See* flounder: summer
flushing rate, 9, 25
food chains, 13–21; DDT in, 88; detrital,
    15–19; grazing, 15, 44; polychlorinated
    biphenyls in, *75,* 76
food web, 14–15, *15*
Fort Edward, 175–176
Foundry Cove, 173, 174
frogs, 78; green, *78;* northern leopard, 78
Fulton, Robert, 120–121
fungi, 16

Gammarus, 53
gastropod, 50. *See also* snails
George Washington Bridge, 9, 134
General Electric (GE), 175–181; Hudson
    Falls plant, *175, 179*
General Motors, 161
Gifford, Sanford, 111
Glacial Lake Albany, 185n2, 185n3
Glacial Lake Hudson, 5
glaciers, 4–5
glucose, 21
goldeneye, common, *82*

goldfinch, American, *85*
goldfish, *72*
Gomez, Estevan, 97–98
goose, Canada, *81*
Great Lakes, 5
gulls, 86–87; great black-backed, *86;* her-
    ring, *86;* laughing, *86;* ring-billed, 86

habitat, 27, 58, 77, 142–143, 147
Half Moon (Halve Maen), 98, 138
harpoon, bone, *95*
Hasbrouck House, 107, *108*
Haverstraw Bay, *3,* 18, 28
Henry Clay, 123
herbivore, 14
herons, 84–85, 171; black-crowned night,
    84–85; in food web, *15;* great blue, 13, 14,
    17, 21, *84;* green, *84*
herring: blueback, *70;* river, 70
Highlands, 4, 5, 104
hogchoker, 65, *68*
home rule, 146, 158
hotlines: for reporting marine animal
    strandings, 189n5 (chapter 6); for report-
    ing pollution, 172
Howe, William, 104, 105
Hudson (city of), 90, 155–157
Hudson, Henry, 98–99; arrival, *97*
Hudson Falls, 173, 175, 177, 179
Hudson-Fulton Celebrations, 133, 138
Hudson North Bay Marsh, *147*
Hudson River: America's river, 108, 112;
    American Heritage River, 159; course, 1,
    5; depth, 4; fjord, 4; geological history of,
    3–6; gorge at Blue Ledge, *2;* income bud-
    get, *20;* length, 2; names, 97–98, 99; oil
    spills, 170; reaches of, 101, 189n5 (chap-
    ter 7); salinity, 9–12; source, 1; strategic
    importance in Revolution, 104, 105, 107;
    stratification, 11–12; therapeutic role,
    116; watershed, 2–3; width, 3. *See also*
    Muhheakantuck; pollution; tides; tribu-
    taries; water supply
Hudson River Conservation Society, 134
Hudson River Estuary Management Pro-
    gram, 157, 158, 165
Hudson River Fishermen's Association, 137,
    150–151. *See also* Riverkeeper
Hudson River National Estuarine Research
    Reserve, 150, 158
Hudson River Park, *143*

Hudson River School, 110–112
Hudson River Valley Greenway, 158–159
Hudson River Valley National Heritage Area, 158–159
Hudson River Waterfront Walkway, *155*
Hudson Submarine Canyon, 4
Hudson Valley: as flyway, 30; as inspiration to artists, 109–114; and literary identity, 112; population diversity, 103, 104. *See also* agriculture; Dutch; English settlement; exploration; sublime
Huguenots, 189n4 (chapter 7)
hydroid, tubularian, *49*
hydroids, 46, 49
hydromedusa, clapper, *45*
hydromedusae, 46
hydrozoan, 45, 49

ice, 31, *32*; harvesting, 119; house, *119*
Ice Age, 4–5
Idlewild, 109, 114
immigrants, 119, 129
Indian. *See* Native American
industries and industrialization, 117–129, 156, 191n8. *See also* transportation
insect, 47–48, 52, 54–55
introduced species, 18, 35. *See also* carp, common; goldfish; loosestrife, purple; mussel, zebra; rat, Norway; swan, mute; water chestnut; water milfoil, Eurasian
invertebrates: definition, 43; benthic, 48–57; as food source, 43, 46, 47, 48, 53, 60, 169; nektonic, 57; planktonic, 44–48
Iona Island Marsh, 150
iron making, 118
Irving, Washington, 101, 112, 114
isopod, 53

jellyfish, 45–46; lion's mane, *45*; moon, *45*
Jervis, John, 128, 191n7
jewelweed, *40*
Juet, Robert, 98–99

Kensett, John, 111
Kidd, Captain William, 103–104
killdeer, *83*
killifish, 73; banded, *73*; in food web, *15*; oil's impacts on, 171; striped, *73*
kingfisher, belted, *87*
Kingston, 106, 146, 165. *See also* Rondout
Kingston Point, *36*

Lake Tear of the Clouds, *1*
lampreys, 41, 61, 64, 188n1
landfill, *98*, 142, *147*, 147–148; disposal of pollution, 163 in, 174, 176, 177, 180
landscape, 99, 109–114; clearing, 117; destruction of, 119, 128, 131; domestication of, 111. *See also* architecture; Downing, Andrew Jackson
lead, 181
leech, 50
light: as limiting factor, 25; penetration into water, 28; and photosynthesis, 13, 21
limiting factor, 24, 25
limulus amebocyte lysate, 58
Livingston, Robert, 102, 103, 120–121
lobster, northern, *34*; fishery, 58; larva, *47*
Long Island, 5, 58, 76, 88
Long Island Sound, 25, 158
loosestrife, purple, *38*
lumbering, 117, 131
luminism, 111, 190n1 (chapter 8)

mallard, *81*
mammals, 89–91
management plans. *See* coastal zone management; estuary management plans
manors, 102–103; map of, *102*. *See also* patroonship
maple, red, *40*
Marathon Battery, 174
marsh, 19–20, 36, 174; detritus in, *16*; high, 37–39, *39*; low, *36*, 36–37. *See also* Hudson North Bay Marsh; Iona Island Marsh; Piermont Marsh; Stockport Flats; Tivoli Bays; wetlands
mayfly, *56*
Melosira, *29*
menhaden, *60*, 62, *70*, 75
merganser: common, *87*; consumption advisory, 189n4 (chapter 6); red-breasted, *82*
midges: Chironomidae, 55; in food web, *15*; phantom, *47*
mills and milling, 117
mink, *90*
minnow, 72–73
Mohawk River, 2, 3
Moina, *47*
mollusk, 50–52, 57; as food, 57–58
moraine, terminal, 5
Mount Marcy, *1*
Mount Taurus, 134

mountain house, 115–116; Catskill, *115*; Cozzen's Hotel, *116*
mouse, white-footed, *89*
mudpuppy, *78*
Muhheakantuck, 7, 93
mummichog, *73*
muskrat, 15, *90*
mussels, 16, 19: blue, *51*, 57; pearly, 50–52, *51*; ribbed, *51*; zebra, 18, 29, 36, 48, 50–52, *61*, 153

Narrows, 5
National Audubon Society, 150
National Environmental Policy Act (NEPA), 140, 141. *See also* environmental impact statement
National Pollution Discharge Elimination System, 166. *See also* State Pollution Discharge Elimination System
Native American, 93–96; chief, *95*; and Henry Hudson, 96, 99; Mahican, 93–94; map of lands, *94*; Munsee, 93–94; place names, 93; relationship with nature, 95
nature: and civilization, 111, 128–130, 139; God's presence in, 109–112. *See also* landscape; sublime; wilderness
Nature Conservancy, 150
New Amsterdam, 100; print of, *98*
New Englander. *See* Yankee
New Jersey: biosolids disposal in, 163; coastal management in, 155; Department of Environmental Protection (DEP), 140, 155, 172; nonpoint source management in, 168; pollution prevention in, 181
New Netherlands, map of, *94*
New York Bight, 23, 25
New York City: audience for painting, 110; leak detection program, 152, *153*; market for natural resources, 117, 119; pirates, 103; Revolutionary War in, 104–105; sewage from, 162–163; and trade, 103, 122; view of, *103*; water supply, 151–153. *See also* New Amsterdam; Westway
New York Harbor: dredging, 148–149; estuary management plan, 157; herons, 84–85, 171; oil spills in, 170; polychlorinated biphenyls in, 177; view of, *103*. *See also* trade
New York State Comptroller, 167
New York State Department of Environmental Conservation (DEC): and Ath-

ens Generating, 144; hotlines, 172; and polychlorinated biphenyls, 175–177, 179, 180; and pollution regulation, 166–168, 181, 182; and St. Lawrence Cement, 156; and wetlands regulation, 149–150. *See also* Hudson River Estuary Management Program
New York State Department of Health: fish consumption advisories, 76; water supply regulations, 152
New York State Department of State (DOS), 156–157
New York State Environmental Quality Review Act (SEQRA), 144, 145, 146
New York State Office of General Services, 150
nitrate, 22, 24
nitrogen, 21–23, 186n5 (chapter 2); cycle, *22*, human inputs, *24*
nonnative species. *See* introduced species
North River, 102, 189n6
North River, 121, *125. See also Clermont*
Northwest Passage, 96–97
nutrient trap, 12
Nyack, 118

oil spills. *See* pollution: oil
oligochaetes, 49–50, 187n2 (chapter 4)
omnivore, 16
osprey, *87;* effects of pesticides on, 87
ostracod, *53*
otter, river, *90*
oxygen, 21, 161; biological demand, 193n1; in water chestnut beds, 35–36
oyster, American, *51;* bar, *58;* as fertilizer, 100; harvest, 57–58; middens, 57

painting. *See* Hudson River School
Palisades, 15; preservation of, 131–133; at Haverstraw Bay, *3;* quarry, *132. See also* Sparkill Gap
Palisades Interstate Park Commission (PIPC), 132–133
Panorama, 112. *See also* Wall, William Guy
park: amusement, 115–116; Bear Mountain, 133, 134; Palisades Interstate, 132–133. *See also* Adirondacks
pathogen, 57, 161, 162, 165
patroonship, 100, 102
Paulding, James Kirke, 112
PCBs. *See* polychlorinated biphenyls

Pediastrum, 30
perch, white, 71; fins of, 66
Philipse, Frederic, 102
phosphorous, 21, 23–24, 186n5 (chapter 2); cycle, 23; human inputs, 24
photosynthesis, 13, 20–21, 21, 25
Phragmites. See reed, common
phytoplankton, 29–31; production by, 18–20, 20, 29
pickerelweed, 37
Piermont Marsh, 15, 27, 150
pipefish, northern, 69
piracy, 103–104
plankton, 28–29. *See also* phytoplankton; zooplankton
plover, semipalmated, 83
pollution: atmospheric, 22, 24, 170; effects on animals, 178–179; nonpoint source, 162, 166, 167–169; oil, 31, 162, 170–173; point discharges of, 162, 165–167; prevention vs. control, 181–182; progress in cleaning, 163, 166–167, 181; and swimming, 133, 136; total maximum daily load, 169–170; toxic, 166, 173–181. *See also* cadmium; hotlines; lead; polychlorinated biphenyls; sewage
polychaetes, 49–50, 187n2 (chapter 4)
polychlorinated biphenyls (PCBs): cleanup of, 173, 175–181; degradation of, 178; in food chain, 75; levels in fish, 75–76; molecule, 175; sources, 175, 177; toxicity, 175, 178–179
pondweed: clasping, 35; curlyleaf, 35; horned, 35
porpoise, harbor, 90
Poughkeepsie, 11, 27; tides at, 7; water supply, 151, 152
Poughkeepsie Railroad Bridge, 128
power plants, 135; and Article X, 144, 145, 192n2, ; Athens, 144–145; Indian Point, 135; Storm King, 134–136, 135
preservation, 131–133. *See also* conservation; environmentalism; Hasbrouck House; Mount Taurus; Scenic Hudson; Storm King
producer, 14
production (productivity), 18, 25; in channel, 28; estuarine, 11–12; of marshes, 36, 37; of submerged aquatic vegetation, 34
Prorocentrum, 30

public trust doctrine, 150
pumpkinseed, 72

quarries and quarrying, 117–118; destruction by, 131–132, 132, 134

railroad, 32, 126–128; Hudson River, 126; Mohawk and Hudson, 126, 127; West Shore, construction of, 129. *See also* transportation
rails, 83, 85; clapper, 85; Virginia, 85
rat, Norway, 89
rattlesnake, timber, 189n2 (chapter 6)
recreation, 116, 133
reed, common, 38
reef, 31
reptiles, 79–80
respiration, 21, 21
Revolutionary War, 104–108, 109; chevaux-de-frise, 104, 106; defensive chain, 105, 106, 107–108; forts, map of, 104, 105; naval battle, 105
Rip Van Winkle Bridge, 28
Riverkeeper, 150–151, 151, 164, 165
roads, 128–129, 133–134, 172; construction of Perkins Memorial Drive, 134; post, 124. *See also* automobile; bridges; Westway
Rockland County, 129, 134
rodent, 89
Rondout, 118
Rondout Creek, 41
rose-mallow, swamp, 38

St. John, 125
St. Lawrence Cement, 155–157
salamander, 78
salt front, 10–11, 152; location of, 11
sandpiper: least, 83; semipalmated, 83; spotted, 83
scaup: greater, 82; lesser, 82
Scenic Hudson, 135, 137, 140; Land Trust, 150
sea grape, 57
sea squirts, 56–57
sea star, common, 56
seahorse, lined, 69
seal: harbor, 91; harp, 91
searobin, 65
sediments, 3, 27, 31–32, 50, 168. *See also* dredging

sewage, 24, 136, 152, 161–165; and algal
blooms, 161; combined sewer overflows,
163, 164–165; and dissolved oxygen levels, 25, 163; and inputs of carbon, 19–20,
20; inputs of nitrogen, 22, 161; pretreatment, 164; and shellfish, 57–59, 156;
treatment plants, *162*, 162–163, 164–165
shad, American, 52, 55, 59, 70; *74*, 144, 175;
fishery, 70, *74*, 76; gills, *62*
sharks, 61, 188n2
shiner: in food web, *15*; golden, *72*; spottail,
72
shipbuilding, 117, 118
shipping, 148, 149, *154*, 157, 170, 172
shipworm, 48
shorebirds, 83–84
shrew, short-tailed, *89*
shrimp: common grass, *54*; sand, *54*; seed,
53
Sierra Club, 132
silverside, Atlantic, 45, *73*
slipper shell, Atlantic, *51*
sloop, 100–101, 120, 126, 190n6. *See also
Clearwater;* shipbuilding; trade
snail fur, *49*
snails, 50; Atlantic moon, 50, *51*; seaweed,
51
snakes, 79–80; garter, 80; northern water, *80*
Sparkill Gap, 5–6, *6*
sparrow, swamp, *85*
Spartina, 38; oil's impacts on, 171
spatterdock, *36, 37*
sponges, 48, 49; boring, *48*; redbeard, *48*
spring peeper, 78
squid, long-finned, 57
stage lines, 124
starfish, 56
State Pollution Discharge Elimination System (SPDES), 166–167, 175
Staten Island, 5
steamboats, 112, 120–121, 122–124, 126,
190n6; and amusement parks, 115–116;
monopoly and *Gibbons vs. Ogden,* 121,
190n3; interior of, *124*; timetable, *123*
Stevens, John, 120
stickleback, fourspine, *73*
Stockport Flats, 150
Storm King, 134–136, *136*; Butter Hill,
114; power plant proposal, 134–136, 141
Storm King Highway, 134, *136*
stormwater runoff, 169

sturgeon, 67; Atlantic, *65, 67,* 74–75, 175;
shortnose, 55, *67*
sublime, 110, 130; Bear Mountain Bridge
as example, *130*; technological, 124,
190n5
submerged aquatic vegetation, 19–20; contributions of carbon, *20,* 34–36
suburbanization, 129
succession, 33
sucker, white, 41
sunfish, red-breast, 72
sunfishes, 71–72; in food web, *15*; gills, *61*;
and polychlorinated biphenyls, *75*
Sunnyside, *113,* 114
Superfund, 173; cadmium cleanup, 173,
174; and polychlorinated biphenyls, 173,
175–181
swamp, 36, *39,* 39–40
swan, mute, *81*
swimming, *133, 154, 164*; and water quality,
165–166
Syracuse, 126

tanning, 119
Tappan Zee, 3, 4, 5
Tappan Zee Bridge, 129, 134
terrapin, diamondback, *79*
thermodynamics, 17
Thompson Island Pool, 177, *178,* 179
three-square, common, *37*
tides: currents, 6, 7–8, 11; cycle, 7–8;
moon's role, 6–7, *9*; neap, 8, *9,* 11; at
Poughkeepsie, 7; range, 8; spring, 8, *9,*
11; sun's role, 8, *9*; time differences, 9,
10; zones of flooding, *33*
Tivoli North Bay, 15, 27, *39,* 150, *154*
toad, American, 78
toadfish, oyster, 64
tomcod, Atlantic, 69
total maximum daily load (TMDL), 169–
170
touch-me-not, *40*
trade, 96, 100
transportation: and industrialization,
120–130; interlocking networks of, *120,
127*; and population growth, 129. *See also*
automobiles; bridges; ferries; railroad;
roads; sloop; stage lines; steamboat; suburbanization; tunnels
treefrog, gray, 78
tributaries, 40–41

Troy Dam, *3*, 8
tugboat, *154*
tunicates, 56–57; golden star, *57*
tunnels, 129–130
turbidity, 3; currents, 4; as limiting factor, 25, 28
turtles, 79; painted, *79*; snapping, 36, *79*

Underground Railroad, 108

Valvata tricarinata, *51*
Van Cortlandt, Stephanus, 102
Verrazano, Giovanni da, 97
vole, meadow, *89*

Wade, William, 112
Wall, William Guy, 111
warbler, yellow, *85*
Washington, George, 104, 106
Watchung Mountains, 5
water chestnut, *34*, 34, *35*, 35–36
water cycle, 1–2, *2*
water flea, 46–47; and polychlorinated biphenyls, *75*. *See also* cladoceran
water milfoil, Eurasian, *35*
water mite, 44, *52*
water moccasin, 79–80
water quality criteria, 166
water quality standards, 165, 166, 170
water supply, 150–153, 186n7; classification for, 165–166
waterfowl, 80–82, 88; foods, 35
watershed, 2–3, 149, 181; and nutrient

inputs, 19–20; protection of, 131; and turbidity, 3
weakfish, 70–71, *71*
West Point, 4, 8, 106–107
Westway, 141–144; area to be filled for, *142*
wetlands, 32–33; perching birds of, *85*; protection, 147–150; regulations, 32, 41, 148–150; values, 147; zones of tidal flooding in, 33. *See also* flat; marsh; swamp; Westway
whales and whaling, 90
whelk, channeled, *51*
wild celery, 13, *34*, 34–35, *35*, 36
wild rice, *37*
wilderness, 111, 112
Willis, Nathaniel Parker, 109, 114, 119
willow: black, *40*; pussy, *40*
windowpane, *68*
Women's Clubs of New Jersey, 132
World's End, 4
worms: in food web, *15*, 16; as indicators of pollution, 50; red-gilled mud, *49*; tubificid, *49*
wren, marsh, *85*
writers, 112–114. *See also* Boyle, Robert; Carmer, Carl; Carson, Rachel

Yankee, 103
yellowlegs: greater, *83*; lesser, 83

zoning laws, 146
zooplankton, 29, 43, 44–48

About the Authors

Stephen P. Stanne has been teaching about the Hudson since 1980, when he joined Hudson River Sloop Clearwater as education director, a job that immersed him in the river both literally and figuratively. In 1999 he became the interpretive specialist for the Hudson River Estuary Program of New York's Department of Environmental Conservation, in partnership with the New York State Water Resources Institute at Cornell University. Mr. Stanne holds a B.A. from Amherst College and a Master of Science teaching degree from Antioch/New England. He resides in New Paltz, New York.

Roger G. Panetta is professor of history and curator of the Hudson River Collection at Marymount College of Fordham University. The Hudson has been a central subject of his teaching, writing, and curatorial work with the Hudson River Museum. He has also edited *Westchester: The American Suburb*, a companion volume for the museum's exhibition of the same title. He has worked with the Beacon Center for Rivers and Estuaries on a Hudson River oral history project. He holds a B.A. in history from Columbia College, an M.A. in American history from Fordham University, and a Ph.D. in American and urban history from the City University of New York. He lives on Riverside Drive in Manhattan.

Brian E. Forist is an environmental educator whose extensive teaching experience includes six years as an education specialist with the Hudson River Sloop Clearwater, teaching on the boat and leading workshops on land. Mr. Forist holds a B.S. from Huxley College of Environmental Studies and an M.S. in environmental studies and elementary education from Antioch/New England. He lives in the Midwest where he is education director at the Indiana Dunes Environmental Learning Center.

Original development of this book was a project of Hudson River Sloop Clearwater, Inc., a not-for-profit, member-supported environmental education and advocacy organization dedicated to restoration and protection of the Hudson River and similar waterways. Its members own and operate the 106-foot sloop Clearwater, launched in 1969 as a floating classroom on the tidewater Hudson. In addition to educational sail programs, the organization provides land-based field trips and classroom presentations, teacher workshops, and curriculum resource materials. Clearwater staff also conduct grass-roots environmental action programs to further the goal of cleaning and preserving the Hudson. Royalties from sales of this book go to Clearwater to support these programs. For more information about the organization, contact: Hudson River Sloop Clearwater, Inc., 112 Little Market Street, Poughkeepsie, New York 12601; telephone 845-454-7673; www.clearwater.org.

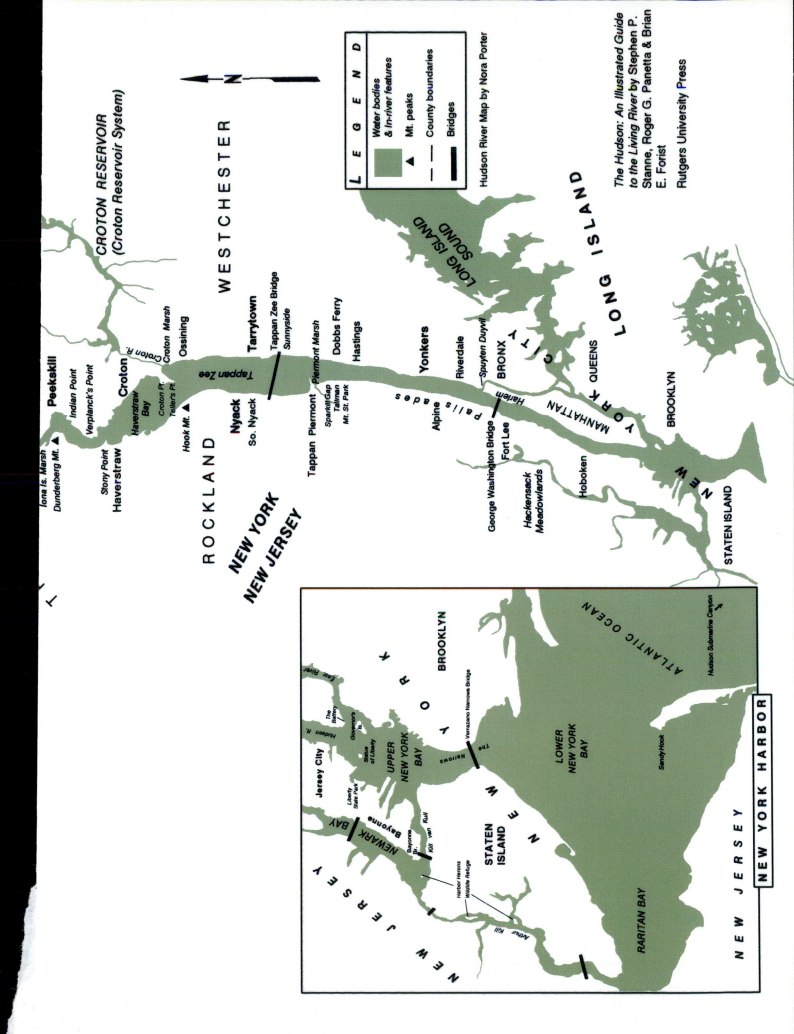

The Hudson: An Illustrated Guide to the Living River by Stephen P. Stanne, Roger G. Panetta & Brian E. Forist

Rutgers University Press

Hudson River Map by Nora Porter

LEGEND

- Water bodies & In-river features
- ▲ Mt. peaks
- County boundaries
- Bridges

CROTON RESERVOIR
(Croton Reservoir System)

WESTCHESTER

N

ROCKLAND

NEW YORK
NEW JERSEY

Peekskill
Iona Is. Marsh
Dunderberg Mt. ▲
Indian Point
Verplanck's Point
Stony Point
Haverstraw
Haverstraw Bay
Croton
Croton Pt.
Teller's Pt.
Hook Mt. ▲
Croton R.
Croton Marsh
Ossining
Tarrytown
Tappan Zee Bridge
Sunnyside
Tappan Zee
Nyack
So. Nyack
Tappan
Piermont
Piermont Marsh
Sparkill Gap
Tallman
Mt. St. Park
Dobbs Ferry
Hastings
Yonkers
Palisades
Alpine
Riverdale
Spuyten Duyvil
BRONX
Harlem
George Washington Bridge
Fort Lee
Hackensack Meadowlands
Hoboken
MANHATTAN
QUEENS
NEW YORK CITY
LONG ISLAND
LONG ISLAND SOUND
BROOKLYN
STATEN ISLAND
NEW

NEW JERSEY

NEW YORK HARBOR

East River
The Battery
Governors Is.
Hudson R.
Jersey City
Statue of Liberty
Liberty State Park
Bayonne Br.
NEWARK BAY
Bayonne
Kill van Kull
Harbor Herons Wildlife Refuge
UPPER NEW YORK BAY
NEW YORK
BROOKLYN
The Narrows
Verrazano Narrows Bridge
STATEN ISLAND
MEN
Arthur Kill
LOWER NEW YORK BAY
Sandy Hook
RARITAN BAY
ATLANTIC OCEAN
Hudson Submarine Canyon